Kwasi Wiredu and Beyond
The Text, Writing and Thought in Africa

Sanya Osha

COUNCIL FOR THE DEVELOPMENT OF
SOCIAL SCIENCE RESEARCH IN AFRICA

CODESRIA

ISBN: 2-86978-150-4
Layout by Hadijatou S. Sané
Cover designed by Ibrahima Fofana

CODESRIA would like to express its gratitude to African Governments, the Swedish
Development Co-operation Agency (SIDA/SAREC), the International Development
Research Centre (IDRC), OXFAM GB/I, the Mac Arthur Foundation, the Carnegie
Corporation, the Norwegian Ministry of Foreign Affairs, the Danish Agency for
International Development (DANIDA), the French Ministry of Cooperation, the
Ford Foundation, the United Nations Development Programme (UNDP), the
Rockefeller Foundation, the Prince Claus Fund and the Government of Senegal for
support of its research, publication and training activities.

Contents

Introduction

The Ghanaian philosopher Kwasi Wiredu is perhaps the greatest living African philosopher, with the possible exception of Paulin Hountondji and V.Y. Mudimbe, and as such, whatever is the focus of his attention is bound to generate widespread interest. Having worked extensively in core areas of traditional philosophy, he has recently published a number of essays on conceptual decolonisation, which are sure to generate extensive debate.

Wiredu's present involvement with conceptual decolonisation certainly broadens the scope of philosophical discourse in Africa beyond the exhausted debate of whether or not it exists. Furthermore, he introduces a much needed multidisciplinarity into African philosophical deliberations. By this one means that it has become imperative to link up with related discursive practices in disciplines such as history, political science, and literature. However, Wiredu has not yet been able to grapple with the full implications of what his project of conceptual decolonisation entails. This study is an attempt to address some of those implications and also limitations.

At this juncture, mention must be made of a few salient facts about Wiredu's philosophical background. His philosophical education was within the British analytic tradition at Oxford during the heyday of Gilbert Ryle and P.F. Strawson. Hume, Dewey and Kant are some of his favourite philosophers. But this tradition of British philosophy has been quite resistant to some of the more progressive currents of continental philosophy. Of this disparity between the French and the Anglo-Saxon traditions of philosophy, O'Farrell notes:

> At the risk of massive generalisation, one can say that in general the tendency on the continent is towards a unified approach to knowledge, to-

wards formulating a satisfactory abstract and all-explaining theory which encompasses science, history, and metaphysics whereas the empirical Anglo-Saxons prefer 'facts' and in general more fragmentary, more patently empirical approaches to knowledge, each discipline and science being content with its own area.[1]

However, the tradition to which Wiredu belongs exhibits what has been called 'the worst excesses of Anglo-Saxon empiricist small-mindedness'.[2] One can see that some of these excesses are manifested in his enterprise of conceptual decolonisation. In fact, Wiredu's equally prominent contemporary, V. Y. Mudimbe, had written about the former's philosophical antecedents in the following manner; 'We shall also refer to Wiredu's very British *Philosophy and an African Culture* (1980), which among other things 'teaches' us that 'it is a fact that Africa lags behind the West in the cultivation of rational inquiry' and indicates that 'the ideal way to reform backward customs in Africa must, surely, be to undermine their foundation in superstition by fostering in the people...the spirit of rational inquiry in all spheres of thought and belief.'[3] As mentioned above, since he fails to include the insights provided by the deconstruction of ethnocentric Western epistemology, the possibilities of his project are immensely undermined. In this regard, other shortcomings may also be discerned.

For instance, Wiredu's handling of the problems of language does not appear to be sufficiently profound. Language, we must note, forms a vital nexus in his project of conceptual decolonisation. In his treatment, language and its attendant cultural dynamics appear rather staid and static, a limitation attributable to an inadequately responsive linguistic philosophy. It is necessary to note some of the theories that have been advanced on the question of constituting meaning. For example:

> Constitutive Graphonomy, the constitutive ethnography of writing systems, attempts to answer their questions by examining the 'objective' meanings of writing as a process of social accomplishment between the participants. Meaning is a social fact which comes to being within the discourse of a culture, and social facts as well as social structures are themselves social accomplishments.[4]

In other words, 'writing comes into being at the intersection of the sites of production and consumption. Although the 'social relationship' of the two absent subjects is usually a function of their access to the 'situation' of the writing, it is in this threefold intersection of situation, author function and reader function that meaning is accomplished'.[5] Finally, we must recognise that:

Language in post-colonial societies, characterized as it is by complexity, hybridity and constant change, inevitable rejects the assumption of a linguistic structure or code which can be described by the colonial distinction of 'standard' and 'variant'. All language is 'marginal', all language emerges out of conflict and struggle.[6]

These are all very vital issues which Wiredu fails to address in any appreciable detail.

As for the question of decolonisation itself, one agrees with Ngugi wa Thiong'o—perhaps the most radical theorist of decolonisation currently working—that it is 'a vast process'. Again, Wiredu does not appear to recognise this, hence the decidedly limited possibilities of his project. One has had to adopt a multidisciplinary approach in this study because of the quite impressive achievements in other fields of study. For example, in literary theory, the discourse of decolonisation has attained sophisticated heights, yet there are still daunting obstacles to be surmounted. Biodun Jeyifo argues:

Historic decolonization having initially enabled the curricular legitimation of African literary study in African universities and schools, the equally historic arrest of decolonisation has swung the centre of gravity of African literary studies away from Africa to Europe and America.[7]

So in the field of literary theory, decolonisation has attained greater levels of problematisation which sooner or later would confront African philosophy. Archie Mafeje, in a thought-provoking monograph entitled *Anthropology and Independent Africans: Suicide or End of an Era*, raises a number of issues pertinent to this study. Being an anthropologist, he carries out a deconstructionist critique of his discipline and needless to say, most of his conclusions are quite striking. One of the problems Mafeje identifies in his discipline is 'the intellectual hegemony of the North, the intellectual immaturity of African anthropologists or the static conception of what anthropology is about'.[8] No matter how 'liberal minded and sympathetic the anthropologist was towards colonised and primitive peoples, he/she was nevertheless responsible for generating ideas which were ideologically useful to the exploiting colonial powers'.[9] However, 'the end of anthropology' was pronounced 'because of its theoretical parochialism and fixation about the primitive world'.[10] To reclaim its future, it was necessary for the discipline to 'undergo a transformation and disengage itself from the colonial system'.[11] Mafeje also argues that the future of anthropology lies in 'interdisciplinary linkages'.[12] He then advocates the virtues of post-modernism in the following terms:

there were glimpses of intellectual projections of the post-modernist writers, who brook no disciplinary boundaries and are intent on exposing the iniquities of western society.[13]

It is one of the central points of this study to apply the same discursive strategy in relation to philosophy. During the course of this piece of work, we shall come to see how Western philosophy is at several instances tainted with ethnocentrism. As such, any discussion on decolonisation will have to confront the question of ethnocentrism in Western philosophical thought. Furthermore, it would also be appropriate to include the deconstructionist approach in the history of Western philosophy to enrich our theoretical insights as regards the question of decolonisation.

In the same vein, the deconstruction of ethnocentric European epistemology is necessary for several reasons. We are informed that:

> Epistemology as the study of mental representations arose in a particular historical epoch..., developed in a specific society, that of Europe, and eventually triumphed in philosophy by being closely linked to the professional claims of one group, nineteenth century German professors of philosophy.[14]

He goes on to say:

> epistemology might not be as universal as it pretends. It is simply one style of thinking out of several possible styles which remained unrecognised because of European political, intellectual, and economic dominance since the sixteenth century.[15]

It is also beneficial for the purposes of this study to note that 'although philosophy departments continue to teach epistemology, there is a counter tradition in modern thought that followed another path. Wittgenstein, Heidegger and Dewey are in agreement that the notion of knowledge as accurate representation, made possible by special mental processes, and intelligible through a general theory of representation, needs to be abandoned'.[16] This study staunchly supports this view. But we must realise 'that deconstruction of epistemology does not imply rejection of truth, reason, or standards of judgement but opens up other possibilities which had been denied—a 'whole teratology of learning'[17] in Foucault's words.

But let us return to the primary subject of this study, Kwasi Wiredu. Professor Wiredu was born in 1931 in Ghana and had his first exposure to philosophy quite early in life. He read his first couple of books when he was in elementary school. These were Bernard Bosanquet's *The Essentials of Logic* and C.E.M. Joad's *Teach Yourself Philosophy* around 1947 in Kumasi, the capital of Ashanti. Logic, as a branch of philosophy, attracted Wiredu because of its affinities to grammar which he liked. He was also fond of practical psychology during these formative years of his life. In 1950, whilst vacationing with his aunt in Accra, the capital of Ghana, he came across another philosophical text which influenced him tremendously. The text was *The Last Days of Socrates* which had the following four dialogues by Plato: The Apology, Euthyphro, Meno and Crito. These dialogues were to influence in a significant way the final chapter of his first groundbreaking philosophical text, *Philosophy and an African Culture* (1980) which is also dialogic in structure.

He was admitted into the University of Ghana, Legon in 1952 to read philosophy but before then he started to study the thought of John Dewey on his own. However, C. E. M. Joad's philosophy had a particularly powerful effect on him. In fact, he used the name J. E. Joad as his byline for a series of political articles he wrote for a national newspaper, *The Ashanti Sentinel*, between 1950 and 1951. At the University of Ghana, he was instructed mainly in Western philosophy and he discovered African philosophy more or less through his own individual efforts. He was to confess that 'the character of my undergraduate education, then was such as to leave my mind a virtual tabula rasa, as far as African philosophy was concerned. The furnishing of my mind in this regard was something I had to do myself.'[18] One of the first texts of African philosophy that he read was J. B. Danquah's *Akan Doctrine of God: A Fragment of Gold Coast Ethics and Religion*. Obviously, his best friend, William Abraham who went a year before him to Oxford University, must have also influenced the direction of his philosophical research towards African thought.

In the summer of 1958, he proceeded to Oxford for his graduate studies where analytic philosophy was the dominant philosophical trend. At Oxford, he was associated with three major philosophers: Gilbert Ryle was his thesis supervisor, Peter Strawson, his college tutor, and Stuart Hampshire, his special tutor. Ryle was already a legendary academic figure at the time having published his *The Concept of Mind* in 1949 and *Dilemmas* in 1954. Both Strawson and Hampshire were still at the height of their productive powers. The former had published *Individuals* in 1959 and went on to publish *The Bounds of Sense* in 1966. Hampshire published *Thought and Action* in 1966, and the two together extended the frontiers of analytic philosophy in Oxford.

Wiredu submitted a thesis entitled *Knowledge, Truth and Reason* before he left Oxford in 1960. Thus, his philosophical antecedents are quite clear. He was trained along the lines established by the analytic school of philosophy and by some of the most prominent members of that school. However, he was to make his distinctive mark in contemporary African philosophy as his two published texts to date demonstrate.

Arguably, his particular contribution to the debate on the origins, status, problematic and future of contemporary African philosophy resides in his formulations regarding what he terms conceptual decolonisation. On this important formulation of his he states:

> By this I mean the purging of African philosophical thinking of all uncritical assimilation of Western ways of thinking. That, of course, would be only part of the battle won. The other desiderata are the careful study of our own traditional philosophies and the synthesising of any insights obtained from that source with any other insights that might be gained from the intellectual resources of the modern world. In my opinion, it is only by such a reflective integration of the traditional and the modern that contemporary African philosophers can contribute to the flourishing of our peoples and, ultimately, all other peoples.[19]

This insight more or less defines Wiredu's attitude and the gestures towards the constitution of contemporary African thought. Also it is an insight that is inflected by years of immersion in the discourse of logical positivism. He confesses gaining entry into the critical discourse that came to be known as African philosophy through his own efforts. Legon and Oxford did not offer courses in African philosophy during his time there. However, he began his reflections of the nature, legitimate aims and possible orientations in contemporary African thought not as a result of any particular awareness of the trauma or violence of colonialism or imperialism but by a confrontation with the dilemma of modernity in the reflective postcolonial African consciousness. This dialectical origin can be contrasted with those of his contemporaries such as Paulin Hountondji and V. Y. Mudimbe. In fact, a younger theorist such as Achille Mbembe would situate the origin of the discursive positionality of the contemporary African consciousness elsewhere. For Mbembe, what he terms, Afro-radicalism and the disciplines of nativism define in a fundamental manner the boundaries of discourse in contemporary Africa.[20] These tendencies are in turn informed by a few crucial events and histories in the African postcolony namely, slavery, colonisation and apartheid. This scenario, essentially defines the complex of situations by which the contemporary African consciousness (or multiplicity of subjectivities) enters into the domain of post-Enlightenment modernity and the problematic politics of self-constitutive identity. It is also a complex of situations that is powerfully mediated by the 'paradigm of victimisation'. The point is, in order to better understand the various discursive complexions and inflections in the thought of a given thinker we have to be aware of the foundational events and gestures behind them.

In relation to Wiredu, the intellectual climate that prevailed in Legon and Oxford was one in which the influence of logical positivism prevailed. Thus, Wiredu did not begin his reflections on African thought with the paradigm of victimisation looming before him but with an adequate mastery of the canons of analytic philosophy and its central preoccupations. This particular discursive moment defines the beginnings of his identity as a thinker after which a family of other identities followed.[21]

At this juncture, perhaps it would be illuminating to pay some attention to the intellectual context in which the body of work by another major African thinker was produced. Paulin Hountondji's *African Philosophy: Myth and Reality,* has been described as perhaps 'the most influential work of African philosophy written in the French language'.[22] V. Y. Mudimbe regards the book as 'the bible of anti-ethnophilosophers' and gives Hountondji the credit of making the philosophical critique of ethnophilosophy a debate of international dimensions.[23] Just as Wiredu had been trained by some of the most prominent names within the analytic tradition of the Anglo-Saxon divide of philosophy, Hountondji was also trained at École normale supérieure of the rue d'Ulm in Paris by some of the accomplished figures of French philosophy in the twentieth-century; Canguilhem, Ricoeur, Derrida and Althusser. Hountondji is particularly forthcoming on the issue of the contributions of his famous teachers to his philosophical development. He has high praise for Derrida, Canguilhem and Althusser in particular. On Derrida, he writes; 'he was a breed apart. Among authors whom he carefully and methodically analyzed—bringing out the cadences of their texts, the texts' inner breath, problems, and challenges, comparing them when necessary to the German or English originals, and expressing himself with exemplary clarity and accuracy'.[24] Having written a dissertation on Husserl himself, Derrida went on to introduce Hountondji to Husserl's *The Phenomenology of Internal Time-Consciousness* and *Logical Investigations.* As for Canguilhem he says; 'Canguilhem, it is well known, has no sympathy for nebulous metaphysics. All the elements that account for the beauty of his writings—rigorous analyses, an austere style, and conceptual rigor—were present in his seminars at Rue du Four'.[25] And on the great and tragic Althusser, he writes:

> Althusser was particularly interested in Spinoza and Rousseau (to whom he devoted two unforgettable seminars) as well as Aristotle and Kant (both of whom he quoted often), Freud, Bachelard, and contemporary thinkers including Lacan, Levi-Strauss, Canguilhelm, and Foucault. It was to this vast learning that we owe his central contribution, which later made him famous: to inject a breath of fresh air into the ideological confines of Marxism (or rather to tear asunder its increasingly closed space and restructure it from top to bottom).[26]

Hountondji went on to write a doctoral thesis on Husserl.[27] In terms of a Western philosopher who has remained an abiding interest for him, Husserl must be singled out. Through his long years of studying Husserlian phenomenology, Hountondji has been able to come up with some significant insights on the topic. Of his numerous insightful perceptions on Husserl's thought, one in particular stands out:

> I paid the greatest attention to Husserl's effort to 'purify the sign'. First, he excluded from his concerns the indicative sign—a material and empirical sign that is neither discourse nor part of discourse—in order to concentrate solely on expression. Next, he excluded from discourse itself those body movements and various gestures that involuntarily accompany speech and still derive from the empirical indication, in order to focus on expression proper—on the linguistic sign which alone is the true bearer of meaning.[28]

After a doctoral thesis on Husserl, Paul Ricoeur, Hountondji's thesis supervisor, wanted him to extend the boundaries of his research on the topic. But he started to contemplate the status of his philosophical research in relation to the kind of audience he wanted to cultivate, the relation between the modes of knowledge he had been trying to articulate and the African continent and the entire question of the geographical location of his academic production. At the same time he was conducting research on Anton Wilhelm Amo, the Ghanaian philosopher who lived and worked in eighteenth-century Germany.[29] Hountondji decided that Amo's work 'could only be part, from the beginning to end, of a non-African theoretical tradition, that it exclusively belonged to the history of Western scholarship'.[30] The extraverted nature of knowledge production in Africa caused him considerable concern and for this reason he stopped further research and plans for publishing on Husserl. With this course-changing realisation, Hountondji decided to make the unremitting critique of ethnophilosophy the centre of his philosophical preoccupation together with an equally robust vigilance against the tendency towards scientific extraversion in Africa. With these concerns in mind, he had mapped out a clear course of action for his philosophical future.

Hountondji argues that ethnophilosophy in general is implicated within the Western anthropological project itself. Hountondji and Marcien Towa are usually credited for the neologism, ethnophilosophy. But in fact, Kwame Nkrumah had used it earlier when he registered for a Ph.D. at the University of Pennsylvania in 1943. However, Hountondji suggests that Nkrumah did not complete the task of adequately defining the term. Hountondji defines ethnophilosophy as 'the extension into the field of thought in general of the inventory of the corpus of the so-called 'primitive' knowledges'.[31] Central to his project is the task of demonstrating that 'ethnophilosophy had a more ancient history that was linked to the history of anthropology in general— that is, to the history of the Western gaze on so-called primitive societies'.[32] Henceforth, the view that theory could only make meaning if it was anchored in practice and henceforth, the stance that the denigration and inferiorisation of the black subject as a result of the violence of colonisation would be the starting points for philosophical reflection and activity. On the definition of his African-centred philosophical problematic, Hountondji writes: 'By African Philosophy, I mean a set of texts: Specifically the set of texts written by Africans and described as 'philosophical' by their authors themselves'.[33] This definitional agenda generated considerable debate in African philosophical circles.[34] Hountondji appears to be so clear regarding the point that the usefulness of African philosophy lies in doing it instead of articulating a foundational discourse to settle once and for all the parameters of debate on the issue. Ultimately, the tendency of scholars of African philosophy to institute a founding discourse that binds Wiredu, Hountondji, Bodunrin and Oruka as practitioners of the same philosophic credo fails.[35] The enormous diversity of their antecedents, discursive orientations, styles and motivational spirits is anything but unitary.

Let us examine motivational impetuses in terms of disciplinary and discursive articulation. According to Hountondji, 'the exclusion practiced by the European scholar becomes when it is taken over by the African intellectual, extraversion'.[36] Indeed, the concept of extraversion which focuses on African modes of intellectual production remains central to Hountondji's reflections. The struggle against intellectual extraversion is crucial because it:

> Has made us waste precious time 'trying to codify a thought that is believed to be given, constituted, instead of simply or quite simply jumping into the water...to think new thoughts'; a movement of withdrawal that is totally unproductive and still makes us, in reality, 'prisoner of Europe', whose respect we still determined to extract, but that leads us to 'petrify', to 'mummify' our cultures 'by making them topics of myths for external consumption'. And what do we find at the end of the road? The same subservience, the same wretchedness, the same tragic abandonment of thinking by ourselves and for ourselves.[37]

For Hountondji, the struggle against intellectual extraversion entailed a vigorous critique of the ethnophilosophical consciousness. Consequently, the 'myths of ethnophilosophy' had to be destroyed because they are also 'the myth of primitive unanimity—the idea that in 'primitive' societies, everyone is in agreement with everyone else—from which it concluded that there could not possibly exist individual philosophies in such societies, but only collective belief-systems'.[38] The ethnophilosophical consciousness is basically unanimist, a term Hountondji borrowed from Jules Romains 'to stigmatize both the illusion of unanimity in the reading of the intellectual history of a given culture, and the ideological exploitation of this illusion for the present and the future'.[39]

Indeed the problem of identity and self-definition has prevailed in African philosophical discourse.[40] Perhaps to have an idea of the intensity of the debates regarding this problem it would be worthwhile to revisit Peter Bodunrin's famous essay on the major orientations of African philosophy.[41] Bodunrin's essay reads like a manifesto for a certain philosophical school which includes Kwasi Wiredu, Paulin Hountondji, Odera Oruka and himself. Following Oruka's equally famous typological grid, Bodunrin posits four major trends in contemporary African philosophy, namely, philosophic sagacity, ethnophilosophy, professional philosophy and the nationalist-ideological trend in African thought.[42] But the reality of the evolution of postcolonial African thought has evinced the rather arbitrary character of this discursive grid. Even the so-called school in which he includes himself and the likes of Wiredu and Hountondji is fraught with so many contradictions that ultimately preclude a singular theoretical description of all of them. Bodunrin, in his famous essay, seems to be more concerned about upholding a certain disciplinary ethic or logic which conforms to the general orientations of analytic philosophy. The question of race, of the traumatised and repressed figure of the black subject, does not appear to be important to him in the way that it is with Hountondji. For him, a racialisation of philosophy, that is, a critique of raciology, amounts to a devaluation, an erasure of philosophy itself. Thus, philosophy, in its most appropriate form must maintain its claim to universality. Bodunrin does not go on to qualify this claim or to grant it the nuance of particularity. Let us now examine how Hountondji mediates between the instance of universality and the necessity for the critique of raciology.

First of all, Hountondji localises the discipline of African philosophy and rids it of any claims to theoretical transparency. According to him, 'African philosophy was first and foremost a European invention, the product of an intellectual history at the intersection of the most diverse of disciplines, notably anthropology, the psychology of peoples, missiological theory, and a good many concerns'.[43] Also, Frantz Fanon's analyses of socio-pathology and forms of collective behaviour under the psychology of colonialism meant more to him than Lacanian psychoanalysis which he infrequently studied. The search for the black subject and his/her insertion at the centre of philosophical deliberation was a quest Hountondji took very seriously. A theoretical fissure appeared in his thought when he made African concerns and authors such as A. Kagame, A. Adesanya, A. Makarakiza, F. M. Lufuluabo, V. Mulago, J. C. Bahoken and F. Eboussi-Boulaga his primary interests. In view of Hountondji's reconfiguration of the discourse/subject dynamic, Bodunrin's rather unproblematised disciplinary positionality becomes even more glaring. In the end, Bodunrin's famous foundational manifesto is perhaps just a little more than a deterritorialised document.

Wiredu's position is somewhat different from either Hountondji's or Bodunrin's. A passage from an interview explains the issue of his institutional relation to African philosophy:

> Prior to 1985, when I was in Africa I devoted most of my time in almost equal proportions to research in African philosophy and in other areas of philosophy, such as the philosophy of logic, in which not much has, or is generally known to have been done in African philosophy. I did not have always to be teaching African philosophy or giving public lectures in African philosophy. There were others who were also competent to teach the subject and give talks in our Department of Philosophy. But since I came to the United States, I have often been called upon to teach or talk about African philosophy. I have therefore spent much more time than before researching in that area. This does not mean that I have altogether ignored my earlier interests, for indeed, I continue to teach subjects like (Western) logic and epistemology.[44]

From the above passage, Wiredu stands closer to Bodunrin than Hountondji in his attitude towards the notion of African philosophy. Here, he appears to take the meaning of the existence of African philosophy for granted. Also lacking is an attempt to de-universalise and hence localise its status. African philosophy appears and sits under the universal rubric provided by Western philosophy and the theoretical space made available for its articulation is derived from the same Western-donated fund of universalism. A crucial theoretical space donated by analytical philosophy provides the occasion for the appearance and consolidation of African philosophy. Terms such as reflective integration and due reflection offer the critical spaces for the theoretical articulation of something whose existence has not yet been concretely conceived. Hountondji suspects these inadequately analysed and problematised critical spaces as ethnophilosophy. In this way, ethnophilosophical practices are much wider and much more entrenched than we often assume. Furthermore, no so-called major orientation of contemporary African philosophy—ethnophilosophy, philosophic sagacity, nationalist-ideology and professional philosophy—remains untainted by the discourse of ethnophilosophy. With hindsight, Bodunrin's critique seems rather overbearing while Hountondji's claim that African philosophy is Western invention makes more sense. Once the critical spaces afforded by terms such as reflective integration and due reflection are appropriated by Wiredu he then turns to texts such as J. B. Danquah's *Akan Doctrine of God: A Fragment of Gold Coast Ethics and Religion* and William Abraham's *The Mind of Africa* which provide the discursive models for an African philosophy. Thus it is not likely that he suffers the extensive trauma caused by the event and violence of the colonial event and the multiple erasures of the black subject under its vast drama.

Consequently, the logic of disciplinarity rather than the compulsions of raciology are more powerful for the formulation of an African philosophy in Wiredu's thought.[45] In contrast, ideologues of blackness and an identitarian politics based on race such as Fanon or Senghor recognised the importance of the currency of race as a crucial factor in not only constituting identity but also in the articulation of speech.

The currency of race for the African or black subject is not only an issue recognised by Hountondji and other major African and black thinkers such as Cheikh Anta Diop, Senghor, Césaire and even Appiah. The histories of raciology are implicated in the far-reaching events of colonisation, apartheid and genocide. The histories of raciology have to do with the very extinction and survival of the black race. Indeed, 'a major element in the European view of mankind was the conviction that 'inferior races' were by nature condemned to extinction: the true compassion of the superior races consisted in helping them on the way'.[46] It is one of the most striking ironies of academic history that one of the most accomplished names of African philosophy— Kwasi Wiredu—has managed to create an impressive body of work that bypasses or at least downplays the currency of race as a crucial and founding element in his work. Instead, a disciplinary ethic seems to be more prominent.

By contrast, Anthony Appiah is derided in African intellectual circles for the very reason of his pronounced cosmopolitanism and because he recognises the importance of race for the black/African subject. Appiah's critique of raciology is exemplary within the entire spectrum of African studies for avoiding the very real danger of nativism and projecting in its place a discourse that carries within its cosmopolitan transnational, transcultural and multi-identitarian attributes. These virtues in his work are not usually admired in many African intellectual circles. Discourses of nativism continue to spring around the African continent as globalisation and localisation foster various ultranationalisms, fundamentalisms, fascisms and particularisms.[47] Hountondji, in contemporary African thought, begins an important critique of the ethnophilosophical consciousness and the cultural dead-end that unanimity fosters. However, he does not pursue the critique of unanimity beyond the immediate boundaries of a narrowly defined identitarian politics. Indeed, he recognises the importance of both Appiah and Mudimbe in extending the critique of unanimism; 'the overdetermination of the concept of Africa is an obstacle to the freedom of the African. Freeing up the future first of all meant reducing this semantic overload, giving back to words their original, simple, and obvious meaning. The reader can easily see, by going through some of Mudimbe's and Appiah's recent works, the extent to which this refusal of geographical refusal is still widely shared today'.[48] Appiah, as Hountondji would grant, carries out a post-anthropological critique of raciology at the moment when the complex histories of the politics of race, nationality, ethnicity confront their transnational and transcultural possibilities.

Apart from this introduction and a brief conclusion, this study comprises six chapters. The first chapter addresses imperialism and the efforts of various Third World scholars in circumventing it. It is interesting to note that Wiredu's project of conceptual decolonisation does not undertake a thoroughgoing critique of imperialism, which is necessary. This chapter also discusses the work of some scholars—Edward Said, Stuart Hall, Paul Gilroy, Henry Louis Gates Jr., Homi Bhabha, Abiola Irele, Gayatri Spivak and a few others—who work within various 'Third World' contexts. It then ends by bringing Spivak into conversation with Niyi Osundare on the issue of post-structuralism. Imperialism is a world-historical process and so is neo-colonialism. Said's famous critique of 'orientalism' marks the moment when postcolonial theory came into existence. Hall's thesis of the recolonisation of the metropole by formerly colonised subjects reconfigures the old colonial order in significant ways. Gilroy's concept of raciology makes important contributions on the question of race.[49] Also, Bhabha's arguments regarding the ambivalence of the colonial encounter have had profound effects on postcolonial studies. So in this chapter, I attempt an examination on colonial discourse that incorporates various sites of resistance-Africa, the west and India—in order to highlight the significance of its world-historical dimensions.

The second chapter explores some of the theoretical perspectives of decolonisation beginning with the work of Frantz Fanon and Walter Rodney. Again these two theorists of decolonisation are brought into conversation, and the central argument in this regard is that Fanon is a more successful theorist of decolonisation since he goes beyond a mere critique of Western imperialism, which is where Rodney stops. More important, any explication of postcolonial theory seems to be incomplete without a discussion—however brief—of Fanon. I also examine the work of the Kenyan essayist and novelist, Ngugi wa Thiong'o and conclude that his project is perhaps the most radical on the African continent. Ngugi wa Thiong'o's point that decolonisation must be conceived as a global project is important in many respects. First, it establishes the interdisciplinarity of such a project. Second, it seeks to address the cultural economy of the decolonisation process. And finally, it serves as a precaution against the colonising tendencies of transnational capital.

The third chapter focuses on two of Kwasi Wiredu's major texts. *Conceptual Decolonisation in African Philosophy* and *Cultural Universals and Particulars* are discussed in some detail. In this chapter we assess in concrete terms the question of conceptual decolonisation and also discuss some of the arguments intended to develop a way of overcoming the limitations of Wiredu's approach. Furthermore, a critique of Wiredu's conceptions of rationality and cultural self-identity is undertaken.

In chapter four, Wiredu's critique of Marxism is examined. Oftentimes, this aspect of his work is overlooked as scholars prefer to focus on his contributions to African philosophy and his experiments in analytic philosophy. In the main, it will be observed that Wiredu is unsympathetic to Marxist philosophy in general.

Chapter five examines the issues of philosophy, politics and post-coloniality as they relate to Wiredu's project of conceptual decolonisation. The segment on philosophy in particular further explores some of the problematics of the philosophy of language that is broached in the course of this introduction. We discuss certain trends in the philosophy of language to show the shortcomings of Wiredu's project. We also propose that his non-party consensual system of politics is unworkable in the contemporary African context, given the availability of more feasible options such as those advanced by the late Nigerian political scientist, Claude Ake and the British historian, Basil Davidson. Finally, I attempt to demonstrate that Wiredu's understanding of post-coloniality is rather restrictive, which, given his customary diligence, ought not to be so. To do this, I employ the insights of theorists such as Stuart Hall and Anthony Appiah.

Chapter six discusses some social realities in Africa that may obtrude in the course of conceptual decolonisation. These social realities concern our knowledge-generating mechanisms and the environment of thought. The present existential conditions are simply appalling. This chapter recounts some of the realities that confront the project of conceptual decolonisation. Finally, it focuses on instances of alternative or 'resistant textuality' in African forms of discourse—Afrocentricism, Soyinka and Appiah—within an extreme context of disinstitutionalisation. This resistant form of textuality compels us to be cautious about generalising the conditions of knowledge production in Africa and to appreciate more local knowledges that manage to circulate in transnational space.

Chapter seven presents the work of a couple of theorists—Achille Mbembe and W. M. J. van Binsbergen—who have been able to offer interesting insights into conditions of existence in what has been described as the African postcolony. Their analyses do more than the usual run of commentaries on the so-called African predicament in that in spite of the harshness of their conclusions and the centrality of African marginality in them, they somehow manage to reinscribe the African condition as worthy of consistent and careful study. Mbembe's theorising of the African postcolony is sometimes found to be problematic by African scholars. It is claimed that his analyses of the postcolonial African condition is often without social-scientific explanation. However, a study of his work is necessary for many theoretical and philosophical reasons. Mbembe has said his work 'builds on critiques already made by, for example, V. Y. Mudimbe (*The Invention of Africa*), K. A. Appiah (*In My Father's House*) and the critiques of ethnophilosophy such as those of Eboussi Boulaga (*La crise du Muntu: philosophie africaine et authenticité*)'.[50] So Mbembe's primary theoretical impulses are basically philosophical. Furthermore, he has initiated the critique of contemporary discourses of nativism and Marxism which he regards as conceptual dead-ends.[51] Whatever reservations mainstream social scientists might have about Mbembe's conceptual novelties, his corpus demands to be read and critiqued for its striking singularity in the field of discourses on Africa.

W. M. J. van Binsbergen on the other hand, offers quite an interesting reading of V. Y. Mudimbe, clearly one of the most gifted theoretical minds in Africa.[52] Binsbergen foregrounds Mudimbe's aggressive and constant multidisciplinarity—linguistics, philosophy, anthropology, novelistic discourse and African historic religion—and the challenges, successes and limitations inherent his conceptual approaches.

This study offers a critique of Western ethnocentrism from a broad historical perspective and then a view of a deconstructed tradition of Western philosophy as it relates to the socio-political contexts of postcolonial African thought. This sort of critique is necessary in order to go beyond a discussion of the merely formal structures of conceptual decolonisation. In between these discursive preoccupations there are discussions on post-structuralism, post-coloniality and Afrocentricity, which, as we shall see, broaden and deepen any project of conceptual decolonisation. Wiredu does very little to avail himself of the numerous insights provided by these vital and related discourses.

Furthermore, this study complicates and rewrites the concept of decolonisation. Ngugi wa Thiong'o points out that decolonisation is a vast process. I totally agree. Indeed there are many versions of decolonisation— 'ideological decolonisation',[53] 'linguistic decolonisation',[54] 'aesthetic decolonisation',[55] 'postmodern decolonisation'[56] and even the de-whitinisation of cyberspace or 'cybernetic decolonisation'.[57] Similarly, there are several forms of colonisation, for example, 'the colonisation of consciousness',[58] and sexual and gendered colonisation.[59] If there are so many forms of colonisation there ought to be several strategies of decolonisation as well. So I examine Wiredu's thesis of conceptual decolonisation and then attempt a rewriting of decolonisation itself by employing categories such as transnationality (Appiah, Mudimbe and even Wiredu himself), liminality (Mudimbe), multiculturality (Appiah, Ngugi wa Thiong'o, Wiredu, Hountondji, Soyinka etc.), multifocality and syncretism. Colonialism was a world historical process[60] and just as racism, it is linked to the continuing expansion of global capital. Thus projects of decolonisation must be equally global in reach and multidisciplinary in discourse such that they can address a wide range of oppressions: political, economic, cultural and aesthetic, institutional, sexual and gendered. The more visible forms of colonisation have led the way to technologised economic globalisation in which in the US 'the Black, Brown, Yellow, Red, female, elderly, gay, lesbian and White working class live the same costs as cheap labour at home as well as in US-dominated Latin American and Pacific rim markets'.[61]

Decolonisation is such a process that extends into the contemporary moment. Of course it would be impossible to undertake a study of all the major intellectuals that pushed for the empowerment of black subjectivities or black and Third World discourse—W. E. B. Du Bois, Anna Cooper, C. L. R. James, James Baldwin, Claudia Jones, Malcolm X, Amiri Baraka, Marcien Towa, Serge Latouche, Theophile Obenga, Samir Amin, Ama Mazama, Kariamu Welsh, Claude Alvares, Aisha Blackshire-Belay, Abu Barry, Gustav Esteva and so many other black intellectuals. However, this study deals with not only black intellectuals. Said, Bhabha, Spivak, Foucault and to some extent Derrida have all provided very important conceptual tools for decolonisation and are discussed in varying detail. This work does not attempt a definitive explanation of decolonisation. Instead, it foregrounds Wiredu's understanding of conceptual decolonisation in order to rewrite the very concept of decolonisation—in its multiple trajectories—in much broader terms.

Notes

1. O' Farrell C., *Foucault: Historian or Philosopher?* London, The Macmillan Press Ltd., 1989, p. 22.

2. Ibid. p. 20.

3. V. Y. Mudimbe, *The Invention of Africa: Gnosis, Philosophy, and the Order of Knowledge*, Bloomington, Indiana University Press, 1988, p. 161.

4. Bill Ashcroft, 'Constitutive Graphonomy', in *The Post-Colonial Studies Reader*, eds. B. Ashcroft et. al., London and New York, Routledge, 1995, p. 298.

5. Ibid. p. 300.

6. Ibid.

7. Biodun Jeyifo, 'The Nature of Things: Arrested Decolonisation and Critical Theory', *Research in African Literatures*, Vol. 21, No. 1, 1990, p. 40.

8. Archie Mafeje, *Anthropology and Independent Africans: Suicide or End of an Era*, CODESRIA Monograph Series 4/96, p. 2.

9. Ibid.

10. Ibid. p. 3.

11. Ibid.

12. Ibid. p. 10.

13. Ibid. p. 11.

14. Ibid. p. 13.

15. Ibid.

16. Ibid. p. 14.

17. Ibid.

18. Kwasi Wiredu in an interview, see *The Third Way in African Philosophy: Essays in Honour of Kwasi Wiredu*, edited by Olusegun Oladipo, Ibadan, Hope Publications, 2002, p. 328.

19. Ibid. p. 337.

20. See Achille Mbembe, 'African Modes of Self-Writing' *Public Culture*, 36/ 2002 and also his 'Ways of Seeing: Beyond the New Nativism', *African Studies Review*, Vol. 44, No. 2.

21. The following list of publications traces Wiredu's discursive preoccupations. The first part is primarily concerned with logic: 'Kant's A priori in Geometry and the Rise of Non-Euclidean Geometries', *Kant Studien*, Nos. 1-4, 1970; 'Truth as Opinion', *Universitas*, March, 1972; 'A Note on Modal Quantification, Ontology and the Indenumerably Infinite', *Analysis*, June, 1972; 'Material Implication and If- then', *International Logical Review*, December, 1972; 'Deducibility and Inferability', *Mind* (New series) 82, Nos. 325, 1973; 'Logic and Ontology, Part 1', *Second Order*, Vol. 2, No. 1, 1973; 'Philosophy, Mysticism and Rationality', *Universitas*, March, 1973; 'On the Real Logical Structure of Lewis', 'Independent Proof' *Notre Dame Journal of Formal Logic*, October, 1973; 'Logic and Ontology Part 2', *Second Order*, Vol. 2, No. 2, 1973; 'To be is to be known', *Legon Journal of Humanities*, 1, 1974; 'What is Philosophy', *Universitas*, 3, No. 2, March, 1974; 'Carnap on Iterated Modalities', *Philosophy and Phenomenological Research*, 35, No. 2; 'Classes and Sets', *Logique et Analyses*, January, 1974; 'A Remark on a Certain Consequence of Connixive Logic for Zermelo's Set Theory', *Studia Logica*, 33, No. 2, 1974; 'Logic and Ontology Part 3', *Second Order*, Vol. 3, No. 2, 1974; 'In Praise of Utopianism', *Thought and Practice*, 2, No. 2, 1975;

'Logic and Ontology Part 4', *Second Order,* Vol. 4, No. 1,1975; 'Truth as a Logical Constant with an Application to the Principle of the Excluded Middle', *The Philosophical Quarterly,* 25, No. 101, 1975; 'Predication and Abstract Entities', *Legon Journal of the Humanities,* Vol. 2, 2, 1976; 'On the Formal Character of Logic', *Ghana Social Science Journal,* May, 1976; 'On 'Reduction ad Absurdum' Proofs', *International Logic Review,* June, 1976; 'Paradoxes', *Second Order,* Vol. 5, No. 2, 1976; 'On Behalf of Opinion', *Universitas,* December, 1976. The following publications have an African-centred problematic as their focus: 'On an African Orientation in Philosophy', *Second Order,* Vol. 1, No. 2, 1972; 'How not to compare African Thought with Western Thought', *Ch' Indaba,* No. 2, 1976. This article was reprinted in Richard Wright ed. *African Philosophy: An Introduction,* Washington D.C. University Press of America, 1977, and Albert Mosley ed. *African Philosophy: Selected Readings, New Jersey:* Prentice Hall, 1995; 'Philosophy and our Culture', *Proceedings of the Ghana Academy of Arts and Science,* 1980; *Philosophy and an African Culture,* Cambridge and New York: Cambridge University Press, 1980; 'Philosophical Research and Teaching in Africa: Some Suggestions', *Teaching and Research in Philosophy: Africa,* Paris: UNESCO, 1984; 'Survey: Philosophy Teaching and Research in English-Speaking Africa', *Teaching and Research in Philosophy: Africa,* Paris: UNESCO, 1984; 'On Defining African Philosophy', T. Serequeberhan, ed. *African Philosophy: The Essential Readings,* New York: Paragon House, 1991; 'Formulating African Thought in African Languages: Some Theoretical Considerations', V.Y. Mudimbe, ed. *The Surreptitious Speech: Presence Africaine and the Politics of Otherness 1947-1987,* Chicago: University of Chicago Press, 1992; 'The Akan Concept of Mind', *Ibadan Journal of Humanistic Studies,* 1983. This article was reprinted in volume 5 of Contemporary Philosophy: A New Survey, G. Floistad ed. Dodrecht: Martinus Nijhoff Publishers, 1987; 'Morality and Religion in Akan Thought', H. Odera Oruka and D. Masolo, eds., *Philosophy and Cultures*, Nairobi: Bookwise, 1983 and was reprinted in Norm Allen Jr. ed. African-American Humanism: An Anthology, New York: Prometheus Books, 1991; 'The Concept of Truth in the Akan Language', P. O. Bodunrin, ed., *Philosophy in Africa: Trends and Perspectives,* Ile-Ife: University Press, 1985; 'The Moral Foundations of African Culture', H. E. Flack and E. D. Pellagrino, eds. *African-American Perspectives on Biomedical Ethics*, Washington D. C.: Georgetown University Press, 1992; 'African Philosophical Tradition: A Case Study of the Akan', *Philosophical Forum,* 24, Nos. 1-3, 1992-93; 'Death and the Afterlife in African Culture', A. Berger et al, eds. *Death and Dying: Cross-Cultural and Multi-Disciplinary Views,* Philadelphia: The Charles Press, 1989; 'On the Question of the Right to Die: An African View', Arthur Berger and Joyce Berger, eds., *To Die or Not to Die?: Cross-Disciplinary, Cultural and Legal Perspectives on the Right to Choose Death,* New York: Praeger, 1990; 'An Akan Perspective on Human Rights', A. Ahmed An-Na' im and Francis Deng eds. *Human Rights in Africa: Cross-Cultural Perspectives,* Washington D. C.: Brookings Institution, 1990; 'Universalism and Particularism in Religion from an African Perspective', *Journal of*

Humanism and Ethical Religion, 3, 1990 and this article was reprinted in D. Kolak and R. Martin eds. *Self, Cosmos and God,* New York: Harcourt, Brace, Javanovich, 1992; 'The Akan Concept of Personhood', H. E. Flack and E. D. Pellegrino, eds. *African-American Perspectives on Biomedical Ethics,* Washington D. C.: Georgetown University Press, 1992; 'Metaphysics in Africa', J. Kim and E. Sosa, eds. *A Companion to Metaphysics,* Oxford: Blackwell Publishers, 1995; 'Custom and Morality: A Comparative Analysis of some African and Western Conceptions of Morals', Albert Mosley ed. *African Philosophy:* Selected Readings, New Jersey: Prentice Hall, 1995; *Cultural Universal and Particulars: An African Perspective,* Indianapolis and Bloomington: Indiana University Press, 1996; 'Can Philosophy be Intercultural? An African Viewpoint', *Diogene* 46, no. 4; With Kwame Gykekye as editor, *Person and Community: Ghanaian Philosophical Studies,* New York: Council for Research in Values and Philosophy, 1992; 'Democracy and Consensus in Traditional African Politics: A Plea for a Non-Party Polity', *The Centennial Review,* 39, No. I, Winter, 1995; 'In Decolonising African Religions', J. Malherbe, ed. *Decolonising the Mind: Proceedings of the Colloquium held at UNISA,* October 1995, Pretoria: Research Unit for African Philosophy; 'Particularistic Studies of African Philosophies as an Aid to Decolonisation', J. Malherbe ed. *Decolonising the Mind: Proceedings of the Colloquium held at UNISA,* October 1995, Pretoria: Research Unit for African Philosophy; and 'Our Problem of Knowledge: Brief Reflections on Knowledge and Development in Africa', I. Karp and Dimas Masolo eds., *African Philosophy as Cultural Inquiry, Indianapolis and Bloomington:* Indiana University Press, 2000.

22. K. Anthony Appiah, 'Foreword', *The Struggle for Meaning: Reflections on Philosophy, Culture and Democracy in Africa*, Paulin Hountondji, Athens, Ohio University Center for International Studies, 2002, p. xiii.

23. V. Y. Mudimbe, *The Invention of Africa: Gnosis, Philosophy and the Order of Knowledge*, Bloomington, Indiana University Press, 1988, p. 158.

24. Paulin Hountondji, *The Struggle for Meaning: Reflections on Philosophy Culture and Democracy in Africa,* 2002, p. 7.

25. Ibid.

26. Ibid. p. 8.

27. The thesis which was defended at the University of Paris X, Nanterre in 1970 is entitled, 'L'idée de science dans les 'Prolegomenes' et la première 'Recherche logique' de Husserl'.

28. Ibid. p. 54.

29. Amo wrote most of his texts in Latin. They include, *Dissertatio inauguralis de jure Maurorum in Europa* (The Rights of Africans Living in Europe), 1729; *Dissertatio de humane mentis apatheia* (On the Impassivity of the Human Mind), 1734; and *Tractatus de arte sobrrie et accurate philosophandi* (On the Art of Philosophising with Sobriety and

Accuracy) 1738.

30. Paulin Hountondji, *The Struggle for Meaning: Reflections on Philosophy Culture and Democracy in Africa,* 2002, p. 73.

31. Ibid. p. 208.

32. Ibid. p. 79.

33. Ibid. p. 97.

34. See in particular these rather well known responses to Hountondji's *African Philosophy: Myth and Reality, Koffi Niamkey,* 'L'impense de Towa et Hountondji', Claude Sumner, ed., *African Philosophy (La philosophie africaine),* Addis Abba, Chamber Printing House, 1980; Oyekan Owomoyela, 'Africa and the Imperative of Philosophy: A Skeptical Consideration', *African Studies Review,* 30, (1) 1987; and Olabiyi Yai, 'Theory and Practice in African Philosophy: The Poverty of Speculative Philosophy', *Second Order,* No. 2, July 1977.

35. See for instance, H. Odera Oruka, 'Four Trends in Current African Philosophy', Alwin Diemer, ed., *Philosophy in the Present African Situation,* Wiesbaden, Franz Steiner, 1981.

36. Paulin Hountondji, *The Struggle for Meaning: Reflections on Philosophy Culture and Democracy in Africa,* 2002, p. 103.

37. Paulin Hountondji, *African Philosophy: Myth and Reality,* Bloomington, Indiana University Press, 1996, p. 50.

38. Paulin Hountondji, *The Struggle for Meaning: Reflections on Philosophy Culture and Democracy in Africa,* 2002, p. 107.

39. Ibid. p. 132.

40. See for instance D. A. Masolo, *African Philosophy in Search of Identity,* Bloomington, Indiana University Press, 1994.

41. See Peter Bodunrin, 'The Question of African Philosophy', *Philosophy,* 56, No. 216, 1981.

42. In the social sciences, these four categories are sometimes collapsed in two main currents. See Achille Mbembe, 'Ways of seeing: Beyond the New Nativism', *African Studies Review,* Vol. 44, No. 2, September 2001 and also his 'African Modes of Self-Writing', *Public Culture,* 36, 2002.

43. Paulin Hountondji, *The Struggle for Meaning: Reflections on Philosophy Culture and Democracy in Africa,* 2002, p. 124.

44. Kwasi Wiredu in conversation with Olusegun Oladipo, *The Third Way in African Philosophy: Essays in Honour of Kwasi Wiredu,* Olusegun Oladipo ed. Ibadan: Hope Publications, 2002, p. 332.

45. Contrast this view with Anthony Appiah's position in which his sophisticated analyses of Wilmot, Blyden and Du Bois makes the question of race crucial for the

formation of African thought. See his *In My Father's House: Africa in the Philosophy of Culture*, New York: Oxford University Press, 1992.

46. Sven Lindqvist, *Exterminate all the Brutes*, trans. By Joan Tate, New York, *The New Press*, 1996, p. 10.

47. Indeed it is arguable that the popularity of the idea of an African Renaissance in South Africa is a new instance of nativism. See for instance, Pieter Boele van Hensbroek's introduction to the *QUEST*, Vol. XV, No. 1-2, 2001 Special Issue on *African Renaissance and Ubuntu Philosophy* suggests that these new forms of nativism are no different from earlier forms such Julius Nyerere's Ujamaa. See also Caspar Schweigman's essay in the volume, 'Ujamaa, a Phantom'.

48. Paulin Hountondji, *The Struggle for Meaning: Reflections on Philosophy, Culture and Democracy in Africa,* 2002, p. 127.

49. See his *Against Race: Imagining Political Culture Beyond the Color Line*, Cambridge, Harvard University Press, 2000.

50. Achille Mbembe, 'On the Postcolony: Interview with Achille Mbembe', *Newsletter of the Wits for Social and Economic Research*, Vol. 1, No. 1, 2002, p. 4.

51. Mbembe criticises Mahmood Mamdani's *Citizen and Subject: Contemporary Africa and the Legacy of Late Colonialism,* Princeton, Princeton University Press, 1996 and also his *When Victims Become Killers: Colonialism, Nativism, and the Genocide in Rwanda,* Princeton, Princeton University Press, 2001 as fostering a discourse of artificial binarism between native and settler, citizen and subject and victim and killer.

52. W. M. J. van Binsbergen, 'An Incomprehensible Miracle: Central African Clerical Intellectualism versus African Historic Religion: A Close Reading of Valentin Mudimbe's Tales of Faith', paper presented at SOAS, University of London, February 2001, http://www.geocities.com/africanreligion/mudi10.htm

53. K. A. Appiah, *In My Father's House: Africa in the Philosophy of Culture*, New York: Oxford University Press, 1992.

54. See for instance, his *Decolonising the Mind*, Nairobi: Heinemann Educational Publishers Ltd. 1986 among his numerous works.

55. Kobena Mercer, 'Black Hair/Style Politics', in Russell Ferguson et al. eds. *Out There: Marginalization and Contemporary Cultures*, New York, Cambridge and London, The New Museum of Contemporary Art and MIT Press, 1990.

56. Masao Miyoshi, 'A Borderless World? From Colonialism to Transnationalism and the Decline of the Nation-State', in Rob Wilson and Wimal Dissanayake eds. *Global/Local: Cultural Production and the Transnational Imaginary,* Durham and London: Duke University Press, 1996.

57. Kali Tal, 'The Unbearable Whiteness of Being: African American Critical Theory and Cyberculture', http://www.kalital.com/Text/Writing/Whiteness.html

58. J. L. Comaroff and J. Comaroff, *Of Revelation and Revolution: Christianity, Colonialism and Consciousness in Africa*, Vol. 1, Chicago, University of Chicago Press, 1991 and *Of Revelation and Revolution: The Dialectic of Modernity on a South African Frontier*, Chicago, University of Chicago Press, 1997.

59. Ann Laura Stoler, Carnal Knowledge and Imperial Power: Race and the Intimate in Colonial Rule, Berkeley: University of California Press, 2002; Anne McClintock, Imperial Leather: *Race, Gender and Sexuality in the Colonial Conquest*, New York and London, Routledge, 1995; and Joane Nagel, *Race, Ethnicity, and Sexuality: Intimate Intersections, Forbidden Frontiers*, New York, Oxford University Press, 2003.

60. Cornel West, 'The New Cultural Politics of Difference', in Russell Ferguson et al. eds. *Out There: Marginalization and Contemporary Cultures*, New York, Cambridge and London, The New Museum of Contemporary Art and MIT Press, 1990.

61. Ibid. p. 25.

1

The (De)Colonising Subject: Speech and Imperialism

Introduction

For the colonised, the colonial encounter has proved to be more than decisive in so many ways. Colonialism not only entailed the seizure of far away lands by the imperial powers of Europe, coupled with the forceful administrative control of the resources of those lands, but also the political, moral and social-cultural dominance of the peoples therein. Since the end of the colonial encounter, entire regions of the world have become geographically re-drawn and politically reconstituted, so that nothing has been the same for the coloniser and the colonised.

Imperialism, needless to say, went hand in hand with colonialism and of course continues even after the decolonisation process. As Ngugi wa Thiong'o, the Kenyan novelist and theorist of culture, in his book, *Moving the Centre* (1993), writes, 'the conquest and subjugation of the entire labour power of other countries by the concentrated capital, or money power, of another country... could never be complete without cultural and hence mental and spiritual subjugation'.[1] Ngugi also argues:

> It is of course true that imperialism, in whatever form and guise, aims at the complete ownership, management and control of the entire system of production, exchange and distribution of the wealth in its home base and those of other nations and territories. This was perfectly clear in the old colonial system.[2]

Here, we note the correlation between colonialism and imperialism, but we should also bear in mind that imperialism continues to survive well after the period of actual colonisation.

But why should philosophy as an academic discipline be concerned with these matters? Philosophy as a formal discipline witnessed its professionalisation in Western Europe, more precisely in the Germany of Kant and Hegel, when colonialism was still in its heyday. The slave trade and colonialism not only led to physical subjugation and humiliation of black peoples, it also resulted in unprecedented mental and intellectual assaults in which an astonishing range of academic disciplines were assembled and deployed for the purpose. In other words, there was intellectual denigration of black peoples in the dominant academic disciples of the time, of which philosophy was one. Anthropology and literature were also involved in this crucial connection. We are also familiar with the now discredited notion that primitive peoples or pre-literate societies have a pre-logical mentality. These erroneous anthropological notions were encouraged within the gamut of Eurocentric academic discourses, including philosophy. Thus, a radical deconstruction of the longstanding Eurocentric and racist bias of philosophy becomes necessary for an African or a Third World subject engaging in philosophy. Two classical examples serve to illustrate this long history of Eurocentric assumptions. David Hume, the British empiricist, in 1735 is noted to have said:

> The Negro is naturally inferior to the whites. There scarcely ever was a civilized nation of that complexion, nor even any individual, eminent either in action or speculation. No ingenious manufactures among them, no arts, no science.[3]

Hegel posited that the African had not reached the height where he:

> ...attained that realization of any substantial objective existence as for example, God or Law in which the interest of man's volition is involved and in which he realises his own being.[4]

In the same vein, he affirms that in:

> this distinction between himself as an individual and the universality of his essential being, the African in the uniform, undeveloped oneness of his existence has not yet attained: so that the knowledge of absolute being, an Other and a Higher than his individual self, is entirely wanting.[5]

Other prominent Western figures such as Thomas Jefferson, a president of the United States of America, and Hugh Trevor-Roper, an eminent historian at Oxford University, have in various ways written pejoratively about the intellectual endowments of the African. The project of modernity and the enlightenment as conceived by the West had as a pivotal concern a discourse of raciology that not only hierarchalised races according to scales of importance but also legitimated the extermination of the so-called inferior races.[6] Kant developed an elaborate raciological discourse in texts like his *Anthropology from a Pragmatic Point of View* (1798) and his 1775 essay, 'On the Different Races of Man.' The point is, race-thinking as Paul Gilroy conceptualises it, is a central feature of Euro-modernity and indeed the entire Enlightenment project. It is simply necessary for Africans and other oppressed Third World peoples to gain entry into the Western archive in order to dislodge the numerous racisms to be found in western scholarship so that they can regain their self-esteem and dynamism. This refers to the needs for acts of intellectual counter-violence. Even at the more basic level, acts of counter-violence against hegemonic oppression have been theorised as essential gestures for restoring a battered and disfigured humanism.[7] Certainly, this is not proving to be an easy endeavour in the wake of neo-colonialism and the unarrested onslaught of imperialism. But these difficulties should in no way discourage us from confronting the issue. The multifaceted problems posed by imperialism are such that Third World nations cannot establish any meaningful existence within the current global system unless a persistent programme of decolonisation in all areas of knowledge production is pursued and completed.

And so in this chapter, I will examine the work of some of the exemplary figures that are presently engaged in dismantling the hegemonic structures of Western discourse. I should mention that their positionalities or subject-positions, strategies, disciplines and levels of consistency are not in the least harmonious. However, it is my belief that it is necessary to establish continuities among their texts since the project of decolonisation is vast as Ngugi wa Thiong'o correctly argues. Furthermore, because of the ever-growing global dimensions of imperialism, the decolonisation process has got to be effected along several fronts spanning several disciplines and regions of the world. In fact, this can be regarded as one of the central arguments of this study. And so I would begin with a critique of the work of the Palestinian polymath, Edward Said, and others like Stuart Hall. Finally, I intend to conclude this chapter with an examination of the work of Abiola Irele. One thing that binds these disparate academic and intellectual figures together is that they are either attempting to deconstruct the structures of dominance within Western scholarship or they are negotiating ways in which to gain entry into the Western archive, thereby reducing the marginality of subjected peoples and minorities from a number of perspectives in terms of class, gender and, of course, race.

Edward Said and the Discourse of Orientalism

Edward Said's *Orientalism* (1978) marks a decisive moment in qualitative Third World discourse and a reconstitution of global academic positions. It also marks the beginning of the entry of postcolonial theory into the academy. Said employs his positionality as an 'Oriental' subject to question and subvert the hitherto inadequately challenged assumptions of Eurocentric discourse on the Orient. In an essay, 'Crisis (in *Orientalism*)' he states:

> *Orientalism* overrode the Orient. As a system of thought about the Orient, it always rose from the specifically human detail to the general transhuman one … *Orientalism,* assumed an unchanging Orient, absolutely different, (the) reasons change from epoch to epoch…[8]

In his book *Orientalism* Said also argues that 'the Orient is an integral part of European material civilization and culture. Orientalism expresses and represents that part culturally and even ideologically as a mode of discourse with supporting institutions, vocabulary, scholarship, imagery, doctrines, even colonial bureaucracies and colonial styles'.[9] Similarly, it is important to note that European imperialism was wholly responsible for the production of the Orient—in political, sociological, military, ideological, scientific and imaginative terms—through an inherent triumphalism. To do this, 'the scientist, the scholar, the missionary, the trader, or the soldier was in, or thought about the Orient, because he could be there, or could think about it, with very little resistance on the Orient's part'.[10]

Orientalism generated a lot of productive debate regarding the colonial/ post-colonial subject. For instance, the Anglo-Indian theorist Homi K. Bhabha argues that the colonial subject is not altogether the defenceless, vulnerable figure Said's discourse describes. Bhabha's main point is that the colonial subject is marked by ambivalence, mimesis and hybridity. Employing deconstructionist argumentative strategies, Bhabha elaborates:

> Hybridity is the sign of the productivity of colonial power, its shifting forces and fixities; it is the name for the strategic reversal of the process of domination through disavowal (that is, the production of discriminatory identities that secure the 'pure' and original identity of authority). Hybridity is the revaluation of the assumption of colonial identity through the recitation of discriminatory identity effects. It displays the necessary deformation and displacement of all sites of discrimination and domination. It unsettles the mimetic or narcissistic demands of colonial power but reimplicates its identifications in strategies of subversion that turn the gaze of the discriminated back upon the eye of power.[11]

Gayatri Spivak's arguments, on the other hand, are in some respects similar to those of Said. In her famous essay, 'Can the Subaltern Speak?' she questions the ability of intellectuals to narrativise the experiences of 'men and women among the illiterate peasantry, the tribals, the lowest strata of urban subproletariat'[12] who have been visited by the 'epistemic violence' of the colonial encounter. Of course mention should be made of the fact that her response is deeply structured by Foucauldian epistemology in its appreciation of knowledge/power relations. As noted earlier, Spivak's position is closer to Said's, while Bhabha problematises the question of colonial subjectification in a more radical manner. This is not to say that Bhabha arrives at a complete theory regarding the colonial subject. What he does instead is to transcend the Manichean allegory (a term coined by Abdul Jan Mohamed to characterise discursive or epistemic binarism) inherent in typical colonial relations involving colonised and coloniser. Bhabha has his own active army of critics. Olakunle George argues that the problem in Bhabha's account of the postcolonial condition is that his 'notion of the mimic man as a figure of menace and transgression is formulated in psychoanalytical terms. However, although Bhabha's critical vocabulary suggests a strictly psychoanalytical delimitation, and although he often appears to circumscribe his explorations and its theoretical purchase within the level of the psyche, his lyricism, especially in his more enthusiastic moments, pushes him squarely onto the level of the sociopolitical.'[13] Benita Parry assesses the debate in the following manner:

> For Spivak, imperialism's epistemic bellicosity decimated the old culture and left the colonised without the ground from which they could offer confrontational words; for Bhabha, the stratagems and subterfuges to which the native resorted, destabilised the affectivity of the English book but did not write an alternative text....[14]

There are other theorists who fault Said's discourse of orientalism. One of such theorists is Samir Amin who writes in his book, *Eurocentrism*:

> The critique of *Orientalism* that Edward Said has produced has the fault of not having gone far enough in certain respects, and having gone too far in others. Not far enough to the extent that Said is content with denouncing Eurocentric prejudice without positively proposing another system of explanation for facts which must be accounted for. Too far, to the extent that he suggests that the vision of Europeans was already Eurocentric in the Middle Ages.[15]

Amin ends up branding Said's critique as 'inverted *Orientalism*'. But perhaps he offers his observations a little too soon. Said's critique of orientalism merely began with the book of the same title. His subsequent text *Culture and Imperialism* (1993) is an impressive elaboration of the thematics explored in *Orientalism*.

As Said writes in the introduction to *Culture and Imperialism*:

> What I left out of *Orientalism* was the response to Western dominance
> which culminated in the great movement of decolonisation all across the
> Third World. Along with armed resistance in places as diverse as nine-
> teenth century Algeria, Ireland and Indonesia, there also went considerable
> efforts in cultural resistance almost everywhere, the assertions of national-
> ist identities, and, in the political realm, the creation of associations and
> parties whose common goal was self-determination and national inde-
> pendence. Never was it the case that the imperial encounter pitted an
> active Western intruder against a supine or inert non-Western native; there
> was always some form of active resistance and, in the overwhelming
> majority of cases, the resistance finally won out.[16]

Said addresses in *Culture and Imperialism* what *Orientalism* leaves out by replying
to his numerous critics. Nonetheless, Bhabha offers the harshest and also the
most complimentary reading of Said since the former's deconstruction of
the colonialist script is essentially a re-reading of the latter. Bhabha argues that
the Orientalist discourse as understood by Said requires further
problematisation in order to get more diversified dimensions of presence as
difference and to make alterity and ambivalence focal points in the counter-
discourse of colonialism. In Bhabha's words:

> colonial power produces the colonized as a fixed which is at once "other"
> and yet entirely knowable and visible. It resembles a form narrative in
> which the productivity and circulation of subjects and signs are bound in
> a reformed and recognizable totality. It employs a system of representation,
> a regime of truth, that is structurally similar to realism. And it is in order to
> intervene within that system of representation that Edward Said proposes
> a semiotic of "Orientalist" power, which in raising the problem of power
> as a question of narrative introduces a new topic in the territory of colonial
> territory'[17]

Another insight of Said that has been appropriated by theorists of the
postcolonial condition relates to his reading of the transition in Victorian
upper-middle-class culture from filiation to affiliation. This socio-cultural
development signified a marked bureaucratisation of both the private and
public realms. It also signalled a more intensive industrialism. Interesting as
this account might be, a particular critic thinks Said does not go far enough.
Anne McClintock argues that 'as the authority and social function of the
great service families (invested in the filiative rituals of patrilineal rank and
subordination) were displaced into the bureaucracy, the anachronistic, filiative
image of the family was projected onto emerging affiliative institutions as
their shadow, naturalized form.'[18] This complicated reading of Said's account

of filiative and affiliative modes of sociocultural institutionalisation makes sense. However, whatever shortcomings that may remain within his work should not be enough to conceal the fact that the insights his impressive corpus afford us into the genealogies of what is sometimes called Third Worldism and imperialism generally, together with the minor and principal subjectivities implicated in both discursive formations, have radically redefined our views and positions regarding the colonial encounter and post-coloniality and their place within the present–day global structure(s). Said's work not only established postcolonial theory as worthy of genuine academic inquiry but also laid the foundations for many of its enduring problematics.

Said recognised that processes of decolonisation need to be multidisciplinary. Second, his deconstruction of the classic colonialist script, the articulation of subject-positions and his new (then) way of reading the power/knowledge connection in relation to colonialist discourse led the way to the subsequent entrenchment of postcolonial theory as counter-discourse.

In the next section, I intend to look into the work of other scholars who have been able to challenge Euro-American centrism in novel ways. It is impossible to cover more than a mere fraction of their work in this chapter, so I will discuss some of the most stimulating theorists in the field.

Third World Scholars in the First World

Stuart Hall has been very instrumental in shaping the climate of debate of leftist ideology in Britain. But his importance is not limited to leftist and progressive ideologising alone. Hall has been important in raising new important questions about what it means to be a black post-colonial British subject. Traditional British scholarship was not equipped to pose these questions and so it fell upon the likes of Hall to do so. He begins his essay, 'The Meaning of New Times', thus:

> How new are these 'New Times'? Are they the dawn of a New Age or only the whisper of an old one? What is 'new' about them? How do we assess their contradictory tendencies—are they progressive or regressive? These are some of the questions which the ambiguous discourse of "New Times" poses.[19]

He goes on to argue that:

> the individual subject has become more important, as collective social subjects—like that of class or nation or ethnic group—became more segmented and 'pluralised'.[20]

This development was brought on by revolutions in the realm of theory, and in discourses such as semiotics, structuralism, and post-structuralism. To give his discourse its distinct theoretical thrust, Hall explains:

'Postmodernism' has a more philosophical aspect. Lyotard, Baudrillard and Derrida cite the erasure of a strong sense of history, the slippage of hitherto stable meanings, the proliferation of difference, and the end of what Lyotard calls the 'grand narratives' of progress, development, Enlightenment, rationality and truth, which, until recently, were the foundations of western philosophy and politics.[21]

At first, classical Marxism provided Hall with a basis to begin his intellectual engagement with the emergent socio-political as well as cultural conditions in Britain that were generating new notions concerning the politics of identity, subjectivity and personal autonomy in the present epoch of virtuality. As an editor of the influential journal, *The New Left Review,* he began a productive interrogation of the existential features of British society. Of him, it has been written:

> Hall's major intellectual contribution does not lie in making definitive statements on theoretical and political issues, but rather in his involvement with a wide range of collective projects, and in his capacity and willingness to take on new issues and to constantly move on, beyond his own previous limits.[22]

This should be apparent enough since as he says, 'I am not interested in Theory, I am interested in going on theorizing. And that also means that cultural studies have to be open to external influences, for example, to the rise of new social movements, to psychoanalysis, to feminism, to cultural differences'.[23] It is my view that any adequately self-critical academic discipline, including philosophy, must take this crucial dictum into total cognisance in order to remain relevant and dynamic. Any academic specialty that fails to heed this credo can only hope for its own stagnation and eventual demise. In fact, this study, if anything else attempts to follow the spirit of this crucial credo.

Let us now examine some of the more concrete accomplishments in Hall's work. Hall has been able to direct fruitful attention to an immensely wide range of radical discourses such as gay and lesbian issues, minority discourse and, of course, Third World affairs. Furthermore, he has been able rearrange the stakes of the debate surrounding the politics of representation in a way by which marginalised groups can articulate more cogent positions. For instance, Hall has demonstrated why the 'black subject cannot be represented without reference to the divisions of class, gender, sexuality and ethnicity'.[24] Thus, in mapping out the new boundaries of cultural studies we are forced to analyse 'the global, historical structures of colonisation, decolonisation and recolonisation'.[25] In this way, Hall has transcended the project itself, thereby placing him ahead of other theorists dealing with the topic. His receptivity to novel frontiers of discursivity also leads him back to his 'not yet completed contestation with Marxist theory'.[26] However, what one finds most pertinent in relation to this study is his view that 'black' is a 'politically and culturally constructed category which cannot be grounded in a set of fixed, transcultural or transcendental racial categories, and which therefore has no guarantees in nature'.[27] This proposition is in accord with the main arguments of this critique of Wiredu's work. Hall undermines the totalising assumptions of the entrenched discourses of raciology by reconfiguring the latent autonomy of the black subject along a multiplicity of lines that are in turn inflected by dynamics of class, gender and sexuality. Whatever the ultimate theoretical limitations inherent in his approach it moves beyond a widespread unanimism that is prevalent in the field. I shall end this discussion of Hall's work with a quotation that captures the nature of his intellectual practice:

> That kind of (all too common) combative polarization of intellectual 'debate', in which one either 'advocates' everything, as a disciple of a certain intellectual position, or automatically 'refuses' and denies in its entirety, once it has been found wanting in some particular respect, offers little prospect of getting us anywhere, and it is greatly to Hall's credit that he offers us such a good model of an alternative intellectual practice.[28]

Paul Gilroy is another theorist of black studies whose sophisticated texts—for instance, *The Black Atlantic*, 1993—reveal with the competent employment of post–structuralist tropes new levels of problematisation regarding the black subject and what it implies in the process of increasing globalisation. Certainly, this discursive positioning makes him an important theorist on black studies from whatever cultural/geographical/ideological divide one approaches the matter. Gilroy argues that the politicisation of the black subject has radically opened up new discursive formations that not only subvert but also transcend the binary logic of classical colonialism. For instance, he posits that:

> Contrasting forms of political action emerge to create new possibilities and new pleasures where dispersed people recognise the effects of spatial dislocation as rendering the issue of origin problematic, and embrace the possibility that they are no longer what they once were and cannot therefore rewind the tapes of their cultural history.[29]

Such views are important to this thesis because they problematise the public sphere in relation to the black subject. In the same vein, he states:

> The sterile idea of origin and the assumption that culture is wholly sedentary lose their special glamour as different scales of enquiry point to other beginnings that require new modes of recognition and new conceptions of movement.[30]

These arguments go against the grain of those put forward by present-day Afrocentrists. Quite interesting and relevant to this study is his argument that: 'the narrative of civilization as progress towards perfection is claimed in the name of an imaginary African homogeneity that mimics the worst aspects of European thinking about self and community'.[31]

Some of Gilroy's views shall be employed much later to deconstruct some of the central propositions concerning conceptual decolonisation. Recently, Gilroy has not only focused on popular black culture and the various levels of its sociological significance but has been carrying out path-breaking studies on the different historical notions of race and its multiple reconfigurations under the operations of power. This sort of critique builds upon the type articulated by Appiah sometime ago.[32] Gilroy carries out an analysis of what he terms race-thinking within the annals of Western modernity and Enlightenment and shows how the so-called Western institutions of rationality were constructed around elaborate experiments in barbarity.[33] The Jewish Holocaust during the Second World War is often singled out as both an event and a process of radical evil within the heart of modernity.[34] Perhaps the most significant aspect of Gilroy's current preoccupations is his theorisations of raciology and its relationship with the idea of cosmopolitan democracy. This particular theoretical conjuncture has a post-anthropological turn that disavows numerous raciological histories while at the same time situating the postmodern condition within their violent and dehumanising radius. The racial beast, we are constantly warned, is alive and well and knocks constantly at our door. Gilroy's admonitions and critique of race-thinking make him one of the most eloquent spokesmen working on the question of race. For instance, he notes that 'the history of racism is a narrative in which the congruency of micro- and macrocosm has been disrupted at the point of their analogical intersection: the human body. The order of active differentiation that gets called "race" may be modernity's most pernicious signature. It articulates reason with unreason. It knits together science with superstition.'[35]

However, the relentless critique of raciological (un)reason and history is not the primary objective. Various forms of nationalism, fundamentalism, intolerant ethnicisms and fascism articulated and supported by the institutions and technologies of the modern nation-state stand in the way of real cultural development and consequently a non-fascistic understanding of the multiple politics of identity and subjectivity. In order to ensure that democracy attains the limits of its possibilities, Gilroy suggests, it must be freed from the metaphysics of race as articulated by the modern nation-state. The 'new' South Africa provides a site to observe how transnational, transcultural and transracial boundaries are being redrawn to establish a postmodern Acropolis such that

might attract Gilroy's interest.[36] Having said that, Gilroy's search for the possibilities for the institution of a cosmopolitan democracy is really worthy of
emulation just as his critique of raciological discourses deserves to be more
widely studied.[37]

Having discussed the scene of black cultural studies in Britain (Stuart Hall
and Paul Gilroy are representative of this tendency), we might broaden the
discussion with a brief survey of an African–American scholar, Henry Louis
Gates, Jr., whose work is also important in this respect. What I find most
interesting about Gates' work is his constant vigilance in relation to the ethnocentrism and even at times racism that is inherent in Western thought generally
and also his vigilance regarding the institutional positioning of minorities in
the US academy. Undoubtedly, his critique of the institutionalised racisms of
Western scholarship has been quite consistent. For instance, he reminds us that
'Kant… was one of the earliest major European philosophers to conflate
"color" with "intelligence", a determining relation he posited with dictatorial
surety".[38] To acquire a fuller understanding of the racist bias of Western philosophy, I shall quote at length a passage from Gates' essay 'Writing, "Race"
and the Difference it Makes':

> Kant, basing his observations on the absence of published writing among
> blacks, noted as if simply obvious that "(Indians) and blacks are lower in
> their mental capacities than all other races". Again, Hegel, echoing Hume
> and Kant, noted the absence of history among black people and derided
> them in failing to develop indigenous African scripts, or even to master
> the art of writing in modern languages.[39]

At this juncture, I should add that the Third World as a concept is employed
in a very fluid manner in this work. Even within the First World there are
Third Worldist elements, and this is why the signifier has to be quite flexible.
From this perspective, Gates is compelling First World America to confront
elements of the Third World—problems created by racism, ethnicity,
multiculturalism and chronic urban poverty—within its own territory.

In spite of the immense success of Gates in the institutional academic
context in the United States, formidable pockets of resistance towards his
work and profile (and that of others like him) exist. For instance, William
Bennett and Allan Bloom, who both represent the new cultural right in the
United States, attack the growing politicisation of what is regarded as the
Western canon and the encroachment of multiculturalism in particular into
the academy.

In justification of his stance Gates argues that:

> The concern of the "Third World" critic should properly be to under-
> stand the ideological subtext which any critical theory reflects and em-

bodies, and what relation this subtext bears to the production of meaning. No critical theory, be that Marxism, feminism poststructuralism, Nkrumah's consciencism, or whatever, escapes the specificity of value and ideology, no matter how mediated they may be. To attempt to appropriate our own discourses using Western critical theory uncritically is to substitute one mode of neocolonialism for another.[40]

Gates concludes by stating that the major preoccupation of the black theorist ought to be 'renaming principles of criticism where appropriate, but especially naming indigenous black principles of criticism and applying them to our own texts. Any tool that enables the critic to explain the complex workings of the language of a text is appropriate here'.[41] At the end of last century, a major debate between Gates and Ali Mazrui raged on the Internet. Gates had produced a film series, *Wonders of the African World* which was read by some critics as an instance of Black Orientalism among other charges. His film series provoked many reactions in disciplines such as theology, African Studies, African History and film studies. Perhaps the major charge levelled against Gates concerns his alleged 'paternalistic possessiveness, ulterior selectivity and cultural condescension, the basic symptoms of a rather dreadful disease, Black Orientalism.'[42] Ali Mazrui argues that the exclusion of Nigeria which is home to three major African ethnicities—Yoruba, Hausa and Ibo—undermines the continental validity of Gates' project. He ends his critique by asking: 'What is going on? What is the agenda? I hope the idea of Black Orientalism is not to sabotage all claims for reparations for Black enslavement.'[43] Gates on his own part argues that a denigration of the African continent was far from his mind when shooting the series. However, he wanted to raise a few unsettling questions the contributions of Africans to the enslavement and sale of their fellow Africans during the Atlantic slave trade and thereby 'bring a dialogue into the open between Africans and African Americans that has long been simmering beneath the surface.'[44]

This brief reading of Gates' work ought to demonstrate why he is important to decolonisation as an intellectual project and from several global/ideological perspectives. His constant assertions that figures such as Francis Bacon, David Hume, Immanuel Kant, Thomas Jefferson and G.W.F Hegel are 'great intellectual Western racialists'[45] provide a more than adequate reason for vigilance. Gates contributions to the problematic of epistemological decolonisation are multiple. First, they question the assumed universal validity of the Western canon as a guide for the whole of human experience including brutally oppressed and repressed collectivities. Second, they include a patient and systematic retrieval of lost and disavowed texts of the African-American experience. And finally, he recognises the institutionally lopsidedness within the US generally as a site to wage another struggle to ensure greater representation for minorities. In other words, institutions are crucial sites to carry out struggles relating to the politics of identity, representation and equity. Furthermore, for African philosophers Gates work establishes the necessity to question in a decidedly unprecedented manner, the long tradition of Eurocentrism in Western thought. Perhaps it is now necessary to review the scene from the perspective of Africans in order to discern some of the arguments that have emerged. In this light, I intend to examine the work of a major African thinker, Abiola Irele.[46]

Distances, Alienation, the Return

I used this word in a double sense. Distance meant first of all geographical distance, the distance from which our scientific, economic, and political dependence is organized.[47]

Abiola Irele has argued that the very phenomenon of conflict among cultures can be a source of human rejuvenation and flourishing. He constantly points out to us how Europe benefited tremendously from the Graeco–Roman evolutionary experience and how the latter was able to further enrich itself with the accomplishments of the ancient Egyptians.

Perhaps as Africans, we are too impatient to adopt Western standards and perspectives as a frame of reference without having imbibed in its totality, the ontological signposts of the modern age. Irele argues that Europe was able to achieve such impressive scientific and technological advancements by cultivating the habit of 'stubborn application'. To become essentially scientific and sufficiently rationalistic, the habits of method, discipline and imaginative inquiry must be cultivated. This is something that took Europe several centuries to master, but it is doubtful whether Africa can really afford such a long period of apprenticeship, given the extremely deplorable socio-political and economic conditions she currently suffers.

Irele argues that in acquiring the ontological characteristics of a particular culture, that is, in securing another mode of interpretation/representation, one is, in the final analysis, immensely enriched. Apart from possessing new semantic/semiotic codes and novel methods of constituting discourses, one acquires, in addition, an altogether different level of experience that cannot be measured in strictly materialist terms.

It is with this frame of mind that Irele plunged into the then exotic area of cultural studies (just as Stuart Hall did) at the onset of his career, one that has been marked by considerable fecundity. Before multidisciplinary studies became the vogue, Irele was already deeply engrossed in them, and this makes him equally at home in the specialties of literary criticism, political thought, the philosophy of science, philosophy and sociology.

In an essay, 'The African Imagination', published in *Research in African Literatures,* Irele states that:

> Despite the undoubted impact of print culture on African experience and its role in the determination of new cultural modes, the tradition of orality remains predominant, serving as a central paradigm for various kinds of expression on the continent.[48]

This view, which connects him with a crucial African reality, is a *problematique* that one hopes other thinkers would explore.

Irele's pronounced cosmopolitanism and powerful immersion in Western culture certainly has its problems. Olusegun Oladipo in his book, *The Idea of African Philosophy* (1992) has taken him up quite strongly on this particular stance. What Oladipo quarrels with in Irele's position is the claim that 'as a matter of practical necessity, we have no choice but in the direction of Western culture and civilization'[49] as regards the continually perplexing issue of Africa's underdevelopment. Oladipo's precise observation is that:

> The answer given by Irele to the important question of what should be the direction of change in Africa, though unequivocal, is very problematic. To say that our movement will have to be in the direction of Western culture and civilization is to say that the goals of that civilization are (or ought to be) our own and that we can achieve these goals by following the path trod by the west.[50]

In essence, Irele may have become totally enamoured of the cultures he has striven diligently to master. In the same vein, Oladipo's charge that Irele's position smacks of an uncritical adoption of Western culture does have its shortcomings. For one, the persistence with which Irele tackles long-standing African problems indicates a seriousness that most certainly goes beyond an uncritical immersion into Western culture.

What one might quarrel with though is Irele's insistence on—for the most part—availing himself of Western theoretical models when African alternatives may provide useful alternatives for particular situations. Indeed, this may seem to be a rather recurrent and paradoxical trope within his corpus. To uncover why this is so, it may be instructive to know his view on the undoubtedly decisive colonial event:

> The colonial experience was not an interlude in our history, a storm that broke upon us, causing damage here and there but leaving us the possibility, after its passing, to pick up the pieces. It marked a sea-change of the historical process in Africa; it effected a qualitative re-ordering of life. It has rendered the traditional way of life no longer a viable option for our continued existence and apprehension of the world.[51]

Now, to assert that nothing, more or less, can be retrieved from traditional culture in the effort to forge a suitable vision of development for Africa has a number of negative implications. Perhaps it is precisely this argument that elicits Oladipo's concern. For Irele, on the other hand, not to discover this necessary strategy (for it is necessary in so many ramifications within and outside intellectual discourse) is somewhat disturbing.

It is true that the colonial encounter was seismic for the African continent but it is also correct that the entry of Western culture into African existence has not completely eroded the organic foundations of African values. To prove the point, as Hall argues, in today's current global dispensation, 'the majority of the population have not yet properly entered the modern era, let alone the post modern'.[52]

Another obvious way of demonstrating this is the rural/urban dichotomy. In spite of the massive rural migrations to urban centres in most African nations, the vast majority of Africans still dwell in rural areas where contact with modernity is often negligible. What this means is that the cosmological structures that govern the outlook of this important majority have a decidedly traditional basis.

But let us take on again the issue of Irele's non-recognition of the epistemological imperatives of traditional cultures. It certainly does no good to his image as a liberal scholar, whose views are ordinarily coloured by a progressive persuasion. In short, there are definite political implications involved in not doing adequate justice to the general outlook of traditional societies. The moment an intellectual excludes that outlook in the invention of a discursive ontology also becomes the moment we must begin to look for the underlying motives for this exclusion. Most certainly, Irele's omission is not of the wilful kind. Instead, it probably stems from his well-intentioned cosmopolitanism as well as his admiration for the more constructive facets of Western civilisation. In this regard, he argues that:

> If we can accept that the scientific and technological civilization which has come down to us historically from Europe can improve the quality of our lives, if we can accept that our modern institutions should be based on political and social ideas articulated elsewhere, there is no reason why we should exclude from our acceptance other valuable areas of experience simply because of their association with Europe.[53]

Even more affirmatively, Irele posits:

> The scientific and technological supremacy of Europe was a historical phenomenon that was both particular and contingent, marked by all the vicissitudes of human experience.[54]

So his fascination for the achievements of Western culture is indeed borne out of the desire to utilize those gains in fashioning a feasible and dynamic paradigm for the enormously beleaguered African continent. Most would argue rightly that this is not altogether possible for several practical reasons. First of all, the degree of scientific and cultural intercourse between the West and Africa is such that the former enjoys a unilateral and indeed hegemonic influence over the latter. By implication, the products of that unequal dialogue are often problematic for Africa's assimilation of them. In the effort to ensure that Africa assimilates the products of this uneven scientific and cultural dialogue, the West itself would also have to be involved.

Consequently, the task of making Africa participate actively in the West–led scientific and cultural adventure of mankind should also entail concrete contributions from the West itself. Irele has not pointed out the need for this in his otherwise remarkable inaugural lecture entitled 'In Praise of Alienation'. The abject existential conditions within the African continent have made it increasingly difficult for her to initiate any sort of dialogue which could have positive global dimensions. Evidently, a far greater understanding of Africa's peculiar historical and contemporary circumstances is required so that more sensitive alternatives regarding development could be evolved.

But what we should have observed is that Abiola Irele's enchantment with the gains of western culture is not merely of the over-indulgent kind. This fascination is constantly turned on the hydra–headed problems that besiege Africa and always with a view to creating an existential paradigm for pulling the continent out of the decadence of post-colony.

Roland Barthes in *Writing Degree Zero* presents his major theoretical formulations on writing and language. The writer inherits a social language which goes a long way in defining his thematic concerns and his mode of signification. Also, he attempts to create an individual style, in other words, the personal stylisation of discourse is indeed a central preoccupation.

When the writer has no substantial fund of inscripted social discourse then there is indeed an enormous problem exemplified by the dichotomy between orality and textuality. This schism has inaugurated a crucial tension in modern African thought and discourse and the modes of address this enduring problematic elicits.

Irele's book of essays, *The African Imagination: Literature in Africa and the Black Diaspora* (2001) explores with great subtlety the foundations of the orality/textuality dichotomy within the different modes of African imaginative expression and the unexpected triumphs that have emerged from this long and disruptive dialectic.

To be sure, the entry of the colonial/postcolonial subject into modernity,

into the Euro-American archive sans scripted text obviously marks the beginning of a particular form of alienation. First, it signals the radical questioning
of a tribal culture, an undermining of its totality, the end of its cosmological
closure in the confrontation with other cultural forms of expression, inscription and subjectification. Second, the entry into the modern library, into modern discourse and once situated within it, inaugurates a season of hesitation
given the prevailing impoverished background of inscripted discourse. Caught
within this discursive nexus, the colonial/postcolonial subject invariably faces
the tyranny of silence which in this case is of a very destructive kind. This kind
of silence is not conditioned by the sort Jean Baudrillard formulates in face
of the 'hyperreality' occasioned by the explosion of postmodernist systems
of communication and advertising. The silence caused by the disorientations
in the age of virtuality is potentially active and subversive.

Silence in the absence of inscripted text is doubly negative. Abiola Irele's
book addresses this silence both theoretically and practically. Irele's effort not
only highlights some of the most notable accomplishments of the African
text (literature) within the continent but also in the diaspora. It is important to
situate this particular academic achievement within its precise context. In Africa,
we are continually assaulted by unending cycles of woes and degradation.
Politics has been downgraded to war in its very lowest form. We cannot talk
of the political field without wincing with disgust, in this sense, failure
reproduces itself as Achille Mbembe has recently argued.

However, Irele's work valorises what is indeed sublime within the African
aesthetic field. The political field has become a veritable theatre of disaster
and cannot be spoken of without embarrassment even though theorists such
as Jean and John L. Comaroff together with Mbembe are beginning to find
ways of performing this difficult task. But in the global market of production the political and the aesthetic fields overlap and are at several instances
inextricably linked. In other words, success in the political field by a particular
nation, region or continent reifies and empowers its aesthetic field.

Consequently, Irele's work marks an interesting trajectory. To write so per-
ceptively and with appreciable dignity about the African aesthetic field without concomitant success in the political sphere gives rise to standards of val-
orisation that the African cultural context in its present formation cannot en-
duringly support. Thus Irele's work stands alone waiting for the much-needed
restoration to take place in the political field so as to acquire its legitimately
deserved social value.

Having made some remarks about the context (or the lack of it) within
which Irele's work might be read we ought to discuss some of its central
issues. The first thing that strikes one is that even within the American acad-

emy where poststructuralism has become a strong tendency and given Irele's customary cosmopolitan orientation, his work continues to valorise African modes of artistic production even when it may be deemed injudicious in terms of career aspirations to do so.

For instance, Irele continually stresses the importance of oral modes of expression when other academics would prefer to dwell on more marketable topics such as postmodernism, globalisation and the cyberspace. But in highlighting the relevance and creative potential of these less valorised domains of discourse Irele introduces us to some crucial aspects of contemporary human culture. Rather than viewing orality as a degraded unprofitable mode of expression, Irele demonstrates how it has become the pivot of a whole range of contemporary African forms of textual expression. Two of his essays in the volume particularly illustrate this view.

Chinua Achebe's *Things Fall Apart* is essentially a subversion of not only a metropolitical worldview but also its mode of signification and language.[55] His recontextualisation of Igbo proverbs and habits of speech within a metropolitan language (English) and frame of reference, the conflation of forms to be found within an oral culture and textual culture created a distinctive literary practice all by themselves and Irele traces the trajectory of this mode of creation together with its lingering impact on African literature.

Also, his essay, 'Study in Ambiguity: Amadou Hampaté Bâ's *The Fortunes of Wangrin*' explores the dilemma of the colonial/postcolonial subject in period of disruptive transition. In this essay, Irele explains the nature of Hampaté Bâ's distinctive genius in traversing the seemingly unbridgeable divide between orality and textuality. Hampaté Bâ begins his text by drawing on the epic traditions of the griots of West Africa which he blends ingeniously with traditions derived from Western textuality. The end result is the creation of an entirely novel mode of discourse. In his mind, Bâ's work, 'produces what by normal canons of judgement would be considered a mixed and even indeterminate genre of the narrative.'[56] Irele demonstrates why this very indeterminacy is the source of the work's most remarkable attributes. In a situation whereby a long established tribal culture is under assault from colonial incursion, new beings, discourses and commodities emerge from the transitional phase. And this transitional phase with all its swift and sudden cultural reversals, the rapid upturning of established tables of values creates room for the most pronounced kind of opportunism, a situation where anything goes.

Indeed some of Africa's most accomplished literary artists have been able to trace the beginnings of socio-political anomie in the continent that offer far more kaleidoscopic images of regression than the theoretical formulations of numerous social scientists. But the failures in the political field may also have affected the visionary gifts of some African literary artists as Irele seems to suggest in the final essay in the volume, 'Parables of the African Condition: The New Realism in African Fiction'. In this essay, Irele turns his critical lens on Kofi Awoonor's *This Earth My Brother*, Yambo Ouologuem's *Bound to Violence* and Wole Soyinka's *Season of Anomy*. Interestingly, Irele is very much concerned with the socio-political conditions under which African texts are produced and how this relates to the question of ideological development. For instance, his chapter on J. P. Clark-Bekederemo discusses extensively the colonial situation and the configuration of historical forces that gave rise to the emergence of modern Nigerian literature. As a piece of cultural criticism, it portrays the personal and collective points of departures together with the structural limitations (both internal and external) that the modern Nigerian literary artist had to surmount in attaining discursive agency and independence. Figures like Chinua Achebe, J. P. Clark-Bekederemo, Christopher Okigbo and Wole Soyinka are the primal exemplars of this socio-aesthetic matrix.

To return to the perplexing homology between literature and politics; Awoonor, Ouologuem and Soyinka in various ways and with differing degrees of success attempt to deal with the growing failure African nation-states were generally experiencing in the political field. And in their various novelistic efforts, the degradation of African political existence seems to have adversely affected their artistic insights. In Irele's view, Ouologuem's *Bound to Violence* does not merit the lofty reputation it enjoys (Appiah for instance wrote a generally positive critique of it in *In My Father's House* (1992) which undoubtedly would boost its canonical status within the African literary archive) because of what he attributes to a 'shallow sensibility.' Similarly, Irele writes regarding Soyinka; 'If, […] *Season of Anomy* fails to satisfy, it is primarily because it does not offer a cogent elucidation of its ostensible political theme. Further, coming from a writer whose dramatic works convey so vivid a sense of specific life, the vagueness of the novel's references—as indeed the inadequate organization of the elements of the narrative—cannot but appear as something of a disappointing performance.'[57]

Irele's book highlights at many moments the tension between the adoption of high theoretical discourse and the vocation of the traditional literary critic as popularised by figures such as F. R. Leavis. His positionality within the U.S. academy definitely necessitates the pursuit of the work of theory or theory as work. Perhaps it can hardly be any other way. But this discursive tension reaches into the body of African textuality where the text as inscribed and constructed in the frame of modernity has a relatively short history. And so this specific mode of (inter)textuality, this mutual engagement and disengagement of both oral and textual forms of expression within the same nexus is essentially constituted along the margins of high theory where the reproduction of texts by texts has been a predominant principle. However, the resolution of this tension can be obtained when the reproduction of texts by texts in Africa becomes a continuous and well established event. Irele's work can also be read as sustained meditation on this discursive dilemma, that is, the problem of producing inscripted discourse within a context of severe epistemic contradictions and reduced collective agency.

One would have to conclude by stating that the *African Imagination* and the quintessential products of African creativity that Irele makes his concerns elicit comforting value in circumstances where the nature of African politics destroys the subjects whose development it is supposed to aid. In other words, when life fails, turn to art.

Having said that, Irele's discursive trajectory raises some crucial theoretical issues which have been alluded to; the orality/textuality dichotomy. Jean-François Lyotard in *The Postmodern Condition* (1984) differentiates between the types of knowledge generated by pre-capitalist societies and post-industrial cultures. The computerisation of existence in post-Fordist societies has entailed the development of a complex network of institutions to produce, classify and disseminate knowledge. Undoubtedly, the individual within this intricate network of institutions and mechanisms of knowledge plays a much more circumscribed role.

On the other hand, knowledge generated by tribal cultures adopts a much different trajectory in the sense that the mechanisms for its transmission are now mostly devalued. Manthia Diawara in his article, 'The Song of the Griot' analyses how the logic of the global economy has evidently led to the commodification of what had previously been a sacred calling but also perhaps caused a devaluation of its historic import. The vocation of the griot as other forms of historico-aesthetic expression such as fuji and juju music forms in Nigeria has succumbed to the imperatives of monetisation. Irele's discussion of orality does not dwell on this development. Rather, it recuperates what is most noble in oral forms of artistic expression and focuses on how these attributes have been crucial to the formation of modern African literature. His analyses of the works of Chinua Achebe, Hampaté Bâ and Wole Soyinka emphasise how the element of orality is indeed central for understanding the unquestioned distinctiveness of their most ground-breaking works.

Now this epistemological stance introduces a new paradoxical twist in Irele's thought. In his previous essays, (see his augural lecture delivered at the University of Ibadan and published in 1987) Irele had argued for the need for the African postcolony to avail itself of the gains of Western modernity.

In embracing the forms of alienation engendered by the disruptive event of colonialism, the African subject's choice is not unique in world history after all human cultures are never completely independent and continue to borrow from each other. This stance generated a lot of debate in African intellectual circles.

Irele has now emerged from that cycle of thought in which he now posits a form of Africanity that has emerged not from a self-absorbed contemplation of the numerous failures in the political field but from a studied interest in the restorative qualities of oral culture as typified by the achievements of Chinua Achebe and Amadou Hampaté Bâ. This opening, this point of entry, points out a way for talking about Africa outside the embarrassing field of politics, within the circumference of a barely identified margin, of acting and speaking on behalf of the continent with an appreciable sense of dignity.

In addition, Irele's recontextualisation of orality/textuality axis obviously forces us to rethink the notion of the author. In his famous essay, 'What is an Author?', Michel Foucault explores the various historical biographies of the author-function. Texts and authors, he argues are defined by specific contextual circumstances. The author-function mode to be found in the constitution of religious texts is different from the one that exists within the scientific community or the artistic field. By extension, texts and authors are in part the inventions of specific fields of activity. Roland Barthes in an equally famous article, 'The Death of the Author' suggests that the diminution of the role of the author is the result of the reader gaining more freedom and autonomy. These views have had a significant impact on poststructuralist theorising. The contextual impasse faced by the author within the Western episteme is markedly different from the kind faced by the postcolonial author.

In the postcolonial milieu, confronted with the silence generated the oppressive architecture of metropolitan modes of expression (*langue*), the postcolonial author either retreats further into the abyss of silence or adopts a form of broken speech (*parole*) which marks the beginning of his insertion into the margins of modernity. It also inaugurates his struggles with the ever present orality/textuality. Irele's contemplation of the orality/textuality matrix has re-established the uniqueness of a particular kind of author. In this way, the Machiavellian silence caused by the trauma of the colonial event is set aside for the proliferation of expressive forms that facilely subvert the centre/periphery distinction in its conventional formation. Silence thus provides multiple opportunities for expressive/explosive freedoms.

Post-Structuralism and Two Third World Arguments

The subalternity of the Third World is not in doubt. The position in which most post-colonials find themselves is certainly not entirely of their own making.

True, all around the subaltern subject are structures of repression and effects of impotence. Nonetheless, agency is never totally absent. But instead of our bemoaning this plight, new structures of negotiation are required to make any meaningful headway in the areas that matter: political, intellectual, cultural, economic, and so on. In other words, new agential spaces have to be found or created. But structures of negotiation are never easy to create. And this seemingly unsolvable problematic is my major preoccupation at this juncture. How does the periphery, that is, the marginal, negotiate with the apparent monologism of Euro-American centrism? How are new subjectivities brought into being in spite of circumscribed and delimiting agential spaces? In other words, how does the subaltern speak?—following the *problematique* Gayatri Spivak has put before us.

Here, I attempt to do an unusual thing, which is to bring into conversation Niyi Osundare's critique of post-structuralism with—one would hope—the rather illuminating insights provided by Gayatri Spivak. I am not merely attempting to use Osundare's position as a lever for promoting Spivak's ideas, rather I want to raise to the fore, the seemingly pervasive spectre of the postcolonial condition and how it structures and delimits the means for agential and discursive action. I want to try to suggest that agency is never totally lacking, indeed agency is always possible and present. I also want to highlight the multiple ways in which the postcolonial reproduces its customary dialectic together with its agential binarisms repeatedly, changing the contexts of its appearance but not quite its powers of seduction and capacities for violence.

First of all, Niyi Osundare's response towards the issue of post-structuralist theorising is a somewhat updated if oblique version of the kind that the three controversial Nigerian literary critics Chinweizu, Jemie and Madubuike launched in *Towards the Decolonisation of African Literature* (1980) on the so-called Western inspired African writers. The arguments of Osundare and the troika, as they are often collectively called, are decidedly strident in their criticisms of Eurocentricism. In philosophical discourse, it is a species of discourse Hountondji would regard as ethnophilosophy.[58] In the social sciences, it would be regarded as a discourse of nativism.[59]

Indeed the monograph that best articulates Osundare's position in relation to post-structuralism is *African Literature and the Crisis of Post-structuralist Theorising* (1993). This monograph is important for several reasons. As mentioned earlier, it typifies a pre-emptory response to Euro-American ethnocentrism and cultural imperialism. But its ultimate usefulness as a theoretic pragmatics ends there. If Osundare accuses Western theory of undue universalism, then his own critique of it does not provide a convincing alternative and constitutes an instance of what Appiah would term reverse racism.

From the very first paragraph, Osundare's frustration with Western theory is clear:

> There is also talk about the "post humanist" era, though we hope in all earnestness that the "post human" society would never arrive.[60]

However, when viewed through the morphology of classical literary criticism, Osundare's reading of the issue exhibits several grave shortcomings. For instance, he says:

> We would be hard-put to tell specifically when "post-structuralism" began—the time and place it was born, its progenitors, its birth–weight, the attending midwives, etc. This is why, despite the several claimants to its originary authorship, we still find it difficult to say in unmistakable terms who the "founders" of post-structuralism were, or, are. There is an inevitable fuzziness, even indeterminacy, about these things which theories of the "post" variety are often too hasty to admit.[61]

Before we proceed, let us contemplate Osundare's apprehension of the arrival of what could be described in Foucauldian terms a post-human era. Michel Foucault's declaration concerning the end of man was and is still easily misconstrued. Foucault's point is that the concept of man is always subject to historical constructions that is, man, 'was a constructed historical concept peculiar to a certain order of discourse, and not a timelessly self-evident principle capable of founding human rights or a universal ethics.'[62] Also, it is important to note that Foucault 'maintained a particularly rigorous commitment [engagement] to a revision of the status of prisoners, and devoted to this the whole of his immense talent as an organizer and an agitator.'[63] In other words, Osundare's notions of what constitutes a 'post- human era' amount to a conceptual misunderstanding in relation to its Foucauldian trope. This point is reaffirmed because it could be easily misconstrued in a postcolonial context where Western notions of humanism (but where they are not often historicised) have a powerful appeal in articulating a wide range of civic positions ranging from confrontations with totalitarianism to the agitations of solidarity networks to build basic institutions of democracy.[64]

Indeed, anyone remotely familiar with recent history of Western theoretical orientations would immediately notice the inaccuracies of those assertions, for example, concerning the supposedly unknown founders of post-structuralism. Furthermore, Osundare does not do enough to understand what exactly the theoretical presuppositions he attacks mean. In short, he frequently conflates post-structuralism and post-coloniality.

Having raised those serious shortcomings in Osundare's critique, it becomes necessary to see if there is indeed a way out of the Third World's subalternity. In this regard, Osundare makes a curiously incomplete reference to Gayatri Spivak's question, 'What is an indigenous theory?'[65] The incompleteness of his response becomes even more troubling when a fuller reading of Spivak is undertaken. Despite criticisms from many quarters about her alleged attachments to Western theory 'Spivak claims not to be interested in proposing an overarching theory either of colonial discourse or of a singular postcolonial text.'[66] Spivak has also been important in the way Said was to opening up the US academy to postcolonial and area studies generally. [67] In spite of the marked discontinuities that are to be discerned in the projects of Third World decolonisation, there are several instances when the very logic of cultural imperialism unifies those discontinuities by the force of its levelling hegemonism. In this regard, the constant tussle between the universal and the particular is never even.

The first major impulse for a Third World subject is to seek active integration into the 'centre', or to construct one that accommodates him/her, that is, to resist any temptation in favour of self-marginalisation. To a certain extent, Osundare is able to accomplish this only for his efforts in the final analysis to be marred by a grave epistemological inconsistency. Take an aspect of the politics that attends his discourse, for example. *African Literature and the Crisis of Post-Structuralist Theorising* was published in a Third World context and is imbued with a pronounced pseudo-revolutionary fervour that many African ethnocentrists would find most appealing. So we find him making a large gesture in this direction and then of course there is the other 'side' (taken to mean the west) to appease or address as the case may be.

This form of appeasement entails an insertion into the jargon of Western critical theory and in spite of a strident Afrocentricism or in spite of the vehement protestations about Western ignorance of African textual morphologies and fields of experience, this insertion obstructs or displaces the earlier one which nods towards an African readership. The insertion into Western theoretical tropes also has its roots in a now common Western textual phenomenon. There is a famous deconstructionist maxim that says you cannot get outside the language of what you intend to critique. As Spivak describes it: 'Deconstruction can only speak in the language of the thing it criticises. So Derrida says, it falls prey to its own critique.'[68] Thus in addressing the issue of African alienation from the perspective of Western critical theory, another equally grave *problematique* that Osundare completely ignores bares itself. He takes for granted the very language and the theoretical presuppositions he employs in his own critique. What this also means is that he has a rather narrow view of post-structuralist theorising.

Let us now return to the question of Third World subjects availing themselves of indigenous theories. More precisely, it would be pertinent to point out how Spivak takes on the indigenous theory question which Osundare raises in his own monograph, if only in an elliptical and partial manner. Indeed, to follow Osundare in this crucial area can only turn out to be a false lead. Spivak was asked, 'What are the possibilities of discovering/promoting indigenous theory?'[69] She replies:

> To construct indigenous theories one must ignore the last few centuries of historical involvement. I would rather use what history has written for me. I am not interested in defending the post-colonial intellectuals' dependence on Western models; my work lies in making clear my disciplinary predicament. My position is generally a reactive one. I am viewed by the Marxists as too codic, by feminists as too male-identified, by indigenous theories as too committed to Western Theory.[70]

In this way, we get a much clear picture of what Osundare fails to demonstrate in relation to Spivak's qualifications. Instead, he continues to follow the beaten track made famous by the likes of the troika of Chinweizu et. al., whose heightened ethnocentrism is the only way for them to make one's disciplinary predicament obvious and to reveal the power of a very particularistic form of identity politics. It also demonstrates that the existing logic of discourses of nativism which haven't advanced very far.[71] And this in turn does not do us much good. The models of indigenous theory that many Third World ethnocentrists have been clamouring for have not emerged. An insightful account and critique of the current wave of the discourse of nativism in Africa was made thus; 'whether it concerns the "political" or the "cultural" discourses on African Renaissance and Ubuntu, the key to fruitful use of these concepts seems to lie in critical debate and creative elaboration of African traditions. Here a "renaissance" is called for in a specific sense. In the European renaissance period the ambition of culture-makers was not to simply reinstate classical values, classical themes and classical ideals, but to surpass them. The promise of an African Renaissance may lie not in a fixation on African heritages as such, but in the ambition to re-appropriate them critically and creatively and so surpass them.'[72] This clamour may be described as 'the glamour of ethnos'.[73] In academic discourse, the anthropological devaluation of the ethnosciences—ethnobotany, ethnozoology, ethnobiology, ethnomineralogy, ethnodemography and ethnolinguistics—as primitive or precolonial knowledges is well known. In fact, the politics of indigenisation has been adopted by politicians and demagogues in many parts of the African continent and transformed into a platform of the most virulent form of anti-intellectualism and xenophobia, which in turn have destroyed virtually all progressive human structures: political, social, cultural, economic, technological and educational. For instance, 'by appealing to Zairians to be themselves, and to reclaim a threatened cultural identity, the "philosophy of authenticity", the state's official doctrine, managed to reduce this identity to its most superficial and abjectly folkloristic level'.[74]

Thus the politics of indigenisation has made irrelevant its intellectual vanguard of which Osundare is a part. Osundare's stance on the question of indigenous theory offers no ready alternatives. The irony is that he stands in undeniable opposition to the totalitarianism of the state, which espouses the ideology of indigenisation if only for propagandistic purposes. For the intellectual caught in this sort of position, the next move ought to be a further problematisation of seemingly irreconcilable scenarios to see if viable options emerge, instead of striving to provide support for an ideology completely vulgarised by the most traumatic kind of authoritarianism. Several Third World intellectuals have not addressed this new angle and have been cut off from a discourse some of them literally built their careers upon. Given the dire political circumstances of postcolony, a more painstaking re-examination of the indigenisation theory is required. There is certainly a significant political dimension to the politics of indigenisation that cannot be ignored or suppressed in a facile manner by the Third World intellectual. This is because indigenisation has been deployed by authoritarian systems to legitimise mediocrity in the realm of culture, corruption and authoritarianism on the part of the state, and to vulgarise the ethos of civil society.

In view of this unacceptable situation, the need to develop an alternative strategy becomes paramount. There is no doubt that the entire dialectic of indigenisation has reached a crisis point wrought by serious political problems. Even if we choose to exclude this important political register, that is, if we elect to restrict the debate within the limits of theory, it will be seen that we are faced with yet another almost insurmountable conceptual aporia. The ethnicisation of discourse also implies a generalised denial of history and a negation of the event of colonialism and its numerous phenomena, both social and textual. In effect, it entails a new theoretical starting point, which most ethnocentrists have been unable to negotiate successfully. To comprehend the extent of this chronic difficulty, we have noted how Abiola Irele presents a graphic description of the colonial encounter and the massive discontinuities it brought in its wake.[75]

Politics of indigenisation, philosophies of authencity, concepts of African Renaissance are all forms of what has been termed camp-thinking. To avoid the pitfalls of camp-thinking, a 'good understanding of the antitoxins that can be discovered and celebrated in crossing cultures – mixing and moving between – provide important resources which today's postcolonial peoples will require if we are to weather the storms ahead.'[76]

Hence, the kind of epistemic rupture 'ethnocentrists of discourse' are advancing is not entirely tenable, because the event of colonialism maintains such a centrality in the existence of all formerly colonised peoples as to invalidate the more extreme forms of romantic glorifications of the African past. Also, 'the concept of postmodernity might provide a useful supplementary means to mark the irretrievable loss of that innocence in truth-seeking and history-writing for which the histories of blacks and Jews in the modern world provide the best, that is the most inhumane, examples.'[77] Just as with deconstruction, the critique of cultural imperialism often falls prey to the language of imperialism that it hopes to subvert, since post-coloniality is in several aspects continuous with colonialism. To trace the lines of any sharp rupture or to delineate the face of any irreconcilable contrast is a great oversimplification.

It is interesting to note that Osundare, like so many ethnocentrists of discourse, is unable to advance beyond the more apparent limits of his critique. What he does instead is to find instances of racism in European texts dealing with the African continent. For example, Osundare writes:

> Rosmarin's reader-response criticism of *Heart of Darkness* is a clear demonstration of the fundamental ethnocentrism of most of post-structuralist theorising, its several blindednesses, and pitfalls; and, in particular of the new metaphysics of readerly power and authority.[78]

Perhaps the aim should not be to unduly privilege any particular reading; in other words, to make any apprehension of a text foundationalist and, in fact, deconstructionist principles warn against the dangers of universalising specific readings of texts; every reading should be tentative, an opportunity to be critical and to maintain vigilance. So for those who are dissatisfied with certain readings there is always the avenue of offering fresh versions.

But there is still the fundamental problem of moving out of the impasse created by the ethnicisation of discourse. This is where the work of Spivak becomes immensely liberating. Spivak reminds us of how the texts of Marx are different from the history of Marxism, which is largely the creation of Marxists and post-Marxists. By extension, the history of Marxism has been put to uses beyond the original intents of Marx's texts and has been made to serve all sorts of local and specific struggles as well as histories. In the process, something other than Marx's texts has been produced. So the problem of misreading or recontextualising texts is not limited to the Third World alone. Texts are used for criticism and action. What then should be our concern is how we are able to generate enough vigilance so as to be sufficiently critical.

Spivak offers yet another example of how even the most enlightened minds could do wanton injustice to texts:

> Habermas makes a lot of sense in the history of the West German political context. He makes a mistake by universalising it. He also makes a mistake by confronting Derrida, whose project is discontinuous with his. How does he do it? By trivialising and canonizing a kind of disciplinary subdivision of labour, in his latest essay, *The Philosophical Discourse of Modernism*, where he chides Derrida because Derrida is not honouring the disciplinary prerogatives of philosophy and literature as they have developed in the European academy since the eighteenth century.[79]

Spivak's criticism of Habermas should not be taken as an uncritical acceptance of deconstructionist morphology. In this regard, she says:

> For a time I felt ferociously angry with deconstruction because Derrida seemed not to be enough of a Marxist. He also seemed to be a sexist. But that's because I was wanting deconstruction to be what it isn't. I realised its value by recognising its limits—by not asking it to do everything for me. I no longer feel that I've got to go out and bat for it in every field. I have very little patience with people who are so deeply into deconstruction that they have nothing else to think about.[80]

Most of the time, the value of critical theory is diminished by its ardent foot soldiers, just as some of the disciples of Nietzsche have put his work to monstrous uses. But this inevitable occurrence should not discourage us from recognising the virtues of critical theory. In a not too disparate connection, Osundare's fear is that:

> Many aspects of post-structuralist theorising have made the humanization of discourse impossible, as a result of the fetishization of the text and its theory.[81]

Then there is an instance when he says, 'misconceptions have not been deconstructed',[82] thereby himself employing a decidedly post-structuralist register. Obviously, Osundare misunderstands a lot of post-structuralist theorising, of which deconstruction is just a 'movement' to employ, in this case a rather awkward term. Citing Derrida, Spivak informs us 'deconstruction is not the exposure of error, it is a vigilance about the fact that we are always obliged to produce truth'.[83] In several instances, Osundare's positionality as an interrogating subject is obscured and one is forced to ask over and over again, to whom does he speak? To be sure, this is a shortcoming he needs to address in a more distinct fashion.

For a postcolonial subject to reach some kind of active accommodation with Euro-American centricism, she/he must discover a way to be "critical", as Spivak argues, and this is important, since we inhabit 'a post-colonial, neo-colonised world'.[84] Nevertheless being "critical" is not the same as pulling down the canons of Western critical theory for the sake of some indigenous theory. The path to what an indigenous theory means is still as nebulous as ever, and the limits of this approach becomes even more evident. To confront the problem of postcolonial theorising in a postmodern milieu, Spivak's approach is simply 'interrupting and "bring to crises" the uncritical edges of totalizing knowledge.'[85]

Having said that, it can be concluded that Osundare's position demonstrates a delimiting theoretical phobia, equivalent to the kind of phobia a Third World subject has towards modern technology, but even more disturbingly, it could serve to foreclose further discursity. We may then pose the question; what mode of textuality does Osundare propose? His position on this is not clearly defined. Certainly Osundare does not appreciate post-structuralist readings of texts. Finally, he does not interrogate the position of post-coloniality from the numerous perspectives such a position must engender. Spivak, on her own part, problematises the position of the post-colonial subject and the disruptive transformations that occur, in addition to offering acceptable post-structuralist textual readings.

It is clear that transversing the theoretical divide between the First and Third World requires discursive sophistication and flexibility, as demonstrated by theorists such as Edward Said, Stuart Hall, Henry Louis Gates, Paul Gilroy, Gayatri Spivak and Abiola Irele. The theoretical problems of Third World subjects in relation to the First World, as raised by Wiredu's project of conceptual decolonisation, demand far more ingenuity than any simplistic binarism can produce.

Notes

1. Ngugi wa Thiong'o, *Moving the Centre*, London, James Currey, 1993, p. 42.
2. Ibid. p. 50.
3. David Hume, cited by Ngugi wa Thiong'o in *Writers in Politics*, Nairobi, Heinemann Educational Books Ltd., 1981, p. 14.
4. Hegel, cited by Wole Soyinka in his Nobel Prize Acceptance Lecture, 1986, and published in A. Maja-Pearce, ed., *Wole Soyinka: An Appraisal*, Oxford, Heinemann, 1994, p. 14.
5. Ibid.
6. See Sven Lindquist, *Exterminate all the Brutes*, trans. Joan Tate, New York, The New Press, 1996, and Paul Gilroy, *Against Race: Imagining Political Culture Beyond the Color Line*, Cambridge, Harvard University Press, 2000.

7. See Jean Amery, *At the Mind's Limits: Contemplations by a Survivor on Auschwitz,* trans. Sidney and Stella P. Rosenfeld, Bloomington, Indiana University Press, 1980.

8. Edward Said, 'Crisis (in orientalism)', in David Lodge, ed., *Modern Criticism and Theory: A Reader,* London and New York, Longman, 1988, p. 279.

9. Edward Said, 'Orientalism' in B. Ashcroft et al, ed., *The Post-Colonial Studies Reader,* London and New York, Routledge, 1995, p. 87.

10. Ibid. p. 90.

11. Homi Bhabha, 'Signs Taken for Wonders' in B. Ashcroft et al, ed., *The Post-Colonial Studies Reader,* London and New York: Routledge, 1995, pp. 34-35.

12. Gayatri Spivak, 'Can the Subaltern Speak?' in B. Ashcroft et al, ed., *The Post-Colonial Studies Reader,* London and New York, Routledge, 1995, p. 25.

13. Olakunle George, *Relocating Agency: Modernity and African Letters,* New York: State University of New York Press, 2003, p. 60.

14. Benita Parry, 'Problems in Current Theories of Colonial Discourse' in *The Post-Colonial Studies Reader* ed. B. Ashcroft, London and New York, Routledge, 1995, p. 43.

15. Samir Amin, *Eurocentricism,* London, Zed Books, 1989, pp. 101–102.

16. Edward Said, *Culture and Imperialism,* London, Vintage, 1994, p. xii.

17. Homi K. Bhabha, 'The Other Question: Difference, Discrimination and the Discourse of Colonialism', in Russell Ferguson et al. eds., *Out There: Marginalization and Contemporary Cultures,* New York, Cambridge and London, The New Museum of Contemporary Art and MIT Press, 1990, p. 76.

18. Anne McClintock, *Imperial Leather: Race, Gender and Sexuality in the Colonial Conquest,* New York and London, Routledge, 1995, p. 45.

19. Stuart Hall, 'The Meaning of New Times', in David Morley and Kuan-Hsing Chen, eds., Introduction to *Stuart Hall: Critical Dialogues in Cultural Studies,* London and New York, Routledge, 1996, p. 224.

20. Ibid. p. 226.

21. Ibid. pp. 227-8.

22. Ibid.

23. 'On Postmodernism and Articulation', an interview with Stuart Hall edited by Lawrence Crossberg in *Stuart Hall, Critical Dialogues in Cultural Studies* eds., D. Morley and K. Chen, London and New York, Routledge, 1996, p. 150.

24. D. Morley and K. Chen, 'Introduction' to *Stuart Hall: Critical Dialogues in Cultural Studies,* 1996, p. 8.

25. Ibid. p. 10.

26. Ibid. p. 17.

27. Ibid. p. 20.

28. Ibid.

29. Paul Gilroy, 'Route Work: The Black Atlantic and the Politics of Exile' in *The Post-Colonial Question* eds. Chambers and Curti, London and New York, Routledge, 1996, p. 22.

30. Ibid. p. 23.

31. Ibid. p. 24.

32. See, *In My Father's House: Africa in the Philosophy of Culture*, New York, Oxford University Press, 1992.

33. See his *Against Race: Imagining Political Culture Beyond the Color Line*, Cambridge, Harvard University Press, 2000.

34. For a recent theorisation of this point, see Alain Badiou, *Ethics: An Essay on the Understanding of Evil*, trans. Peter Hallward, London and New York, Verso, 2001.

35. Paul Gilroy, *Against Race: Imagining Political Culture Beyond the Color Line,* Cambridge, Harvard University Press, 2000, p. 53.

36. See Phillipe-Joseph Salazar, *An African Athens: Rhetoric and the Shaping of Democracy in South Africa,* London and New Jersey, Lawrence Erlbaum Associates, 2002.

37. Fortunately, scholars such as Anthony Kwame Appiah and Achille Mbembe are seriously working on various discursive possibilities to achieve this end.

38. Henry, Louis Gates, Jr., *Loose Canons: Notes on the Culture Wars,* New York and Oxford, Oxford University Press, 1992, p. 60.

39. Ibid. p. 61.

40. Ibid. p. 69.

41. Ibid. p. 79.

42. 'Editorial: The Mazrui-Gates Debate', *AfricanUpdate*, Vol. VII, Issue 1, (Winter 2000) http://www.ccsu.edu/afstudy/updtWin2k.htm

43. Ali Mazrui, 'Black Orientalism? Further Reflections on "Wonders of the African World"' *AfricanUpdate*, Vol. VII, Issue 1 (Winter 2000), http://www.ccsu.edu/afstudy/updtWin, 2k.htm

44. Henry Louis Gates Jr., 'A Preliminary Response to Ali Mazrui's Preliminary Critique of "Wonders of the African World,"' *AfricanUpdate*, Vol. VII, Issue 1, (Winter 2000), http://www.ccsu.edu/afstudy/updtWin, 2k.htm

45. Ibid. p. 73.

46. Some conventional African philosophers may disagree with this view. But I would rather argue that there is a certain systematicity in Irele's work. For example, his first published book, *The African Experience in Literature and Ideology*, Bloomington, Indiana University Press, 1990, is a consistent thematisation of the struggles for textual articulation and representation in modern African literary criticism and the politics of identity and epistemic counter-violence in postcolonial Africa. In this way, his work goes beyond being just of a piece of culture critique. It is instead, an articula-

tion of an African textual presence and also an ideological reflection on the reasons for such an articulation.

47. Paulin Hountondji, *The Struggle for Meaning: Reflections on Philosophy, Culture and Democracy in Africa,* 2002, p. 232.

48. Abiola Irele, 'The African Imagination' in *Research in African Literatures,* Vol. 26, No. 1, Spring, 1995, p. 56.

49. Olusegun Oladipo, *The Idea of African Philosophy,* Ibadan, Molecular Publishers, 1991, p. 92.

50. Ibid.

51. Abiola Irele, *In Praise of Alienation,* inaugural lecture delivered in 1982 and published privately, Ibadan, 1987, p. 15.

52. D. Morley and K. Chen, 'Introduction' to *Stuart Hall, Critical Dialogues in Cultural Studies,* 1996, p. 14.

53. Abiola Irele, *In Praise of Alienation,* 1987, p. 30.

54. Ibid. p. 31.

55. At a more specific level, it can be read as a creative as well as epistemic rewriting of texts such as Joseph Conrad's *Heart of Darkness,* New York and London, W. W. Norton, 1988.

56. Abiola Irele, *The African Imagination: Literature in Africa and the Black Diaspora,* New York, Oxford University Press, 2001, p. 86.

57. Ibid. p. 233.

58. See Paulin Hountondji, *African Philosophy: Myth and Reality,* Bloomington, Indiana University Press, 1996 and also his *The Struggle for Meaning: Reflections on Philosophy, Culture, and Democracy in Africa,* Athens, Ohio University Center for International Studies, 2002.

59. See Achille Mbembe, 'Ways of Seeing: Beyond the New Nativism', *African Studies Review,* Vol. 44, No. 2, 2001 and also his "African Modes of Self-Writing", *Public Culture,* 36, 2002.

60. Niyi Osundare, *African Literature and the Crisis of Post-Structuralist Theorising,* Ibadan, Option Books and Information Services, 1993, p. 1.

61. Ibid. p. 2.

62. Alain Badiou, *Ethics: An Essay on the Understanding of Evil,* New York and London, Verso, 2001, p. 5.

63. Niyi Osundare, *African Literature and the Crisis of Post-Structuralist Theorising,* Ibadan, Option Books and Information Services, 1993, p. 6.

64. Wole Soyinka says in a famous quote of his, 'justice is the first condition of humanity', see his prison memoirs *The Man Died,* London, Penguin, 1972 and a more recent volume, *The Burden of Memory, The Muse of Forgiveness,* New York, Oxford University Press, 1999.

65. Gayatri Spivak, *The Post-colonial Critic: Interviews, Strategies, Dialogues,* London and New York, Routledge, 1989, p. 135.

66. Olakunle George, *Relocating Agency: Modernity and African Letters*, 2003, p. 63.

67. On this point see her book, *Outside in the Teaching Machine*, New York and London, Routledge, 1993.

68. Gayatri Spivak, *The Post-colonial Critic: Interviews, Strategies, Dialogues,* London and New York, Routledge, 1990, p. 69.

69. Ibid.

70. Ibid.

71. Discourses of nativism continue to emerge, perhaps the most famous of the new kinds is the concept of an African Renaissance and Ubuntu Philosophy which rose out of the ideologies of black empowerment in post-apartheid South Africa. Indeed, Julius Nyerere's Ujamaa in some respects constitutes an earlier and perhaps also more sophisticated variant of the discourse of nativism. On these specific issues, see *QUEST: An African Journal of Philosophy,* Vol. XV, No. 1-2, 2001 which is a special issue on African Renaissance and Ubuntu Philosophy.

72. Pieter Boele van Henbroek, Introduction, *QUEST: An African Journal of Philosophy,* Vol. XV, No. 1-2, 2001, p. 7.

73. Paul Gilroy, *Against Race: Imagining Political Culture Beyond the Color Line,* 2000, p. 96.

74. Paulin Hountondji, *The Struggle for Meaning: Reflections on Philosophy, Culture and Democracy in Africa*, 2002, p. 112.

75. See his inaugural lecture, *In Praise of Alienation* 1987, pp. 1-36.

76. Paul Gilroy, *Against Race: Imagining Political Culture Beyond the Color Line,* 2000, p. 93.

77. Ibid. p. 96.

78. Niyi Osundare, *African Literature and the Crisis of Post-Structuralist Theorising,* 1993, p. 13.

79. Gayatri Spivak, *The Post-colonial Critic: Interviews, Strategies, Dialogues,* 1989, p. 111.

80. Ibid. pp. 33-134.

81. Niyi Osundare, *African Literature and the Crisis of Post-Structuralist Theorising,* 1993, p. 10.

82. Ibid.

83. Gayatri Spivak, *The Post-colonial Critic: Interviews, Strategies, Dialogues,* 1989, p. 12.

84. Ibid. p. 166.

85. Olakunle George, *Relocating Agency: Modernity and African Letters*, 2003, p. 63.

2

Weapons of Victimage:
Decolonisation as Critical Discourse

Rodney and Fanon: A Dialogue

Fanon's strong words, though excessively Manichean, still describe the feelings and thoughts between the occupying British Army and colonised Irish in Northern Ireland, the occupying Israeli Army and subjugated Palestinians on the West Bank and Gaza Strip, the South African Army and oppressed Black South Africans in the townships, the Japanese Police and Koreans living in Japan, the Russian Army and subordinated Armenians and others in Southern and Eastern USSR. His words also partly invoke the sense many Black Americans have toward police departments in urban centres. In other words, Fanon is articulating century long heartfelt human responses to being degraded and despised, hated and hunted, oppressed and exploited, marginalised and dehumanised at the hands of powerful xenophobic European, American, Russian and Japanese imperial countries.[1]

In the concluding segment of the previous chapter, I brought Niyi Osundare into conversation with Gayatri Spivak in order to advance some views regarding post-structuralism and Third World positionalities. This chapter similarly begins with a conversation between Walter Rodney and Frantz Fanon.

Fanon and Rodney were both concerned with the future of Africa but from somewhat disparate perspectives. Here, I argue, if only tentatively, that Fanon does more to transcend the limitation of his time and text. Rodney on the other hand is more or less solely preoccupied with presenting the historical imperatives that led to the underdevelopment of the African continent. The point, though is, an historical excursus on Africa may indeed also address itself to the future, something Rodney's text does not quite succeed in doing in spite of the immense possibilities of doing so.

Africa is widely known to be the poorest continent in the world and this discouraging position compels us to constantly re-evaluate what efforts Third World theorists and researchers have made from colonial times to the present to address this unfortunate state of affairs.[2] During the colonial era and the period immediately after the attainment of independence, engaging theoretical postulations regarding the African developmental quest were advanced. Indeed it could be argued that at the time there was greater ideological experimentation and perhaps confidence than what followed after the general euphoria surrounding the advent of independence.[3] Since it may be affirmed that 'the end of ideology' syndrome is also noticeable within the African context, even as the same problems regarding the continent's development persist, we may revisit the entire issue again with the hope that new ways of understanding might emerge.

Our analyses of the two primary texts in question, Walter Rodney's *How Europe Underdeveloped Africa* and Frantz Fanon's *The Wretched of the Earth* focus on the different ways in which they articulate black subjectivity and their momentary limitations. One would have to call them momentary, because any consideration of underdevelopment ought to be addressed within the framework of developmental potential. In other words, while a nation may be underdeveloped today, it does not preclude the eventuality of development in the future. Furthermore, within the confines of that conjectural space another *problematique* arises which may be formulated thus: how has eventual development occurred if it does truly occur? Or how have the truths of the texts corresponded with the trajectories or histories of actual development? These are questions that do not immediately lie within the scope of this discussion. Another interesting point is that both theorists of decolonisation/ underdevelopment discussed here, in a bid to find a catharsis for their wholly justified anger, are unable to avoid venturing into the field of pure conjecture, of metaphysics, as it were. They are both naturally implicated in the type of discourse (that is, the counter-violence Fanon so eloquently theorises) the bondsman vents against the monolith of domination. Also in instances, especially in Rodney's text, anger becomes an emotion of pure rebellion.[4] But as I have remarked, this can be regarded as natural, considering the urgent demands on the theorists, both conceptual and practical.

This reading of Rodney does not intend to be exhaustive because as with any text, we are compelled to interpret it in as many ways as possible. We have to sift through its multiple layers of meaning and discursive possibilities in the light of how new realities are revealed to us, and within those as yet undecided limits, we are bound to discover that our construct of the transcendental signified (in relation to the text), or the archaeology on which we situate our understanding of the text, will of necessity remain indeterminate. We are confined, in other words, to evaluate the text from within and without. In this respect, extra-textual considerations such as morality, politics and ideology come into play. However, the most tempting way to read the text is to situate it within its historical specificity, that is, within the highpoint of decolonisation.

Rodney has a strong bias in favour of socialist ideology, and his analysis of underdevelopment as a historical phenomenon in Africa is informed by a copious application of Marxist methodology, an approach he had obviously hoped would present in more searing terms the ravages of imperialism and economic exploitation in Africa. Since Rodney wrote his opus, we have witnessed the collapse of communism in Eastern Europe and, more specifically the USSR, the foremost workshop of its praxis.

A significant portion of Rodney's text serves as a major strategy for raising black consciousness. It is also a strident counter-discourse to the ravages of colonialism and its continuing forms of exploitation. This basically Euro-American directed critique—which lacks a critical discourse targeted at contemporary Africa—and the anger that Rodney displays in depicting the ravages of the European colonial adventure, are opposite sides of the same coin, that is, the coin of ethnocentrism. But unfortunately he does not indicate how capable Africa is of responding to the prerequisites of development and the challenges of decolonisation. He also does not indicate precisely how much productive capability she has left, which in my view restricts his understanding of the complex, uneven and often violent dialectics of decolonisation. The violence of decolonisation is now evident in the postcolony in the way the postcolonial state has inherited, and become overwhelmed by, the brutalities of the colonial state.

More pertinently, a major circumstance to have changed since the publication of Rodney's book is the collapse of communism as already mentioned. Indeed he is very liberal in his application of Marxist ideology in analysing the factors responsible for Africa's underdevelopment.[5] Marxism serves as the key to the platform on which to launch his crusade for social and political reconstruction or, in this particular instance, decolonisation. Nonetheless, his assessment that: 'A glance at the remarkable advance of socialism over the last fifty years will show that the apologists for capitalism are spokesmen of a social system that is rapidly expiring'[6] is no longer tenable. Rodney does not stop there in eulogising the virtues of socialism. He also writes: 'Socialism has re-instated the economic equality of communism, but communalism fell apart because of low economic productivity and scarcity'.[7]

But as we shall observe later on, he turns the very basis of his Marxist critique against itself. Furthermore, Rodney's reading of Marxism is decidedly partial. Samir Amin states that: 'Marxism was formed both out of and against the Enlightenment, and as a result, is marked by this origin and remains an unfinished project'.[8] Furthermore, Amin informs us that Marx:

> leaves his manuscripts dealing with the "Asiatic mode of Production" in an unsystematic state, showing them to be incomplete reflections. Despite these precautions, Marxism succumbed to the temptation to extrapolate from the European example in order to fashion a universal model.[9]

Consequently, Stuart Hall 'identified marxism as an obsolete and reductivist system of thought'.[10] The same passage continues: 'It was necessary to go beyond its limitations in order to understand contemporary culture'.[11] Rodney exemplifies the figure of Third World for whom Marxism became the ideology of universal redemption, but nonetheless he remains popular for his unsparing but honest critique of Western imperialism and capitalist modes of exploitation.

It is also interesting to note how Rodney employs a moral evaluation of the phenomenon of imperialism. The United States is castigated as 'the most underdeveloped country in the world for practising external oppression on a massive scale while internally there is a blend of exploitation, brutality and psychiatric disorder'.[12] From this perspective, the issue of underdevelopment is given an ethical dimension, and not only in terms of man's poor mastery in handling his environment, well-being and material condition. Development in this case also refers to the realm of morality.[13] Like several other Afrocentric writers Rodney is of the view that 'the Christian Church has always been a major instrument for cultural dominance'.[14] If we are to go by his moralising with regard to the question of underdevelopment/decolonisation, Africa too cannot be exempted from criticism.

Let us now examine Rodney's liberal application of Marxian methodology to African historical circumstances. He writes that Marxists 'are very progressive because they were concerned with the concrete conditions of Africa rather than with the preconceptions brought from Europe'[15] and such a view does not address Samir Amin's quite valid objections to traditional Marxism.[16] But in fact there are far more nuanced readings by Walter's contemporaries. For instance, 'whereas Fanon distinguishes between the analysis of a struggle for liberation (first phase) from the promotion of socialism (second phase) Senghor tends to define African socialism as just a stage in a complex process beginning with Negritude and oriented towards a universal civilization. He emphasizes three major moments: Negritude, Marxism, and universal civilization.'[17]

In addition, Frantz Fanon recognises that Marxism has to be modified when dealing with a colonial situation, which surely is an advancement from Rodney's position. More precisely, Rodney is less cautious in his application of the Marxist ideology.

Jean-Paul Sartre in his preface to Fanon's *The Wretched of the Earth* says that Europe needs to be decolonised, a gesture that is not only charitable from the humanistic angle, but also one of immense theoretical value. Elsewhere, Sartre argues that 'the Negro creates an anti-racist racism. He does not at all wish to dominate the world; he wishes the abolition of racial privileges wherever they are to be found; he affirms his solidarity with oppressed of all colours. At a blow the subjective, existential, ethnic notion Negritude passes as Hegel would say, into the objective, positive, exact position of the proletariat.'[18] Samir Amin has coined a term for the proposed Third World reinsertion into the global system— 'delinking'—which entails a severance of the periphery from the hegemonic metropoles.[19] On his own part, Fanon also stresses the need for Africa to embark on decolonisation. In this connection, it may be argued that Africa invariably looks towards the West, the same site that perpetrated the 'crime of colonialism',[20] and sees her (Africa's) distorted image, contorted by misgovernment, ethnic destruction, starvation, disease and genocidal conflicts. Furthermore, Sartre's view that 'Europe is springing leaks everywhere....The ratio of force has been inverted, decolonisation has begun...'[21] is far from being the entire truth of the matter.

More importantly, Fanon equates decolonisation with radical change. In other words, it is 'simply the replacing of a certain "species" of men by another species of men'.[22] He goes on to say that decolonisation is 'a programme of complete disorder'.[23] Therefore, from this perspective, the colonised is saddled with the endeavour of carrying out processes that would amount to nothing less than revolutionary change or outright violence. From all available evidence, this has not been possible within the African continent. This distressing reality is further worsened by the mistake, made so often, of equating the conditions of Third World development/decolonisation struggles with certain seemingly related stages in the European evolutionary process. In her book *Colonialism and Alienation* Renate Zahar cites C. Bettelheim, where he debunks this widely held assumption:

These countries industrialized today, were not economically dependent. Their production was not structured in such a way that it had to accommodate hypertrophied sectors closely linked to overseas markets and strongly penetrated by foreign capital. These economies neither developed nor stagnated in consonance with upward or downward trends of one raw material or another, of some primary agricultural product on the world market. They were not subject to heavy external commitments (interest, dividends, or royalties payable to foreign capitalists), and their nascent industry did not have to compete with powerful, well-established industries dominated by the same big capital which controlled their own natural resources… Even though these economies might show a low level of industrialization, they were not deformed or unbalanced but on the contrary integrated and centred upon themselves.[24]

Perhaps it is with this renewed awareness that some prominent circles within Africa have started to advocate a programme of reparations.[25] But certainly this reading of the two distinct (Western and the Third World) historical evolutionary taxonomies has done little to diminish the immense dichotomy between them, and instead the West continues to enjoy an unrestrained pace of development while the Third World stagnates. Of course, this is a rather crude explanation does not account for all the components within the scenario and so this assessment should be regarded as only a manner of speaking. However, Samir Amin puts it in the following terms:

The subsequent unfolding of the history of the capitalist conquest of the world showed that this conquest was not going to bring about a homogenization of the societies of the planet on the basis of the European model. On the contrary, this conquest progressively created a growing polarization at the heart of the system, crystallizing the capitalist world into fully developed centers and peripheries incapable of closing the ever widening gap, making this contradiction within "actually existing" capitalism—a contradiction insurmountable within the framework of the major and most explosive contradiction of our time.[26]

Apart from the picture of general stagnation and even retrogression, another distressing spectre looms, the spectre of violence. In this regard, Renate Zahar's observation on the colonised subject is still relevant to our contemporary world. She argues:

Excluded from all social institutions, cut off from his own history, deprived of his own language and all possibilities of untrammelled self-expression, the colonised is left with two alternatives: open revolt or withdrawal to his own family and traditional institutions and values, such as the family and religion, which have already been divested of their former vital functions by the contact with colonialism.[27]

The two alternatives just advanced do not offer conclusive strategies for decolonisation or Africa's numerous existential problems. Take for instance the choice of revolt. Revolt in this case could only bring greater discomfort to the already prostrate populations of Africa. Africa is most vulnerable to the implacable forces of contemporary globalisation. Perhaps this position needs to be clarified. The West, which most Third Worldists would regard as the 'enemy', has entered into a new and more complex relationship with the Third World; hence the manicheanism of actual colonialism, that is, the rigid dualism of the entire situation has given way to a much more intricate play of relations in which such sharp contrasts no longer exist. Yet, in this fresh set of relations between the centre and the periphery, the hegemonic dominance of the former continues to prostrate the latter. The battle line is no longer clear, yet its site is always a source of vehement contestation. Therein lies the crisis as regards the issue of violence. Given the two unpalatable alternatives offered by Zahar, there exists nothing short of an excruciating loss of will or at best a futile groping in the woods. Furthermore, this unfortunate situation is to be found in the domain of the practical as well as the theoretical.

Fanon uses the advocacy of violence for his programme of decolonisation and as a strident apocalyptic injunction for the oppressed peoples of Africa to make a severance from the set-backs of their history.[28] On the threat of imminent violence, he writes, 'the look that the native turns on the settler town is a look of lust…to sit at the settler's table, to sleep in the settler's bed, with his wife if possible. The colonized man is an envious man.'[29] Fanon's account of the colonial situation is inflected by a spectre of overt sexual violence and as McClintock notes, 'both colonizer and colonized are here unthinkingly male, and, the Manichean agon of decolonization is waged over the territoriality of female, domestic space.'[30]

Fanon's worst fears have become chronic realities in terms of the multi-faceted dimension of stagnation and decrepitude to which the entire African continent has been plunged. More importantly, the spirit of the Fanonian programme of decolonisation and by extension radical reform has been impeded, at least for the moment, by certain circumstances such that can be observed as a seemingly unbridgeable schism between theory and praxis, between the concrete and the abstract. In this way, the concrete dimensions of his project of decolonisation remain incomplete. But Fanon continues to be vital to reflections and projects of decolonisation. Indeed he is important to Bhabha and his genius lies in the fact that 'he may yearn for the total trans-formation of Man and Society, but he speaks most effectively from uncertain interstices of historical change: from the area of ambivalence between race and sexuality: out of an unresolved contradiction between culture and class: from deep within representation and social reality.'[31] As the Western postmodern metropole, 'the end of Man'[32] was being proclaimed, Fanon saw a different conceptual scenario:

> It is a question of the Third World starting a new history of Man, a history which will have regard to the sometimes prodigious theses which Europe put forward, but which will also not forget Europe's crimes, of which the most horrible was committed in the heart of man, and consisted of the pathological the pathological tearing away of his functions and the crumbling of his unity…For Europe, for ourselves and for humanity, comrades, we must turn over a new leaf, we must work out new concepts, and try to set afoot a new man."[33]

Within the same conceptual history from whence the Foucauldian end of man emerged there is also the desire for a new birth of man drawing inspiration from the Jacobin imaginary. For Gilroy, Fanon is 'both beneficiary and victim of Europe's progress in its blood-stained imperial mode.'[34] Just as apartheid went on to destroy the social link within the entire geo-body, European racism undermined the universality of man as an entity. Part of Fanon's significance as a theorist of decolonisation lies in his reading of this rupture in the universal order of Man. As Gilroy points out, 'his words articulate a reminder that between the fortified encampments of the colonizers and the quarters of the colonized there were other locations. These in-between locations represent, not disability or inertia, but opportunities for greater insight into the opposed worlds that enclosed them.'[35]

So indeed, to limit Fanon's significance to the period of the rupture with colonialism is to reject a crucial part of the labour of instituting engaging strategies for decolonisation/reconstruction against the backdrop of a suitable intellectual framework. Decolonisation in the Fanonian sense implies active participation by and radicalisation of the masses of Africa. This has not occurred and this is why I argue that his programme of decolonisation is incomplete. The forces of reaction have blocked the avenues through which the masses can receive his message. They are simply dispossessed of the necessary avenues for enlightenment. This assessment needs to be clarified and to do so entails a critical examination of the prevailing conditions in the African postcolony. This is a task I intend to take up later in the study. But for now, let us restrict ourselves to reading Fanon in a much narrower way.

The bourgeoisie to whom Fanon constantly directs his admonitions has succeeded most effectively in sequestrating the routes to his message. By those routes, I mean, denying the underclass the right to qualitative education. The bureaucratisation of terror and the homogenisation of subjectivity are only two methods by which African political elites induce collective disempowerment. The bourgeoisie too has suffered immensely through this act of oppression in which the violence engendered by it is in turn unleashed upon it. Pursuing a similar course of argument, it can be said that it is those to whom his message is not immediately directed—the bourgeoisie—who have hindered the realisation of his project and these are the collaborators of imperialism and the local surrogates of neo-colonialism.[36] One should make a qualification here, which Amin has already made, that:

> The very term imperialism has been placed under prohibition, having been judged to be "unscientific". Considerable contortions are required to replace it with a more "objective" term like "international capital or "transnational capital".[37]

He continues:

> Imperialism is precisely an amalgamation of the requirements and laws for the reproduction of capitals; the social, national, and international alliances that underlie them; and the political strategies employed by these alliances.[38]

Nonetheless, the Fanonian programme of decolonisation and by implication violence has not been fully realised, at least, in the field of practical politics. This incompleteness of Fanon's programme affects every African in practical terms. Secondly, as I stated in the beginning of this discussion, this shortcoming can be redressed, since the project of decolonisation is a continuous process. One thing however is certain, and this is that the colonial situation as regards the question of decolonisation and strategies for subversion is immensely different from the post-colonial epoch, given the radical transgressions within the entire dialectical process and the globalisation and technologisation of new means of terror and domination. Revolutionary change, at the point it might have occurred during the colonial era, did not come about. Instead there were mere perfunctory signals of revolt and, need one add, cosmetic reforms, although one is aware that some nations in Africa experienced the fiercest battles against foreign domination. In the light of the play of relations to be found in the post-liberation era, a new theory of decolonisation and consequently reconstruction is required, one in which some of the central propositions of Fanon's theory would have to be modified. We must also not forget that Fanon was concerned with the demands of praxis just as he was with those of theory, and the latter can only succeed to the extent to which the former is implemented. However it is agreed that 'it was Frantz Fanon who first provided a systematic framework for the political analysis of racial hegemonies at the level of black subjectivity.'[39]

I shall now make some comparative remarks about Rodney's text and Fanon's. Fanon recognises the gulf between theory and praxis, that is, the apparently insurmountable gulf between those opposing polarities and hence he seeks to negotiate this schism by overt political action and revolutionary practice. In essence, his text is a programme of action, an injunction to violence directed at the then unliberated peoples of Africa to break the reign of colonialism. Fanon's text also provides a blueprint for a new society. Consequently, his programme of decolonisation/subversion—and it is a programme in the very widest sense of the term—is devoid of nihilism as so often happens when rebels decide to act, to paraphrase Albert Camus on the question of revolutionary practice. Violence, in Fanon's programme, is merely the prelude to reconstruction and psychic rehabilitation, since he was aware that only decisive action could enforce the aspirations of colonised peoples. In addition, categories such as race, class and sexuality are central to Fanon's analysis. His pioneering work has also been responsible for the emergence of important notions in postcolonial theory such as ambivalence in which theorists have read off scenarios 'where the disavowal of difference turns the colonial subject into a misfit- a grotesque mimicry or "doubling" that threatens to split the soul and the whole, undifferentiated skin of the ego. The stereotype is not a simplification because it is a false representation of a given reality. It is a simplification because it is an arrested, fixated form of representation that, in denying the play of difference (that the negation through other permits), constitutes a problem for the representation of the subject in significations of psychic and social relations.'[40]

Rodney, on the other hand, only gives an account of colonialism and imperialism, even though he is able to construct a theory that is an elaborate analysis of the historical configurations that created colonialism and underdevelopment. But his text stops short of further theoretical articulation. This is a crucial distinction to emphasise. An African reading Rodney's text, whether on the continent or in diaspora, is invariably outraged by his presentation of the catastrophic disruptions inflicted by colonialism upon his history together with his sense of self. While Rodney is able to write a graphic account of European imperialism as well as African underdevelopment, he is unable to construct a full-blown theory of decolonisation. The unmasking of the disruptive dynamics of colonialism might more usefully include a concrete programme of reform, if the subversion of foreign domination is to be achieved. One is not charging Rodney with total failure, but only suggesting that his text fails to realise its full potentialities. Nonetheless, this does not diminish his importance in exposing the centuries of disastrous colonialism Africa has had to endure.

In the next section, we will examine the work of Ngugi wa Thiong'o, who, it may be argued, is one of the most important theorists of decolonisation that Africa has produced, in addition to being one of the greatest novelists on the continent. Ngugi's ideas on decolonisation have been collected in various anthologies of essays and they provide an invaluable source of reflection for any serious discussion on the topic.

Ngugi wa Thiong'o and the Decolonisation Process

Ngugi wa Thiong'o's conception of decolonisation is one of the most radical to be conceived on the African continent. Not only is Ngugi wa Thiong'o one of Africa's foremost creative artists, he is also a formidable theorist of culture and has published several books on questions of race, class and, of course, imperialism.

The range of Ngugi wa Thiong'o's project of decolonisation is a product of his long study of the dynamics of colonialism and its attendant phenomena. He began by questioning the neo-colonial educational arrangement in Kenya as far back as the late sixties when he was still a young scholar. In his important book *Writers in Politics* (1981), he states:

> Let us not mince words. The truth is that the content of our syllabi, the approach to and presentation of the literature, the persons and the machinery for determining the choice of texts and their interpretation, were all an integral part of imperialism in its classical colonial phase, and they are today an integral part of the same imperialism but now in its neo-colonial phase.[41]

Ngugi goes on to examine the relationship between literature and society and how this linkage in turn radically affects a people's cultural orientation. A central assertion of his is that 'literature was used in the colonisation of our people'.[42] To transform this situation, it is then necessary to employ literature for the subversion of imperialism. Throughout *Writers in Politics*, Ngugi maintains a decidedly Marxist ideological stance and so his analyses of the forces that control the economy, politics, education and culture are based upon the socialist conception of class and society.

At the early stages of his career, Ngugi had reasoned:

> For the last four hundred years, Africa has been part and parcel of the growth and development of world capitalism, no matter the degree of penetration of European capitalism in the interior. Europe has thrived, in the words of C.L.R. James, on the devastation of a continent and the brutal exploitation of millions, with great consequences on the economic political, cultural and literary spheres.[43]

Colonialism gave way to neo-colonialism, which Ngugi defines thus:

> Neocolonialism… means the continued economic exploitation of Africa's total resources and of Africa's labour power by international monopoly capitalism through continued creation and encouragement of subservient weak capitalistic structures, captained or overseered by a native ruling class.[44]

In turn, this compromised ruling class makes defence pacts and other unequal agreements with its former colonial overlords so as to secure its grip on political power. The masses, for their part, are effectively alienated from the structures of power.[45] Ngugi urges that 'we must insist on the primacy and centrality of African literature and the literature of African people in the West Indies and America'[46] so as to present a unified front against cultural and psychological effects of global imperialism. In this regard the oral literature of our people is of particular importance. Secondly, he states that:

> Where we import literature from outside, it should be relevant to our situation. It should be the literature that treats of historical situations, historical struggles, similar to our own.[47]

This is a point Ngugi stresses repeatedly in his numerous texts, and one reason that his conception of decolonisation can be recognised to be not only radical but also broad in the range of its discursive investments. As such, his understanding of decolonisation has an undoubtedly global dimension, as will be discussed later. Furthermore, Ngugi agrees with Fanon that decolonisation is a radical process in which the oppressed masses all over the world would have to 'adopt a scientific materialistic world outlook on nature, human society and human thought'.[48] Hence it is not enough to indulge in 'a glorification of an ossified past'.[49] Indeed, he is always critical of the more unsavoury aspects of traditional cultures, as well as of imperialism. As he posits:

> The embrace of western imperialism led by America's finance capitalism is total (economic, political, cultural); and of necessity our struggle against it must be total. Literature and writers cannot be exempted from the battlefield.[50]

As Ngugi's decolonisation project is concerned with imperialism on a global scale, consequently, he stresses the need for oppressed people all over the world to unite in order to confront it. Ngugi describes the situation in the United States thus:

> The ruling robbing minority has always been Euro-American. The Afro-American has, by and large, been part of the robbed working majority. But the Afro-American worker has been the most exploited, the most oppressed section of the working majority. Racism and racist theories

have been effectively used by the ruling Euro-American minority of robbers and thieves to divide the robbed majority—Afro-American, Euro-American, Asio-American—by bribing the Euro-American working class with titbits of the loot cruelly robbed from the Afro-American workers, and also by feeding the Euro-American worker with spurious fascist notions of racial superiority and the Afro-American worker with equally spurious notions of racial inferiority.[51]

However, he identifies two major consciousnesses within the American social system, the one positive and the other negative. The negative tendency, according to Ngugi, is represented by the position of figures like Phyllis Wheatley and Booker T. Washington, who in turn have been followed by figures like Martin Luther King Jr., James Baldwin, Ralph Ellison, Whitney Young, Eldridge Cleaver and 'other thinkers and spokesmen who have allied themselves with the consciousness of the exploiting and oppressing minority'.[52] The other tendency, which is the positive one, according to him, is represented by the position of the following activists and thinkers: Benjamin Banneker, David Walker-Douglass, Du Bois, Paul Robeson, Richard Wright, Malcolm X and George Jackson. How he arrived at his classifications and illustrations is not explained.

Nevertheless, Africa remains Ngugi's primal ideological battleground. More importantly, his book *Decolonising the Mind* (1986) carries the discourse of decolonisation even further. In a statement at the beginning of the book he declares, '*Decolonising The Mind* is my farewell to English as a vehicle for any of my writings; from now on it is Gikûyû and Kiswahili all the way'.[53]

Indeed, it can be said that language forms the major thrust of *Decolonising the Mind*. Obi Wali, the Nigerian critic, broached the all-important issue in 1963 and this stance had a tremendous impact in the field of literary productions and literary studies generally. From this it could be argued that African writers and literary theorists have not only been in the forefront of the decolonisation process but have also defined the stakes and trajectories of the debate. African philosophers have a lot to gain from those writers and literary theorists who foresaw some of the problematics they (African philosophers) are now addressing.[54] Obi Wali's now-famous thesis was that:

> The whole uncritical acceptance of English and French as the inevitable medium of educated African writing is misdirected and has no chance of advancing African literature and culture. In other words, until these writers and their western midwives accept the fact that any true African literature must be written in African languages, they would merely be pursuing a dead end, which can only lead to sterility, uncreativity, and frustration… (African literature lacks any blood and stamina) because it is severely limited,

to the few European-oriented few college graduates in the new universities of Africa, steeped as they are in European literature and culture.

The ordinary local audience with little or no education in the conventional European manner and who constitute an overwhelming majority has no chance of participating in this kind of literature.[55]

Ngugi reminds us that Abiola Irele believes that indigenous African texts, that is, writing in African languages, constitute 'the classical era of African literature'.[56] So one can understand why decolonisation as a topic in literary and cultural studies is bound to be extremely beneficial, that is, it promises to be a fertile area of discourse.

In *Decolonising the Mind*, Ngugi continues to draw attention to the corrupting power of Western imperialism and the equally detrimental political and economic subservience of the African neo-colonial bourgeoisie, which in turn leads to 'a culture of apemanship and parrotry enforced on a restive population through police boots, barbed wire, a gowned clergy and judiciary'.[57] But as mentioned earlier, language remains his primary concern, and the following lengthy quotation (from *Decolonising the Mind*) reflects this:

> Why, we may ask, should an African writer, or any writer, become so obsessed by taking from his mother-tongue to enrich other tongues? Why should he see it as his particular mission? We never asked ourselves: how can we enrich our languages? How can we "prey" on the rich humanist and democratic heritage in the struggles of other people in other times and other places to enrich our own? Why not have Balzac, Tolstoy, Sholokov, Brecht, Lu Hsun, Pablo Neruda, H.C. Anderson, Kim Chi Ita, Marx, Lenin, Albert Einstein, Galileo, Aeschylus, Aristotle and Plato in African languages. And why not create literary monuments in our own languages?[58]

Ngugi not only poses these vital questions but also sets out to address them squarely in the realm of practice. Herein lies his significance as a radical theorist of decolonisation. We have noted that since the late 1970s he had started composing his novels, plays, children's books and even academic essays in Gĩkũyũ. Nonetheless, this approach has its shortcomings as one hopes to demonstrate later.

Ngugi goes on to argue that:

> Language was the most important vehicle through which power fascinated and held the soul prisoner. The bullet was the means of the physical subjugation. Language was the means of the spiritual subjugation.[59]

He also avers that language possesses a dual character, since it is both 'a means of communication and a carrier of culture'.[60] In more ways than one he emphasises the role of culture in the evolution of language as the store of a people's collective identity, memory and development. He puts it in the following terms:

> Language carries culture, and culture carries, particularly through orature and literature, the entire body of values by which we come to perceive ourselves and our place in the world.[61]

Another point Ngugi makes is that colonialism sought to dominate a people's productive forces and distributive capabilities and in so doing it also controlled 'the entire realm of the language of real life'.[62] Thus the imposition of a foreign language on a people 'could never as spoken or written properly, reflect or imitate the real life of that community'.[63] Furthermore, Ngugi argues that the colonial education most formerly colonised regions came to adopt was fraught with serious defects, since it was culturally alienating. Accordingly:

> Since culture does not just reflect the world in images but actually, through those very images, conditions a child to see that world in a certain way, the colonial child was made to see the world and where he stands in it as seen and defined by or reflected in the culture of the language of imposition.[64]

The colonial child then was compelled to view his own indigenous languages through the lens of 'low status, humiliation, corporal punishment, slow-footed intelligence and ability or down right stupidity, non-intelligibility and barbarism'.[65] However, formerly colonised peoples were often at pains to adopt languages of imposition, which usually meant English, French, Spanish or Portuguese. The adoption of these metropolitan languages often provided sites of intense contestation. In other words they were indelibly marked by resistance and/or ambivalence on the part of the colonised. This resistance gave rise to new African languages like Krio in Sierra Leone and Pidgin in Nigeria.[66]

This brings us to what one would consider to be the most radical proposition that Ngugi makes as regards the question of decolonisation. He simply asks for the jettisoning of European languages of colonial imposition in favour of indigenous African languages. For Africans who continue to write in a European language, it is his view that they are merely creating 'another hybrid tradition, a tradition in transition, a minority tradition that can only be termed as Afro-European literature'.[67] Those who fall into this category include Chinua Achebe, Wole Soyinka, Ayi Kwei Armah, Sembene Ousmane, Agostino Neto, Sedar Senghor and several others. At this juncture, it should be pointed out that Ngugi's classification of Euro-African literature would also have to include texts written by Africans in European languages in the fields of political science, sociology, anthropology and, of course, philosophy. Unfortunately, this study also falls within this unenviable category.

In 1977 Ngugi states that he made what could be regarded as 'an episte-mological break'[68] with his past by his active involvement with the Kamiriithu Community and Education and Culture Centre. This break was decisive be-cause it sought to connect the masses of Kenyan people with a truly indig-enous theatrical practice.

If both *Writers in Politics* and *Decolonising the Mind* are shaped by a decidedly socialistic persuasion as well as a revolutionary fervour, the same cannot be said of Ngugi's recent book, *Moving the Centre* (1993). In his preface to the book he declares:

> I am concerned with moving the centre in two senses at least. One is the need to move the centre from its assumed location in the West to a mul-tiplicity of spheres in all the cultures of the world. The assumed location of the centre of the universe in the West is what goes by the term Euro-centricism, an assumption which developed with the domination of the world by a handful of Western nations.[69]

He continues:

> Moving the centre in the two senses—between nations and within na-tions—will contribute to freeing of world cultures from the restrictive walls of nationalism, class, race and gender. In this sense, I am an unre-pentant universalist. For I believe that while retaining its roots in region and national individuality, true humanism with its universal reaching out, can flower among the peoples of the earth, rooted as it is in the histories and cultures of the different peoples of the earth.[70]

These two excerpts form the predominant thrust of *Moving the Centre*. More importantly, Ngugi equates the ideological struggles to 'move the centre' with a vast decolonisation process that transformed global geo-political relations at the end of the Second World War. The book, to be sure, is subtler than his previous books and more aware of the seemingly endless chains of reaction created in the wake of the globalisation process. Obviously, as he states, 'the fax, the telex, the computer, while facilitating communications, also mean the instant spread of information and culture across national boundaries'.[71] Ngugi never allows important new configurations to evade his attention, which ex-plains his continuing relevance to the decolonisation process. Equally, Ngugi remains a powerful theorist of Third Worldism as the following extract should evince:

> The twentieth century is a product of imperialist adventurism, true, but also of resistance from the people of the Third World. The resistance is often reflected in the literature of the Third World and it is an integral part of the modern world, part of the forces which have been creating and

are still creating the heritage of a common culture. They come from Asia. They come from South America. They come from Africa. And they come from the oppressed national sectors and social strata in North America, Australasia and Europe. The Third World is all over the world.[72]

This is a definition that cuts across the entirety of his corpus. On some grounds, Ngugi has still not shifted his arguments. For instance, he affirms that 'despite the hue and cry about reductionism, nativism, backwardlookingness from the Europhonist opponents of this development, writing in African languages still holds the key for the positive development of new and vital traditions of literature as we face the twenty-first century'.[73] However, this objective is far from being realised due to several grave problems as Ngugi himself notes:

> Writing in African languages has many difficulties and problems. Problem of literacy. Problems of publishing. Problem of lack of a critical tradition. Problems of orthography. Problems of having very many languages in the same country. Problems of hostile governments with a colonised mentality. Abandonment by some of those who could have brought their genius—demonstrated by their excellent performance in foreign languages—to develop their own languages.[74]

Even Ngugi himself has not found a way to circumvent these numerous problems and this in my opinion remains the greatest shortcoming of his theory of decolonisation. The greatest irony is that he now wages his struggles against neo-colonialism from the site of the greatest capitalist power in the world-the US- and he now needs Western capital to facilitate the articulation of his views in institutional bases that are largely funded by the West. However, in many instances in *Moving the Centre*, we see him achieving admirable theoretical dexterity such as when he argues for cross-fertilisation among languages and cultures. Then, finally, it is encouraging that Ngugi notes:

> It is important to remember that social intellectual processes, even academic disciplines, act and react on each other not against a spatial and temporal ground of stillness but of constant struggle, of movement, and change which brings about more struggle, more movement, and change, even in human thought.[75]

It is views such as this that have made him the subject of this discussion. But Ngugi himself acknowledges the difficulties of translation and that the status of a particular language is dependent on the influence of the people who speak it.

Having examined various theories of decolonisation with particular relation to Africa, it would certainly be useful to know how repressed/marginalised groups elsewhere confront the prevalence of Euro-centricism.

In this respect, we shall look at India and Brazil. The case of India is particularly interesting because of the high level of theoretical sophistication attained there, while Brazil is important because it is the nation with the second largest black population in the world.

Perspectives from Elsewhere

We shall now move on to examine processes of decolonisation outside Africa. Decolonisation in India has attained immense theoretical complexity, as evinced by the ambitious project launched by the Subaltern Studies Group. This project attempts to rewrite Indian colonial history in order to privilege the various epistemic perspectives of the subaltern classes in the Indian subcontinent. It is the belief (as formulated by Ranajit Guha) of the Subaltern Studies Group that:

> The historiography of Indian nationalism has for a long time been dominated by elitism—colonialist elitism and bourgeois—nationalist elitism... sharing the prejudice that the making of the Indian nation and the development of the consciousness–nationalism which confirmed this process were exclusively or predominantly elite achievements. In the colonialist and neo-colonialist historiographies these achievements are credited to British colonial rulers, administrators, policies, institutions, and cultures: in the nationalist and neo-nationalist writings—to Indian elite personalities, institutions, activities and ideas.[76]

To be sure, this project has laudable intentions, but several obstacles mar its ultimate viability. One problem Gayatri Spivak associates with the project is that of representation.[77] In this way, Spivak employs a 'post representationalist vocabulary'[78] as advanced by Michel Foucault and Gilles Deleuze to deconstruct the essentialist politics of representation adopted by the Subaltern Studies Group. Her exact words are:

> In the slightly dated language of the Indian group, the question becomes, How can we touch the consciousness of the people? With what voice–consciousness can the subaltern speak? The project, after all, is to rewrite the development of the Indian nation. The planned discontinuity of imperialism rigorously distinguishes this project, however old-fashioned its articulation, from "rendering visible the medical and juridical mechanisms that surrounded the story..."[79]

As mentioned above, the politics of representation as elaborated by poststructuralist theorists (Foucault, Derrida, Deleuze) mars much of the general appeal of the project. Spivak claims that 'certain varieties of the Indian elite are at best native informants for first-world intellectuals interested in the voice of the other'.[80] Of course this is a situation that applies to all intellectuals engaged in the task of decolonisation all over the world. The way out of this impasse would then be to 'insist that the colonised subaltern subject is irretrievably heterogeneous'.[81] To act otherwise would be to project an essentialist mode of representation that blurs even further the positionalities of the subaltern classes. This is the problem Spivak incisively identifies. However, this does not detract from the fact that, on the whole, the question of decolonisation in India has reached an appreciably high level since the postcolonial intellectuals are now compelled to learn their privilege as their loss.[82] Not even Ngugi wa Thiong'o addresses this vital point, as is the same all over the African continent. What Spivak demonstrates to us is that it is not enough to make a case for the subaltern classes from an intellectual point of view. We must also be sufficiently concerned with the politics of representation so that we shall not be reproducing the very excesses of imperialism we are seeking to subvert.

The politics of representation is a problem that has got to be confronted within the colonial situation itself and also within processes of decolonisation. The question of the subaltern being unable to speak can be read along several lines. It can begin at the point of confronting a raciologically inflected academic discourse and institutional infrastructure. This theoretical racism has been found in Kant, Hume and Hegel and reappeared in Husserl as a member of the Subaltern Studies Group points out:

> There was one version of this argument in Husserl's *Vienna Lecture of 1935*, in which he proposed that the fundamental difference between 'oriental philosophies' (more specifically, Indian and Chinese) and 'Greek-European science' (or as he added, 'universally speaking: philosophy') was the capacity of the latter to produce 'absolute theoretical insights', that is, 'theoria' (universal science), while the former retained a 'practical universal' philosophy and hence 'mythical-religious' character. This 'practical-universal', philosophy was directed to the world in a 'naïve' and 'straightforward' manner, while the world presented as presented as a 'thematic' to theoria, making possible a praxis whose aim is to elevate mankind through universal scientific reason.[83]

The studies that emerged from the work of the Subaltern Studies Group also warn against the homogenisation of experiences within subalternity. For instance, Spivak in her feminist readings of the genealogies of decolonisation avers, 'in modern India, there is a 'society' of bonded labour where the only means of repaying a loan at extortionate rates of interest is the bond-slavery. Family life is still possible here, the affects taking the entire burden of survival. Below this is bonded prostitution, where the girls, women abducted from bonded labour or kamiya households are thrust as bodies for absolute sexual and economic exploitation.'[84] In India, the process of decolonisation also reconfigured the 'woman question' at the heart of the modern nation-building project. Although some might argue about the merits of the essentialising gesture of this move, it can also be argued that it brought woman into the interstice between the private and the public and rearticulated her as both figure and discourse in the shadowy threshold of the public sphere. In other words, it brought into crisis the in-between that Fanon identifies as a site for the articulation of renewed struggles against hegemonic dominance and oppression. In the space—although filled with silence—created for her within the agenda of the nation-building project and the processes and discourses of decolonisation a schema of discursive binarisms was created for her; inner/outer, spiritual/material, home/world, and feminine/masculine. In this male-created schema, she is also meant to be the custodian and possessor of spiritual and God-like qualities which were meant to preserve and encourage a certain notion of domesticity.[85] In the Indian case, European racism and imperialism led to a counter-articulation of nationhood along a series of frontiers. We must remember that colonial entailed the coercive creation of new subjects, life-worlds, commodities, services, desires and subjectivities.[86] Thus processes of counter-articulation against these new configurations had to be equally vast and comprehensive as the more astute theorists of decolonisation have argued.[87]

In Brazil also, Eurocentrism and racism are problems that face every black subject. So it is not surprising that the discourse of Negritude is still continuing there. However, Femi Ojo-Ade argues for a modified version of the Negritudist ideology as opposed to the 'monolithic or monopolitic'[88] version propagated by Leopold Sedar Senghor. We recall Wole Soyinka's famous retort against the Senghorian version of Negritude: 'I don't think a tiger has to go around proclaiming its tigritude'.[89] Perhaps why black Brazilians find Negritude appealing is because they are faced with the same problems that the likes of Senghor address, namely:

> The realities of racism. The relevance of struggle and revolution. The responsibilities of everyone claiming to represent the black race.[90]

Furthermore, black Brazilians have to exist daily with the entrenched official 'policy of de-negrification and de-Africanization'.[91] And so within this situational matrix, Femi Ojo-Ade argues for the relevance of Negritude within the Brazilian context. It is claimed that Negritude as couched in its classical form has been plagued with accusations of 'lack of "objectivity" of "emotionalism" and "sentimentality", of the necessity for "logical, scientifically correct reasoning"'.[92] But Abdias do Nascimento, a prominent black Brazilian author and ideologue of Negritude, counters these accusations by imploring Africans:

> not to engage in detailed academic discussion but rather to reflect on questions of historical and immediate importance to the destiny of the African Worlds… African scholars and thinkers (must) remove themselves from the minutia of current research engagements in order to discuss the broader concerns…we have a responsibility to consider in the interests of our people.[93]

Consequently, 'Abdias uses the notion of Negritude as springboard for the African-Brazilian liberation struggle'.[94] Let us revisit some of the claims and arguments being made against Negritude. Indeed, Soyinka has modified some of his earlier views on the concept but his reservations against Leopold Sedar Senghor remain:

> Senghor appears compelled to query deep into the humanism of the oppressed to escape the undeniable imperatives in the present with an excursion into pristine memory, and forge, from within its parity and innocence, an ethos of generosity whose lyrical strength becomes its main justification.[95]

Within the scope of an ironical gesture, Soyinka reaffirms the claims about a Senghorian conception of Negritude's emotionalism and sentimentality but later names Jacques Roumain, Etienne Lero and Rene Despestre as representing 'the non-negotiable sector in the province of Negritude.'[96] In the same gesture in which he denounces Senghor as an apostle (and a 'failed priest') of Negritude, he expresses faith in some lesser known members of the Negritudist creed. V. Y. Mudimbe argues that the alienation caused by colonialism gave rise to African discourses of otherness and authenticity of which the concepts of Negritude and black personality are direct off-shoots.[97] The violence of colonisation had military, political, cultural, economic and religious dimensions including an assault on psychic consciousness. Thus: 'Negritude becomes the intellectual and emotional sign of the opposition to the ideology of white superiority.'[98] Mudimbe does discern undue emotionalism and sentimentality in Negritude as Soyinka does. Instead, according to him,

> 'Negritude is the "warmth" of being, living, and participating in a natural, social, and spiritual harmony. It also means assuming some basic political positions: that colonialism has depersonalized Africans and that therefore the end of colonialism should promote self-fulfillment of Africans. Thus Negritude is simultaneously an existentialist thesis (I am what I have decided to be) and a political enterprise. It also signifies a political choice: among European methods, socialism seems the most useful for both cultural reassessment and socio-political promotion.'[99]

Mudimbe is able to situate Negritude as an ideology of otherness within an elaborate as well specific historicity; the backdrop of Marxism, African socialism, a cosmopolitan humanism and reinscriptions of African mutualism. Within this broad and at the same time specific compound of discourses, Negritude becomes a necessary and perhaps even unavoidable tool of decolonisation. The black subject is invariably faced with a welter of epistemic, cultural, economic and institutional hurdles which constantly threaten to make, mar and remake him/her while he/she must contest, bypass or transform these external hegemonies. Soyinka's positionality as a postcolonial African subject means he invariably has to confront a similar set of issues but rather than employing a Senghorian repertoire of discursive tropes he has chosen to deploy a different register of rhetorical practices. But both Senghor and Soyinka are confronted by the varying and multiple problematics of the postcolonial condition which rather than divide them should unite them in the understanding of a particular, relentless violence.

Paul Gilroy displays a sympathetic understanding of this violence and his reading of Senghor's set of circumstances and positionality points the way towards the formulation of a truly cosmopolitan ethic. According to Gilroy, Senghor:

> the Senegalese poet, statesman, resistance fighter, socialist, and influential theorist of Negritude, hybridity, and cultural intermixture is a convenient representative of the generation of colonial intellectuals who faced fascism on the battlefield and then used their confrontations with it to clarify their approaches to freedom and democracy, culture and identity. Senghor's work exhibits a similar pattern in which fervent humanism is combined with, but somehow not contradicted by, a romantic ethnic particularity and an appreciation for cultural syncreticism and transcultural symbiosis.[100]

Thus, the Senghorian politics of identity makes sense to many African-Brazilians. There is obviously the need for solidarity among African-Brazilians, and efforts have been made in this direction, except that they are not effective enough. The Brazilian socio-political system evidently constitutes a great disincentive. African-Brazilians are placed at the lowest rungs of the economic hierarchy, and so they have very little access to sustained qualitative education. Unemployment among them is also high, and a large majority of them reside in favelas (slums).

Recent studies of urban life in Brazil have pointed out the emergence of new models of spatial segregation and the radical transformation of public space and culture.[101] Even as some have noted that heterogeneity is here to stay, 'the transformations going on at the level of the urban environment represent an attack of a different kind. They reject the principles of openness and equality, and take inequality and separation as their values.'[102] These new urban spatial configurations are also leading to the criminalisation of the poor of which black Brazilians form a predominant part.[103] In other words, these exclusionary geographies of spatial inequality have deep racial implications as well.

In addition, African-Brazilians are effectively excluded from the legislative organs of the state and the centres of political activity. There is an overwhelming necessity to confront the numerous structures of oppression in Brazilian society by African-Brazilians. There is also the need to construct effective linkages with the African continent itself, since the forces of colonialism and neocolonialism are products of a Pan-European adventure. We are faced with two major problems in this respect, first of all, the differences in outlook between Africans and African-Brazilians. Ojo-Ade puts it thus:

> The ground gained in the past by the invading forces of Christianity and Islam continue to be reinforced in Africa while diasporan Africans are clinging to an Afrocentric religiosity as a means of survival.[104]

This difference is vital and cannot be overlooked. The other problem pertains to the political situation of blacks in Brazil. Ojo-Ade informs us that 'there remains a lack of strong dedicated and focused leadership able to offer the people a sense of purpose and the strength to take charge of the state'.[105] And so given this situation, decolonisation as a conceptual project has several daunting obstacles to scale. We will recall that Ngugi termed decolonisation 'a vast process' which entails linking up with similar struggles worldwide.

In the next chapter, we shall examine the work of the subject of this study, Kwasi Wiredu. Of course, his position is in several instances fundamentally different from some of the ones we have considered so far. However, similarities exist, and examining some of them would help in more ways than one for the observations to be projected in the subsequent chapters.

Notes

1. Cornel West, 'The New Cultural Politics of Difference', in Russell Ferguson et al. eds., *Out There: Marginalization and Contemporary Cultures,* New York, Cambridge and London, The New Museum of Contemporary Art and MIT Press, 1990, p. 25

2. The literature on African underdevelopment in the domain of the social sciences is copious. See the following works for example: Claude Ake, *A Political Economy of Africa,* Harlow, Longman, 1981, *Social Science as Imperialism,* University of Ibadan Press, 1979 and also his *Revolutionary Pressures in Africa,* London, Zed, 1978; Samir Amin, *Le Développement inégal. essai sur les formations sociales du capitalisme périphérique,* Paris, Editions de Minuit, 1973; and Thandika Mkandawire and Adebayo Olukoshi,

eds. *Between Liberalisation and Oppression: The Politics of Structural Adjustment in Africa,* Dakar, CODESRIA, 1995.

3. The following works are representative of this African historical moment: Nnamdi Azikwe, *Renascent Africa*, London, Cass, 1969; Kwame Nkrumah, *I Speak of Freedom: A Statement on African Ideology,* London, Heinemann, 1961 and also his *Consciencism*, London, Heinemann, 1965; Julius Nyerere, *Ujamaa: Essays on Socialism,* London, Oxford University Press, 1968; and L. S. Senghor, *On Socialism*, trans. Mercer Cook, New York, Praeger, 1964.

4. It is noted that Rodney's text was hurriedly composed but it is still an important text because of the tremendous impact it has had on Third World struggles against various forms of external oppression.

5. The embarrassing volte face of many African Marxists in the wake of steep ideological challenges is well known. Paulin Hountondji's final word on the impasse of Marxists in Africa; 'I have written…that instead of this Marxism in tablet form that so many of our compatriots swallowed like a panacea, of this closed system that had answers to everything, we must recognize that the debate in Marxism has always been in reality plural and contradictory.' *The Struggle for Meaning: Reflections on Philosophy, Culture and Democracy in Africa,* 2003, p. 183.

6. Walter Rodney, *How Europe Underdeveloped Africa*, London, Boyle L'Ouverture Publications, 1972, p. 8.

7. Ibid. p. 20.

8. Samir Amin, *Eurocentricism*, London, Zed Books, 1989, p. 119.

9. Ibid. p. 120.

10. Stuart Hall cited by Colin Sparks, in 'Stuart Hall, Cultural Studies and Marxism', *Stuart Hall, Critical Dialogues in Cultural Studies*, Eds. D. Morley and K. Chen, London and New York, Routledge, 1996, p. 78.

11. Ibid.

12. Walter Rodney, *How Europe Underdeveloped Africa,* 1972, p. 22.

13. It is interesting to note that the Nobel Prize-winning economist, Amartya Sen has reintroduced the ethical and humanistic to the current debates on development.

14. Walter Rodney, *How Europe Underdeveloped Africa,* 1972, p. 35.

15. Ibid. p. 46.

16. Discourses of decolonisation in Africa have been described to be marked by two major tendencies: nativism and Marxism. Achille Mbembe's work *On the Postcolony,* Berkeley, University of California Press, 2001 sets itself the task of overcoming these conceptual blocks.

17. V. Y. Mudimbe, *The Invention of Africa: Gnosis, Philosophy, and the Order of Knowledge*, Bloomington, Indiana University Press, 1988, p. 93.

18. Jean-Paul Sartre, *Black Orpheus*, Paris, Présence Africaine, p. 59.

19. Samir Amin, *Eurocentricism*, Zed Books, 1989, pp 116–117.

20. Jean-Paul Sartre, Preface to *The Wretched of the Earth,* Middlesex, Penguin Books, 1963, p. 21.

21. Ibid. p. 23.

22. Frantz Fanon, *The Wretched of the Earth*, Middlesex, Penguin Books, 1963, p. 27.

23. Ibid.

24. C. Bettleheim, cited by Zahar R. in *Colonialism and Alienation: Concerning Frantz Fanon's Political Theory,* Benin, Ethiope Publishing Corporation, 1974, p. 8.

25. For a sophisticated treatment of the problematic of reparations see, Paul Gilroy, *The Black Atlantic: Modernity and Double Consciousness*, Cambridge, Harvard University Press, 1993. See also Wole Soyinka, *The Burden of Memory, The Muse of Forgiveness,* New York, Oxford University Press, 1999.

26. Samir Amin, *Eurocentricism*, 1989, p. 75.

27. R. Zahar, *Colonialism and Alienation*, 1974, p. 24.

28. For a detailed account of Fanon's thought on violence see Dipo Irele's *The Violated Universe: Fanon and Gandhi on Violence*, Ibadan, Critical Forum in conjunction with New Horn, 1993.

29. Frantz Fanon, *The Wretched of the Earth*, 1963, p. 30.

30. Anne McClintock, *Imperial Leather: Race, Gender and Sexuality in the Colonial Conquest*, 1995, p. 355.

31. Homi Bhabha, *The Location of Culture*, London, Routledge, 1994, p. 40. For a critical engagement with Bhabha's views on Fanon see Henry Louis Gates Jr. 'Critical Fanonism', *Critical Inquiry,* 17, Spring, 1991.

32. See Michel Foucault, *The Order of Things,* London, Tavistock, 1972.

33. Frantz Fanon, *The Wretched of the Earth*, 1963, pp. 254-55.

34. Paul Gilroy, *Against Race: Imagining Political Culture Beyond the Color Line*, 2000, p. 71.

35. Ibid.

36. For a much more nuanced assessment of this stance, a study such as Jean- Francois Bayart et al's, *The Criminalisation of the State in Africa*, London, James Currey, 1997 should do.

37. Samir Amin, *Eurocentricism*, 1989, p. 75.

38. Ibid.

39. Kobena Mercer, 'Black Hair/Style Politics' in Russell Ferguson et al. eds., *Marginalization and Contemporary Cultures*, New York, Cambridge and London, The New Museum of Contemporary Art and MIT Press, p. 250.

40. Homi K. Bhabha, 'The Other Question: Difference, Discrimination and the Discourse of Colonialism' in Russell Ferguson et al. eds., *Out There: Marginalization and Contemporary Cultures*, p. 80.

41. Ngugi wa Thiong'o, *Writers in Politics*, Nairobi, Heinemann, 1981, p. 5.

42. Ibid.

43. Ibid. p. 11.

44. Ibid. p. 24.

45. Ibid.

46. Ibid. p. 90.

47. Ibid.

48. Ibid. p. 31.

49. Ibid.

50. Ibid. p. 73.

51. Ibid. p. 125.

52. Ibid. p. 134.

53. Statement at the beginning of Ngugi wa Thiong'o's *Decolonizing the Mind,* Nairobi, East African Educational Publishers Ltd, 1986.

54. See for instance, Kai Kresse's article, 'The Problem of How to Use African Thought-On a Multilingual Perspective in African Philosophy', *African Philosophy*, Vol. 12, No. 1, March 1999 which expresses a similar view.

55. Obi Wali, cited by Ngugi wa Thiong'o in *Writers in Politics,* 1981, pp. 55-56.

56. Abiola Irele, cited by Ngugi wa Thiong'o in *Moving the Centre*, London, James Currey, 1993, p. 20.

57. Ngugi wa Thiong'o, *Decolonizing the Mind*, 1986, p. 2.

58. Ibid. p. 8.

59. Ibid. p. 9.

60. Ibid. p. 13.

61. Ibid. p. 16.

62. Ibid.

63. Ibid.

64. Ibid. p. 17.

65. Ibid. p. 18.

66. Ibid. p. 93.

67. Ibid. pp. 26-7.

68. Ibid. p. 44.

69. Preface to Ngugi wa Thiong'o's *Moving the Centre*, 1993, p. xvi.

70. Ibid. p. xvii.

71. Ibid. p. 13.

72. Ibid. p. 18.

73. Ibid. p. 21.

74. Ibid.

75. Ibid. p. 29.

76. Ranajit Guha, cited by Gayatri Spivak in 'Can the Subaltern Speak?', *The Post–Colonial Studies Reader,* London and New York, Routledge, 1995, pp. 25-6.

77. Gayatri Spivak in *'Can the Subaltern Speak ?'*, 1995, p. 26.

78. Ibid. p. 27.

79. Ibid.

80. Ibid. p. 26.

81. Ibid.

82. This is a point G. Spivak makes.

83. Dipesh Chakrabarty, 'Postcoloniality and the Artifice of History: Who Speaks for the "Indian Pasts?"' *A Subaltern Studies Reader: 1986-1995*, Ranjit Guha, Minneapolis: University of Minnesota Press, 1995, p. 226.

84. Gayatri Chakravorty Spivak, *Outside in the Teaching Machine,* New York and London, Routledge, 1993, p. 73.

85. See Partha Chatterjee, 'The Nation and Its Women', *A Subaltern Studies Reader: 1986-1995* Ranjit Guha, Minneapolis, University of Minnesota Press, 1995.

86. For a particularly insightful body of work on the various dimensions of colonialism see, John L. Comaroff and Jean Comaroff, *Of Revelation and Revolution: Christianity, Colonialism and Consciousness in South Africa*, Vol. 1, Chicago: Chicago University Press, 1991 and also *Of Revelation and Revolution: The Dialectics of Modernity on a South African Frontier*, Chicago: Chicago University Press, 1997.

87. Arjun Appadurai explores some of the subtler and deeper dimensions of British colonialism in India in his book, *Modernity at Large: Cultural Dimensions of Globalisation*, Minneapolis, University of Minnesota Press, 1996.

88. Femi Ojo-Ade, *Being Black, Being Human*, Ile-Ife, Obafemi Awolowo University Press, 1996, p. 262.

89. Wole Soyinka, cited by Janheinz Jahn in *Neo-African Literature: A History of Black Writing,* New York, Grove Press, 1968, p. 226.

90. Femi Ojo–Ade, *Being Black, Being Human*, 1996, p. 262.

91. Ibid. p. 264.

92. Ibid.

93. Abdias do Nascimento, cited by Femi Ojo-Ade in *Being Black Being Human,* 1996, pp. 264-5.

94. Femi Ojo-Ade, *Being Black Being Human*, 1996, p. 265.

95. Wole Soyinka, *The Burden of Memory, The Muse of Forgiveness,* New York, Oxford University Press, 2000, p. 105.

96. Ibid. p. 164.

97. V. Y. Mudimbe, *The Invention of Africa: Gnosis, Philosophy and the Order of Knowledge*, 1988, p. 92.

98. Ibid. p. 93.

99. Ibid.

100. Paul Gilroy, *Against Race: Imagining Political Culture Beyond the Color Line,* 2000, pp. 91-92.

101. See Teresa P. R. Caldeira, 'Building Up Walls: The New Pattern of Spatial Segregation in Sao Paulo', *International Social Science Journal* 147, 1996.

102. Teresa P. R. Caldeira, 'Fortified Enclaves: The New Urban Segregation', in James Holston, ed., *Cities and Citizenship*, Durham, Duke University Press, 1999, p. 127.

103. Ibid.

104. Femi Ojo-Ade, *Being Black, Being Human,* 1996, p. 274.

105. Ibid. p. 270.

3

Kwasi Wiredu and Fanon's Legacy

The Beginnings

Kwasi Wiredu, the Ghanaian philosopher, has helped in defining the contemporary boundaries of what we call African philosophy. Hitherto, the question of the very existence of African thought had been problematic.[1] Using his ethnic group, the Akan, as a major frame of reference, Wiredu problematises the tradition/modernity dichotomy in a way that indicates the binarism can be productively transcended.[2] By developing a critical consciousness concerning both modernity and tradition it is possible to arrive at a fruitful conceptual fusion indicative of the direction that the liberation of the postcolonial subject from the difficulties of coping with the modern world might take. As Wiredu argues, the postcolonial subject should not be undermined by unnecessary drawbacks of tradition.

Wiredu's importance is underscored in Olusegun Oladipo's *Philosophy and the African Experience: The Contributions of Kwasi Wiredu* (1996). Oladipo demonstrates that Wiredu is exemplary among present day African thinkers in diligently searching for a synthesis between traditional African cultures and the gains of Western-spawned modernity, in order to enable Africa to secure a more prominent place in the modern world. Wiredu's programme spans epistemology, politics, ethnicity and the questions of identity. Wiredu's numerous discursive interests necessitate the interdisciplinary approach of this study.

Since African philosophy (in its modern articulation) has a relatively short history of textuality, that is, as a documented construct, it would be instructive to determine how Wiredu has been able to overcome this fundamental problem. In several ways he represents a vital link between his philosophical predecessors such as Nkrumah, Senghor, Sekou Toure and Nyerere, and the poststructuralist contributions of his fellow compatriot, Anthony Kwame Appiah. However, this link is more complex than it appears. For instance, Wiredu's grounding in the workings of philosophical analysis, that is, Anglo-Saxon positivism, distinguishes him from Senghor, Nyerere and Nkrumah. Wiredu's philosophical interests overlap with those of thinkers like his compatriot, Appiah, even though their discursive practices are considerably dissimilar. The ways in which their discursive practices differ is a subject to be tackled in the following chapter. Indeed, a crucial part of this study is to attempt to trace the various discursive and interdisciplinary (re)readings these overlappings motivate.

Apart from Oladipo's book on Wiredu, D.A. Masolo's *African Philosophy in Search of Identity* (1994) has a rather lengthy section on Wiredu. But Masolo's reading of his Ghanaian counterpart is essentially limited to the latter's views on truth, and most of his discussions are concentrated on Wiredu's *Philosophy and an African Culture*, which as a text does not offer an elaborate rendering of Wiredu's views on conceptual decolonisation and its numerous transdisciplinary problematisations. Therefore, in this chapter we shall undertake a preliminary critique of Wiredu, although chapter four contains the nucleus of most of my arguments. But before we go any further, it would certainly be of assistance to undertake a brief reading of Oladipo's book on Wiredu.

Philosophy and the African Experience: The Contributions of Kwasi Wiredu is expository in nature, although it provides an introduction to Wiredu's project of conceptual decolonisation. However, Oladipo offers one memorable criticism of Wiredu's work. He argues that 'his neglect of politics and economics on aspects of the African social reality which have played a significant role in determining the nature and course of African development (under-development)'[3] leaves a lot to be desired. This study will address some of the subjects Wiredu does not address in relation to conceptual decolonisation.

The first part of this chapter deals with a 1995 volume of essays, entitled *Conceptual Decolonisation in African Philosophy* (selected and introduced by Olusegun Oladipo) and a few other major articles by Wiredu that are of relevance to this study. The second part brings Wiredu into conversation with Oladipo on the issues of rationality and self-identity. The final part offers a reading of Wiredu's last volume of essays, *Cultural Universals and Particulars* (1996), which is an extended version of the thematics explored in *Conceptual Decolonisation in African Philosophy*.

The volume *Conceptual Decolonisation in African Philosophy* is an apt summation of Wiredu's philosophical interests with a decidedly African problematic to date. For those who are familiar with his landmark philosophical work, *Philosophy and an African Culture*, published first in 1980, this volume should serve as a fertile source for greater elucidation.

In the second essay of the volume, entitled 'The Need for Conceptual Decolonisation in African Philosophy', Wiredu writes that 'with an even greater sense of urgency the intervening decade does not seem to have brought any indications of a widespread realization of the need for conceptual decolonisation in African philosophy'.[4] The intention at this juncture is to examine some of the ways in which Wiredu has been involved in the daunting task of conceptual decolonisation. Decolonisation itself is a painful ordeal because it necessitates the destruction of certain conceptual attitudes that inform one's worldviews. Secondly, it usually entails an attempt at the retrieval of a more or less fragmented historical heritage. As observed in the previous chapter, decolonisation in the Fanonian sense is a necessity for all colonised peoples and, in addition, 'a programme of complete disorder'.[5] However, we are talking of decolonisation here as a matter of a purely practical interest. This is not to say that Fanon had no plan for the project of decolonisation in the intellectual sphere. Connected with this project as it was then conceived was a struggle for the mental reorientation of the colonised African peoples. It was indeed a programme of violence in more senses than one.

But with Wiredu, there is not an outright endorsement of violence, for decolonisation in this instance amounts to conceptual subversion, if one may be permitted the use of the expression. As a logical consequence we might as well stress the difference between Fanon's conception of decolonisation and Wiredu's. Fanon can be regarded as belonging to the same philosophical persuasion that harbours figures like Nkrumah, Senghor, Nyerere and Sekou Toure, 'the philosopher-kings of early post-independence Africa',[6] as Wiredu calls them. This is so because they had to live out the various dramas of existence and the struggles for self and collective identity at more or less the same colonial/postcolonial moment. Those 'spiritual uncles' of professional African philosophers were engaged, as Wiredu tells us, in a strictly political struggle, and whatever philosophical insight they possessed was put at the disposal of this struggle, instead of a merely theoretical endeavour. Obviously, Fanon was the most astute theoretician of decolonisation of the lot. In addition, for Fanon and the so-called philosopher-kings, decolonisation was invested with a Pan-African mandate (panafricanism) and political appeal. We must note in full this vital disparity with what we shall soon demonstrate to be the Wiredu conception of decolonisation. But whether we accept it or not,

Africans generally will have to continue to ponder the entire issue of decolonisation as long as our sense of selfhood remains obscured, our economies in a state of prostration, and our social and political institutions plagued by chronic disintegration. This, in a way, is a legacy foreseen by Fanon.

There is however a fashionable dimension to the question of decolonisation that is now engaging the attention of Third World scholars and researchers on Third World issues. As we know, the end of colonialism in Africa and other Third World countries did not entail the end of imperialism and the dominance of the metropolitan countries. Instead, the politics of dominance assumed a more complex, if subtle form. African economic systems floundered alongside African political institutions, and as a result, all manner of major and minor crises have been engendered which will still have to be addressed for a long time to come.

Let us look briefly at the intellectual aspect of the problem of decolonisation, for that is what primarily concerns us. A segment of post-colonial theory involves the entry of Third World scholars into the Western archive, as it were, with the intention of dislodging the erroneous epistemological assumptions and structures regarding their peoples.[7] This, one might argue, is another variant of decolonisation. Wiredu partakes of this type of discourse, but sometimes he carries the programme even further. We shall now look at how he does this. He affirms:

> Until Africa can have a lingua franca, we will have to communicate suitable parts of our work in our multifarious vernaculars, and in other forms of popular discourse, while using the metropolitan languages for international communication.[8]

This conviction has been a guiding principle with Wiredu for several years.[9] In fact, it is not merely a conviction; there are several instances within the broad spectrum of his philosophical corpus where he tries to put it into practice. Two of such attempts are his essays 'The Concept of Truth in the Akan Language' and 'The Akan Concept of Mind'. In the first article, Wiredu informs us that 'there is no one word in Akan for truth'.[10] Similarly, we are told that 'another linguistic contrast between Akan and English is that there is no word 'fact'.[11] For reasons of economy I shall cite an extract I deem to be the central thesis of the essay; Wiredu writes that he wants 'to make a metadoctrinal point which reflection on the African language enables us to see, which is that a theory of truth is not of any real universal significance unless it offers some account of the notion of being so'.[12]

Wiredu's argument faces several problems which make his notion of decolonisation seem a little suspect, due mainly to what one may regard as a

sign of epistemological hesitation. In many respects, Wiredu is only comparing component parts of the English language with the Akan language and not
always with a view to drawing out 'any real universal significance' as he says.
The entire approach seems to be irrevocably restrictive. But before we go on,
it is of considerable importance to stress a distinction that Wiredu does not
appear to constantly bear in mind. One is not saying that he is totally unaware
of it, but that he doesn't put it consistently in the foreground of his reflections. This is the distinction that lies between an oral culture and a textual
one.[13] Most African intellectuals usually gloss over this difference, even though
they may acknowledge it. The difference is indeed very significant, because of
the numerous imponderables that come into play. Abiola Irele has been able
to demonstrate the tremendous significance of orality in the constitution of
modern African forms of literary expression.

First of all, we have to admit the rudimentary forms of documentation
and knowledge storage within an oral culture. The scope for discursive reflection is circumscribed by the very constraints of orality, while the discursivity
attendant within a modern inter-textual situation is also too evident. Once
again, we have the discursive dichotomy that characterises the distance between tradition and modernity. Confronted with the stereotypes of the colonial script, the post-colonial subject may react violently against most notions
of 'Westernity' or modernity as conceived solely by the West, or may adopt a
dogmatic recourse to indigenous culture (*nativism* and *ethnophilosophy*). It is this
kind of simplified response to the classical colonial script that further frus-
trates efforts at decolonisation.[14]

To be sure, Wiredu has not adequately interrogated the distance between
orality and textuality. Because if he has sufficiently done so, he would not be
too confident about the manner in which he thinks he can dislodge certain
Western philosophical structures embedded in the African consciousness.
Postcolonial theorising has brought to the fore the multiple dilemmas of this
theoretical and existential matrix. This complex of problematics has been
described in the following manner:

> The term postcolonialism is prematurely celebratory and obfuscatory in
> more ways than one. While some countries may be postcolonial with re-
> spect to their erstwhile European masters, they may not be postcolonial
> with respect to their neighbours. Yet neo-colonialism is not simply a re-
> peat performance of colonialism, nor is it a slightly more complicated,
> Hegelian merging of tradition and colonialism into some new, historic
> hybrid. More complex terms of analyses of alternative times, histories
> and causalities are required to deal with complexities that cannot be served
> under the single rubric of postcolonialism.[15]

Herein lies another problem with the issue of conceptual decolonisation: where do we establish the limits? Does decolonisation end with the conceptual structures that concern formerly colonised peoples, or does it approach or seek to contest all Western epistemological structures that indicate a tendency towards global dominance and universality? If the second aspect of the question is the case, then the disruption/subversion/repelling of epistemic violence at once becomes a central theme in Wiredu's conception of decolonisation, since we have accepted the unlimited scope of the decolonising operation. Wiredu is a careful philosopher and he constantly stresses the view that:

> If we approach ... the philosophic suggestions of other cultures (as, for example, those of the Orient) in the spirit of due reflection, being always on the look out for any conceptual snares, perhaps we can combine insights extracted from those sources with those gained from our own indigenous philosophical resources to create for ourselves and our peoples modern philosophies from which both the East and the West might learn something.[16]

'Due reflection' is the key expression, (or what he has defined as reflective integration elsewhere)[17] but one would have to admit that it is a rather problematic one, for the very meaning of what is to be so classified is a highly philosophical matter.[18] Wiredu illustrates some instances in which he mentions how the process of due reflection could be applied, which we shall look at later. But let us be forewarned that not all the instances are altogether satisfactory. Any reflective activity upon a given concept or situation in the effort towards decolonisation is an extremely hazardous task for the mere reason that there are no readily available criteria, indeed, conceptualising the difficulties of postcolonialism is never easy. In other words, all such debates can only be resolved empirically or pragmatically, and the methods by which they are resolved are beyond any concise or predetermined approach.

Another essay by Wiredu, entitled 'The Akan Concept of Mind' (published much earlier than *Conceptual Decolonisation in African Philosophy*), is also an attempt of conceptual recontextualisation, to employ a more suggestive expression this time. Wiredu begins by stating that he is restricting himself to a study of the Akans of Ghana in order 'to keep the discussion within reasonable anthropological bounds'.[19] His objective is a modest but nevertheless an important one, since it fits very well with his entire philosophical project which, as we have noted earlier, is concerned with ironing out philosophical issues 'on independent grounds' and possibly in one's own language and the metropolitan language bequeathed by the colonial heritage.[20]

So we are to proceed gradually, traversing the problematic interfaces between various languages in search of satisfactory structures of meaning. As mentioned earlier, even if this approach is a modest one, it is also a highly engrossing one. The immediate effect is a radical diminishing of the entire concept of African philosophy, a term which under these circumstances would become even more problematic. The consequence of Wiredu's position is that to arrive at the essence of African philosophy, we would have to deconstruct its monolithic structure to make it more context-bound. First, Africa as a geographical entity would require further deconstruction. Second, a new thematics to mediate between the general and the particular would have to be found. Third, the critique of unanimism and ethnophilosophy would have to be driven onto higher and often highly contested grounds. Finally, the days of epistemological complacency would definitely be over. This is an issue if not a problem that will invariably confront the African philosopher when she adopts the Wiredu approach.

Furthermore, in dealing with the traditional Akan conceptual system, or any other, for that matter, we must always bear in mind that we are relating to 'a folk philosophy, a body of originally unwritten ideas preserved in the oral traditions, customs and usages of a people'.[21] Wiredu is fully aware of this, but what leaves a lot to be desired is the manner in which he negotiates the wide expanse between the realities of a textual culture and those of an oral one. Orality and textuality are not the same thing.[22]

We should, however, look more closely at his article 'The Akan Concept of Mind', which is the subject of this part of our discussion. Wiredu again enumerates the ways in which the English conception of mind differs markedly from that of the Akan, due in a large part to certain fundamental linguistic dissimilarities. Another major point he raises is that 'the Akans most certainly do not regard mind as one of the entities that go to constitute a person'.[23] It is interesting to know this, but where does it lead? After reformulating traditional Western philosophical problems to suit African conditions, it remains to be seen how African epistemological claims can be substantiated using the natural and logical procedures available to African systems of thought. Cannot this conceptual manoeuvre degenerate into a dead-end of epistemic nativism?

Furthermore, in spite of all claims to the contrary, behind every quest for decolonisation is the quest to diminish in overt terms the presence of the Other. In addition, there is essentially a latent desire for epistemic violence, as well as difficulties concerning the negotiation of linguistic divides. In the following quotation, for example, Wiredu attempts to demonstrate the significance of some of those differences:

> By comparison with the conflation of concepts of mind and soul prevalent in Western philosophy, the Akan separation of the 'Okra' from

'adwene' suggests a more analytical awareness of the sanctification of human personality.[24]

We need to substantiate more rigorously claims such as this, because we may also be committing an error in establishing certain troublesome linguistic or philosophical correspondences between two disparate cultures and traditions.

Another crucial if distressing feature of decolonisation as advanced by Wiredu is that it always has to measure itself up with the colonising Other, that is, it finds it almost impossible to create its own image so to speak by the employment of autochthonous strategies. One is not asserting that decolonisation has to always avail itself of indigenous procedures, but isn't the very concept of decolonisation concerned with breaking away from imperial structures of dominance in order to express a will to self identity or presence? To be sure, the Other is always present, defacing all claims to full presence of the decolonising subject. This is a contradictory but inevitable trope within the postcolonial condition. The Other is always there to present the criteria by which one is adjudged either favourably or unfavourably. There is no getting around the Other as it is introduced in its own latent and covert violence, in the hesitant counter-violence of the decolonising subject and invariably in the counter-articulations of all projects of decolonisation.

Let us return to the problem raised earlier, of relating an oral culture to one in which established forms of textuality prevail. In an oral culture one observes mainly static conceptual modes (especially when they are inscribed in the heart of modernity and its technologies) and consequently the entire discursive potential of such a community is severely restricted when compared to a culture of textuality. To buttress this point, one notices that in presenting the Akan concept of mind, Wiredu has only a few related specialised concepts at his disposal. The problem as suggested earlier arises primarily from the conflation of oral and textual discourses.

Wiredu's more recent attempts at conceptual decolonisation have been quite interesting. An example of such an attempt is the essay 'Custom and Morality: A Comparative Analysis of some African and Western Conceptions of Morals'. He is able to explore at greater length some of the conceptual confusions that arise as a result of the implantation of Western ideas within the African mindset. This wholesale transference of foreign ideas and conceptual models has caused the occurrence of severe cases of identity crises and, to borrow a more apposite term, colonial mentality. Indeed, one of the aims of Wiredu's efforts at conceptual decolonisation is to indicate instances of colonial mentality and determine strategies by which they can be minimised. So he makes a lot of sense when he argues that polygamy in a traditional setting amounts to efficient social thinking but is most inappropriate within a modern framework.[25] In this way, Wiredu is offering a critique of a certain traditional practice that ought to be discarded on account of the demands and realities of a modern economy.

In the same vein, he demonstrates how the Western idea of ethics regarding marriage differs immensely from the Akan conception. To be precise 'Christianity, as it came to us in Africa through the missionaries, proscribed premarital sex, as totally incompatible with morality'[26] but on the other hand among the Akans, "considerable mutual knowledge between both principals, including 'carnal' knowledge, is regarded as a commonsensical requirement".[27] He concludes this line of argument by affirming that 'in regard to this notion of the dependence of morality on religion, we encounter a rather striking contrast, for it does not even make sense in the Akan context'.[28] This essay, one may add, provides engaging ideas, the reason being that the theoretical models employed are able to engage practical considerations in a fruitful manner.

Wiredu's discussions of Akan conceptions of courtship, marriage and morality within the context of postcolonial modernity invariably lead to other related issues: ideologies of sexuality, questions of gender, raciology, nano-politics, biopolitics, the care and technologies of the self and the entire dilemma of ethics.[29] Again, postcolonial studies have made tremendous strides in these various directions. Once on the postcolonial frontier, race, sex and power become a combustive mix. Several studies have demonstrated that the colonial regime seized, broke down and transformed the cosmoses of the tribal cultures it colonised (one says this bearing in mind the tropes of resistance, hybridity, ambivalence and transgression inherent in the colonial condition).[30] Wiredu's analysis of power would have been richer if he had included a Foucauldian dimension or better still, perspectives from postcolonial theory. Postcolonial theory informs us that the colony was projected and disavowed as anachronistic space. This particular technology of power disavowed, 'feminised' and vilified all devalued collectivities; Jews, blacks, women, the industrial working class, criminals and the poor. As such, 'in the colonies, black people were figured, among other things, as gender deviants, the embodiments of prehistoric promiscuity and excess, their evolutionary belatedness evidenced by their 'feminine' lack of history, reason and proper domestic arrangements.'[31]

Wiredu writes that premarital sex was allowed in the traditional Akan context. However, Christianity frowned against the practice. But what Wiredu does not depict is the full impact of the comprehensive colonial logic and its multiple violences. In most colonial situations, discovery, sex, power and conquest are often intertwined. When Christopher Columbus and Amerigo Vespucci visited the 'New World' these overlapping logics had free rein. Joane Nagel, in a recent study of colonial conquest and its ethnosexual dimensions writes:

> Columbus viewed the native people as naïve and childlike in their nudity, simple in their spirituality, primitive in their technology, and cooperative in their dealings. In contrast to Columbus's Eden, Vespucci's mundus novus was more like Sodom and Gomorrah, filled with cruel torturers, depraved cannibals, treacherous men, and licentious women; the inhabitants of the new world were dangerous, duplicitous, promiscuous, and incestuous. The only two points of agreement between the men's account are revealing. Both Columbus and Vespucci found the people they encountered, particularly the women, to be quite attractive, especially those with light skin; and both men congratulated themselves and their crews on their civilized, Christian treatment of the natives.[32]

The attitudes of Columbus and Vespucci towards the natives depict a clear picture of the operations of a colonial technology of power and the racial and sexual ecology it helped in legitimating. The Christian scrutiny of local sexual mores was far more penetrating than Wiredu's account of the colonial encounter suggests: 'the Franciscans disapproved of sexual intercourse between anyone other than married men and women in anything other than the 'missionary position', since as the seventeenth-century theologian Tomas Sanchez stated, this was the 'natural manner of intercourse.'[33] In time, as the colonial intrusion become secure in its reach and more solid at its foundations, natives and the colonised 'were metaphorically bound in a regime of surveillance, collectively figured by images of sexual pathology and racial aberration as atavistic throwbacks to a primitive moment in human prehistory, surviving ominously in the heart of the modern, imperial metropolis. Depicted as transgressing the natural distributions of money, sexual power and property and thereby as fatally threatening the fiscal and libidinal economy of the imperial state, these groups became subject to increasingly vigilant and violent state control.'[34] These views from postcolonial theory and sexology are very relevant to Wiredu's account of marriage, courtship and sexual mores in the traditional Akan context and they also deepen our understanding of the multifaceted dynamics of the colonial conquest and its subsequent relations. Here, Wiredu's exertions indicate other fertile directions for African philosophy even though he doesn't go far along them but the mere fact he draws attentions to an important and also often repressed trope at the centre of the colonial encounter is encouraging enough.

However, one cannot ascribe a similar attitude to his essay 'Democracy and Consensus in African Traditional Politics: A Plea for a Non-Party Polity'. In this essay Wiredu argues that the:

> ...Ashanti system was a consensual democracy. It was a democracy because government was by the consent, and subject to the control, of the people as expressed through the representatives. It was consensual because, at least, as a rule, that consent was negotiated on the principle of consensus (By contrast, the majoritarian system might be said to be, in principle, based on consent without consensus.).[35]

When Wiredu broaches the issue of politics and its present and future in postcolonial Africa, then we are compelled to visit a whole range of debates and discourses especially in the social sciences in Africa which arguably are more directly concerned with questions pertaining to governance, democracy and the challenges of contemporary globalisation. The next section will examine the problems of governance in contemporary Africa while at the same time focusing on the common challenges posed by the current wave of globalisation.

Postcolonial Africa continues to contend with the same old problems: poverty, illiteracy, disease, inhumane authoritarian state structures and genocidal conflict situations. All these problems are in turn compounded by the widespread collapse of several national economies and state apparatuses. Within the contemporary global system, the general state of affairs in the distressed African continent bestows upon it a singularity (exceptionalism?) not to be found in other regions of the world. Other regions, cultures and geopolitical blocs struggle to establish and define larger roles for themselves inside the current global structure while Africa recedes continually from a world order propelled by complex systems of information technology, transnational capital and entities and a series of international arrangements and institutions that are by and large a product of contemporary processes of globalisation.

The intensive technologisation of contemporary human experience necessitates that Africans scholars and Africanists rethink terms such as marginalisation, imperialism and hegemony in view of the new kinds of stratification caused by high-level digitalisation and global capitalism. These twin forces are creating spectres, scenarios and conditions which, to be sure, have outstripped our existing conceptual models.

Globalisation: And Where Does Africa Fit In?

For purposes of clarity and focus, I shall suggest that the events of the millennial moment have further excluded Africa in a way existing epistemologies do not describe. And this is why we have to reconsider terms such as marginalisation, imperialism and hegemony from a highly particularistic stand-point. The production of capital, knowledge(s), cultural formations and new modes of human activity without any meaningful let alone significant contri-bution by the African continent calls for an urgent retheorisation of lack, absence and passive agency. This is needed to clarify African realities and options in the face of processes of digitalisation and capitalisation that have vastly redefined and expanded the common field of human experience as conceived and understood by the West.

Also, if Africa is not a significant participant in the contemporary global order then how can it partake in the problems, futures and advantages en-shrined in it? What precisely are the new discoveries, languages, values and institutions that are products of processes of contemporary globalisation? Are these discoveries, languages, values and institutions not developments forged by the West and civilisations who genuinely share Western values? The point is that since Africa is not a major global player, those Western-inspired developments would prove rather problematic for African digestion. But even in spite of the continued and systematic relegation of the African conti-nent from processes of contemporary globalisation, forms of existence are being produced within the continent that call for a retooling of existing meth-odological approaches. If for example, populations of African nations in-crease while industrial and agricultural output diminishes in direct relation, what strategies of survival have emerged and in what contexts and forma-tions? How would those strategies of survival impact on the general under-standing of processes of contemporary globalisation in their acceptable and digestible formations? These are questions that obviously require a deepening and broadening of existing methodological projects.

The expansion of capital within the African continent has always been a slow and irregular affair because of a condition Samir Amin terms, 'capital-ism without capitalists.'[36] The trajectories of transnational capital have always managed to further exclude and marginalise Africa. The point would be to examine what formations the very structures of exclusion have generated and what these might mean from local and global standpoints. Also, there is the need to reposition and reconceptualise knowledges relating to the condi-tions that reproduce Africa's continued marginalisation. This section cannot address the full implications of these general questions, rather, it would only attempt to further highlight the epistemological imperatives of Africa's con-tinued marginalisation from processes of globalisation and the forms of organisation that have emerged in the continent that bypass and/or subvert those very processes.

Theorists such as Claude Ake[37] and Achille Mbembe have stressed that the postcolonial state in Africa shares similar characteristics with the colonial one in its random and widespread economy of violence and arbitrariness. In addition, we must remember that the nation-states of Africa themselves are a product of the arbitrariness of the colonial intervention.[38] They, in other words, were constructed as superimposed structures of force without sensitive correlation with local conditions. As such, the vast struggles and the mechanisms of stabilisation that produced nation-states of the West are largely absent within the African context. By mechanisms of stabilisation, one means the development of a capitalist system alongside a mercantile class, the emergence of a robust civil society and the multiple and general stratification of society into distinct formations. In other words, there was development and differentiation within society at the same time. This scenario is largely absent within the context of Africa's historical evolution.

In Africa, because of the economy of violence on which the colonial and postcolonial states were constructed the question of rights became indistinguishable from the brute fact of power, the force of the 'commandement' as Mbembe terms it. Furthermore, the question of raising feasible options for development among the postcolonial political elite did not arise. During independence and after, the absence of a productive sector and also a material base necessitated a blind struggle for power. As such, the rules of political competition were never free and fair and in this way a taxonomy of Hobbesianisation was instituted within the political and economic realms. Ake described the scenarios thus:

> Political power was everything: it was not only access to wealth but also the means to security and the only guarantor of general well-being. For anyone outside the hegemonic faction of the political elite, it was generally futile to harbor any illusions of becoming wealthy by entrepreneurial activity or to even take personal safety for granted.[39]

In view of this situation, the political elites operated within what one might call on ideological vacuum. In more precise terms, the development paradigm which they advocated was a mask for the struggles for the consolidation of political power. Thus the development paradigm was not meant to serve the purpose of development.

From this perspective, the very question of rights and ownership within the African context assumes a peculiar angle. Mahmood Mamdani draws on an important distinction between 'ethnic' and 'civic' spaces and how these categories have impacted on the general understanding of various rights and obligations in Africa.[40] Not only have those categories affected the attitudes and practices towards rights and obligations, they have also influenced in a profound manner the trajectories of projects of democratisation and modernisation within the continent.

Africa is marked tragically by two essentially oppositional series of binarisations: precolonial and postcolonial, premodern and modern, ethnic and civic, universals and particulars and so on. And so we see feudalistic tendencies enshrined in, and struggling within apparently modern discourses, institutions and frameworks. Consequently, the productions, products and taxonomies that emerge from this conceptual mesh are neither here nor there. Or might one say they are in the main feudalistic in view of their rudimentariness and inchoateness. This is why the following scenario is evident in the political realm:

> The state in Africa has been a maze of autonomies of form and content; the person who holds office may not exercise its powers, the person who exercises the powers of a given office may not be its holder, informal relations often override formal relations, the formal hierarchies of bureaucratic structure and political power are not always the clue to decision-making power. Positions that seem to be held by persons are in fact held by kinship groups; at one point the public is privatized and at another the private is 'publicized' and two or more political systems and political cultures in conflict may coexist in the same social formation.[41]

Undoubtedly, the existence of these contradictory practices within the same social formation has wide-ranging implications not only for the proper functioning of law and order but also for the comprehension of how rights and obligations are construed in such a context. In the conflation of 'civic' and 'ethnic' ideologies, mentalities and practices, employing purely Western models and approaches to the tasks of socio-political organisation within the African context unusually proves to be inadequate and unrepresentative.

What is more, the state in Africa is still at a very rudimentary stage of development and this is even more so in comparison to countries of South East Asia. Due to the fact that political power in Africa is associated with monetary wealth, the productive sectors that are normally independent of the state have been stifled. This deliberate emasculation of independent productive sectors of the economy has intensified the processes of brutalisation within the political realm to the detriment of general social cohesiveness and a truly independent civil society. Thus, a pathology of Hobbesianisation characterises much of Africa both within the public and private spheres. Claude Ake describes the pathology in the following manner:

> In much of Africa, the public sphere is a contested space where strangers converge to appropriate for their interest groups whatever is in offer,

including the power of the state. Every interest group is out for itself; each wants to appropriate and privatize state power to its own benefit. The issues of national interest, public interest, or even public policy scarcely arise. When they exist, they are lost in the contradiction between the manifest and latent functions of policy.[42]

In other words, the state in Africa exists within a realm of lawlessness. Again this condition has profound implications for Western theories and models of socio-political organisation. Recall that the Lockean model of the social contract was meant to institute a mode of social accord that not only promoted and protected private property and initiative, it also sought to reinforce the rights of the individual within the collective. This model has been modified and refined over centuries in the West but its basic tenets remain the same.

On the contrary, what obtains in Africa are the emergence of forms of 'private indirect government',[43] new violent technologies of domination (that exist outside the realms of legitimacy and institutionalised norms and practices) in addition to the continued gangsterisation of the military and law enforcement agencies. If the state dispenses an economy of death as Mbembe argues that very economy has in turn been appropriated by the larger society and rechannelled with even greater devastation. For the state, the values of democracy, accountability, transparency, consensus building and the rule of law have never been central. Instead, strategies of authoritarianism and self-perpetuation are infinitely more important and so African populations have never properly acquired the habits and attitudes enshrined within the Lockean compact and the tenets inherent in the ideals of the Enlightenment.

Samuel P. Huntington argues that post-Cold War era is being dominated by a 'clash of civilizations'.[44] Regrettably, Africa is not regarded as the centre of a major civilisation. Undoubtedly, the advent of the colonial event in Africa not only disrupted a previously stable mode of relations but it also disallowed the basis for the emergence of a genuinely productive material system. Colonial administrative authorities ensured that a truly independent class of capitalists or entrepreneurs was not produced.[45] The absence of a vibrant economic kingdom meant the struggle for a material base had to waged within the political kingdom where most of the economic resources are concentrated. This condition has invariably defined the trajectories of the state in Africa up till the present times. And states and societies around the world are products of specific historical configurations. The dominance of Western ideas and models of organisation have led to the near universalisation of them.

But Huntington warns us to exercise caution against this pervasive universalisation. He points out the ideologies that defined the outcome of the twentieth century namely 'liberalism, anarchism, corporatism, Marxism, communism, social democracy, nationalism, fascism, Christian democracy',[46] are all products of the Western civilisation. And yet the West seeks to universalise the values behind these ideologies on a world scale. To be sure, local factors outside the Western civilisation are always working to subvert and transform those universalised values and ideologies. This is why his thesis of dividing the world into seven or eight civilisations seems attractive at least initially in spite of the reaction contained in his central arguments.

Africa's peculiar civilisational perspectives have meant that superimposed Western models have had to be reconfigured to suit local conditions. And the products of those processes of recontextualisation have been marked irreducibly by hybridity, mimesis and eclecticism.

At this juncture, let us focus on processes of contemporary globalisation and then examine how Africa is or is not affected by the expansion of global capitalism. Increasingly, protests and counter-discourses to contemporary globalisation are undergoing more robust articulation. Activists of the antiglobalisation movement claim that contemporary globalisation has reached its point of crisis and that the system in its present form is now a source of delegitimisation.[47] They argue in addition that globalisation has failed to deliver its promises and that it is not in a position to do so anyway. Even more disconcerting is the claim that the transnational corporation is the prime mover of contemporary globalisation and that it is the cause of widespread and unparalleled environmental degradation. At the political level, it is pointed the liberal democratic models as practiced by Western countries have in fact being converted into plutocracies because of their corruption and domination by corporate capital.[48] Anti-globalists in turn advocate a widening and deepening of processes of political participation and the reform of the institutions that mediate those processes.

Implicated in globalisation processes is the US quest to dominate and militarise space.[49] Noam Chomsky warns us that the US Space Command is about to push the arms race into a more complex stage. Regarding the nature of their project he writes:

> The space command isn't really concerned about the danger that we might blow up the world. That's a small problem. What they're interested in is something different. They're interested in providing the basis for U.S. military action, including first strike if needed. But more important, they're protecting U.S. based investment and commercial interests. And they give an analogy. They say that the militarization of space is very much like the development of navies. The British navy ruled the seas in order to protect British investments and commercial interests.[50]

Thus the U.S. Space Command is the military arm of Corporate America and its collararies. It aims for full-spectrum dominance of space with the aid of its vast technological expertise and any challenge from any potential adversary would be met by even more massive militarisation.[51] Chomsky also points out that since the West took over the Russian economy more than a decade ago the result has been economic collapse.[52]

More radical anti-globalists argue that the globalisation of poverty and the employment of debt as a weapon of control by the U.S. is a deliberate strategy conceived as far back as 1948.[53] In that year, George Kennan, the State Department imperial planner had written:

> We have 50 percent of the world's wealth, but only 6.3 percent of its population. In this situation, our real job in the coming period is to devise a pattern of relationships which permit as to maintain this position of disparity. To do so, we have the dispense with all sentimentality ...[We] should cease thinking about human rights, the raising of living standards and democratization.[54]

In this way, the relationship between the Bretton Woods institutions and U.S. Space Command was forged. And while this relationship has promoted the interests of corporate America on a global scale, it has resulted in escalating levels of poverty elsewhere. Advances in technology have brought about a continuing process of dematerialisation and miniaturisation whereby regions such as Africa even in its status as a producer of raw materials have experienced even greater peripheralisation and pauperisation. With the possible exception of South Africa, the continent is excluded from the debates and actions meant to check the erosion of workers' rights and the ravages of global capitalism on the welfare state and its previous abilities to provide benefits in education, healthcare and public infrastructure. But even in South Africa, the unions are clearly losing their dynamism and diversity and are beginning to resemble their American counterparts.[55]

Antiglobalists also argue that the mantra of neoliberalism is certain to further dispossess the underclass. In precise terms:

> As neoliberalism expands, conflicts between unions and their own rank-and-file members are apt to grow. From South Africa to the United States, since the initial social upheavals in which they emerged, unions have survived by accommodating to the dominant economic order. This has meant adopting an informal structure and culture that denies rank-and-file members control over union affairs, in the workplace, at the bargaining table, in the halls of government, and on the streets.[56]

What this means is that corporate globalisation is aiming for a complete feudalisation of economic life within the current global order.[57]

Activists are also pushing for a transnational revolutionary movement to campaign for corporate accountability and protests have begun to demand a radical restructuring of the World Trade Organisation (WTO), the International Monetary Fund (IMF) and the World Bank in order to address the needs of people and also the environment.[58] But by and large, these protests and activities have an insignificant African input. This is because Africa has become 'a strategic ghetto'.[59] The ghettoisation of the African continent is a product of several factors. First, an elemental exclusion from the new technological order has meant that it has not been able to develop the new structures of relations and make the radical questioning of corporate globalisation possible. In other words, not only is Africa removed from the centres of debate, its technological disadvantages prevent it from even apprehending the various ramifications to technicalities of that debate.

Electricity, which for instance, is taken for granted in other regions of the world is still a big problem in most parts of Africa. Thus this excludes it from the digital network that interconnects other regions of the globe and further entrenches its ghettoisation. The genocidal conflicts that plague many nation-states of Africa also means there are more urgent concerns that preoccupy African governments and peoples other than the serious threats posed to the environment by corporate globalisation.

As a result of the new structures of feudalisation being erected by corporate capital and its various institutional advocates and support systems, corporate globalisation has been described as a 'system ruled by the law of the jungle: a war in which everyone fights everyone, and may the strongest, the most ferocious, the most ruthless win.'[60] In addition, it is a system 'responsible for the accelerated destruction of the environment; for air, land, and water pollution; as well as for the green house effect that could produce an ecological disaster of unimaginable proportions in a matter of a few years.'[61]

These are all very serious matters that should concern Africans as they do other people but because of the continuing ghettoisation and immiseration of the African continent they do not as they ought to. Africa is not considered fit for dollarisation as has been carried out in Ecuador, El Salvador, Guatemala and Panama. Chinweizu, the radical Nigerian public intellectual reminds us that George Bush had said 'we need Africa, but not with the Africans'.[62] He also points out that the dynamics of the post Cold War era have marked Africa for extinction and adds that 'the Black World must quickly and durably put together a collective security alliance to protect itself and its civilisation.'[63] There are many actions Africa needs to take in order to survive and many of these are widely known.[64] But the reality is that the numerous internal problems and contradictions, the crises of many nation-states, death, disease and poverty all make the possibilities of forging a really viable alliance exceedingly dim. Achille Mbembe captures the regression in which Africa is enmeshed:

> We must speak of Africa only as a chimera on which we all work blindly, a nightmare we produce and from which we make a living and which we sometimes enjoy, but which everywhere deeply repels us, to the point that we may evince toward it the kind of disgust we feel on seeing a cadavar.[65]

Neither this spectre nor this positionality enables Africa to meet the challenges of corporate globalisation let alone its own numerous internal contradictions. Left within its ghetto, Africa's chances of survival are indeed very minimal. The problems within the ghetto are enough to cause its total disintegration. But before the advent of this disintegration, other forms of life and death are emerging. The final part of this section examines some of the features of these forms.

Forms of Life and Death in the Ghetto

It is obvious that the Lockean compact of socio-political organisation is in deep distress in many parts of Africa. Recall the creation of territorial boundaries by the Congress of Berlin in 1884 introduced a form of territoriality that was alien to the existing forms prior to colonisation. The forms of territoriality introduced by colonisation have never been stable. The very artificiality of their construction is reflected in the various kinds of conflict that plague the continent from those based on ethnically motivated struggles to those based on the unclear perceptions of the nation-state itself. The nation-state as a product of colonisation is often a terrain of acrimonious dispute.

The historical forces that contributed to the stabilisation of the nation-state in the West are different from these that [de]constructed Africa. The legacies that have stabilised that nation-state in the West include Greek philosophy, rationalism, Roman law, Latin Christianity, and the tradition of the rule of law.[66] But even in the West, these legacies are under threat as immigrants of vastly disparate backgrounds decide to make the West their home.

Also, those vital legacies have not been central to the formation of the nation-state in Africa. In the specific case of Africa, the nation-state is a product of a form of territoriality whose foundational principle depends on force and arbitrariness. That is why the nation-state in Africa is largely unstable. The notion that the transference or exportation of Western institutions, practices and values is bound to lead to Westernisation is being invalidated. Rather than bringing triumph, the assumed dominance of neoliberalism after the collapse of communism at certain grave moments, exhibits signs of exhaustion. With this state of affairs, non-Western cultures are in the process of fashioning new mechanics of existence and for the most part, these mechanics are informed by values and modes of behaviour that draw some of their ontological features from a world shaped by disorienting forms of postmodern conflict.[67]

These forms of post-modern conflict assume many colorations. Because the state no longer possesses a monopoly of force and because its legitimacy is everywhere contested, 'strange' informal technologies of domination have emerged. Warlordism and the rise of ethnic militias have become a common occurrence. The struggles over the construction and possession of identities have also assumed alarming proportions as a result of the basically non-ideological depoliticisation of the political realm.[68] In other words, the struggles of identity have become disconnected from traditional conceptions of sovereignty and citizenship. In the absence of the traditional conceptions of the construction of consciousness, subjectivity and modes of belonging, the fabrications of personal and collective identities are in turn defined by forces and agents devoid of traditional notions of legitimacy. The church, the crime syndicate, the Islamic brotherhood, the neighbourhood vigilante group or the ethnic association also possess the instruments and powers for the construction of personal and collective identity since both the state and the nation are failing.

The failed state on its part, attempts to conjure a dramaturgy of excessive histrionics at the point of its absent legitimacy. Nothing no longer binds the subject-citizen to the state or nation in concrete terms. The postcolonial African state has enough to cope with contending with debt dependency, absent social services and public infrastructure and declining gross domestic production. These problems erode its ability to monopolise force and maintain law and order.

For the subject-citizen, the state in the circumstances being described loses its attraction and s/he begins to look for other forms of community and belonging. In the postcolony, the matter of life and death is then judged more or less by chance.[69] In this case, s/he (the subject-citizen) may find himself/herself within any kind of association whether legitimate or illegitimate. As mentioned earlier, these associations include religious sects, ethnic militias, non governmental organisations etc. The point is that the state is no longer the sole arbiter of personal and collective identity in the classical Hegelian sense. Identities are now assuming a multiplicity of characteristics: disaporic, transnational and of course purely and narrowly sectarian.

In Africa, where the state has never had a secure foundation the implications of its final loss of legitimacy are numerous. First, it opens up a terrain in which a variety of actors and social formations struggle to fill the vacuum. Second, the emergent structure of social relations and institutions which in turn are products of processes of disinstitutionalisation and informalisation[70] may not bear exact resemblance with the eroded structures and institutions. Third, we can point to the existence of new technologies and agencies of domination outside the collapsed state order. Fourth, new forms of marketisation and regions of commerce are also springing up. Fifth, the subject-citizen in the face of the collapsed state apparatus and new forms of political and economic disempowerment has to redefine his/her status without the manifest support of the dissolved psychosocial and political order. Even within this broad range of implications, he/she has to contend with a variety of conundrums that make everyday life as previously lived no longer applicable.

In sub-Saharan Africa, the banalisation of death is more or less an accepted fact of existence. In Rwanda, the Democratic Republic of Congo, Angola, Burundi, Somalia, Liberia, Sierra-Leone, Sudan and Nigeria events bear this out. For instance in Nigeria even after the civil war (1967–70), low intensity conflict is a fact of life with the perpetual disturbances in the Niger Delta region, religious conflicts in most of the North and now the crises resulting from the activities of several ethnic militias.[71] In the case of Nigeria, its sheer size, population density and luck has kept it from full scale internecine conflict up till now. But this is not to claim that its luck will hold out, things might change.

South Africa which is now seen as the leading nation within the African continent also has to cope with crucial problems which if improperly handled may diminish its influence. These problems include substantial black unemployment, the negative forces of global capitalism and the large influx of illegal immigrants who put tremendous pressure on its services and resources. It also has to deal with the threat of ghettoisation which is a reality everywhere in the postcolony.

In most parts of Africa, the loss of legitimacy of the nation-state and its multiple structures and institutions have resulted in processes of disinstitutionalisation and informalisation with new agents and associations struggling to usurp the place and functions of old legitimate orders. Some of these agents and associations operate within ideological contexts that are sometimes antithetical to the interests and orientations of the traditional nation-state. Thus notions relating to citizenship, nationhood and nation-building, ownership, territoriality and so on have come under onslaught. Within the context of regression in the postcolony and global capitalism all these various concepts have to be reconceptualised bearing in mind the changes and challenges brought on by processes of disinstitutionalisation and informalisation. In Africa, the state is usually neither Lockean nor Hegelian. It is instead a fabrication of force and for its survival maintains an economy of terror.

Thus the bestowal of rights, benefits and obligations on the subject-citizen is more often than not an act of whim and arbitrariness. Nowhere is this more evident than in the numerous kinds of authoritarian formations basking within or outside traditional structures of legitimacy that characterise Africa. The privatisation of public authority obviously has telling implications on the rights and potentials of the individual. What the individual owns and the means by which s/he owns it have to contend with the personalisation of public authority. In other words, constitutionalism and the rule of law as observed in consolidated democracies hardly exist in most parts of Africa. Thus, the question of rights, civic order and political stability relates to the mechanics of force since authorities normally operate within structures of normlessness.

But the structures of normlessness within which the state in Africa thrives are not only what determine the various fortunes of private and public life. We also have to bear in mind that the average African subject is marked by a series of binary epistemologies; civic and ethnic, colonial and postcolonial, tradition and modernity etc. all of whose borderline demarcations must not be taken for granted since they are themselves subject to overlapping determinations and of course sometimes subvert their defined rigidities and boundaries.

Finally, we have to be alert to the changes now taking place in the postcolony. Indeed these changes are profound for the collapse of state orders and cannot be dismissed lightly. The emergent social formations and actors of the post-statist (dis)order in Africa may eventually go a long way in determining the open questions of citizenship, territoriality, morality, belonging and of course ownership. Perhaps more than with corporate globalisation, Africa has to contend with the rapid disintegration of its old orders and the challenge of replacing them with viable ones. This is the conclusion one is tempted to draw as post-statist social formations and (dis)order grow into prominence.

Obviously, the institution of these new social formations awash with all the various kinds of uncertainties imaginable—both conceptual and practical—necessitates a reconceptualisation of a wide array of issues. What would be the fate of the human subject within the matrix of these violent permutations? How will social (dis)order emerge and from what precise mechanisms of power? What will be the primary impetus behind these new technologies of domination? These are questions that ought to be the focus of inquiry in this transitional phase. In addressing them, it is likely that we shall be able to fathom the shape of the dynamics to come. In addition, we shall be in a position to anticipate the effects of crucial phenomena that might well decide the fate(s) of the African subject and continent.

For Wiredu however, a different set of concerns regarding political life in Africa is addressed. According to him, political party structures are to be replaced by non-party consensual politics. Nothing captures the urgency of this conviction more than the remark that 'far from the complexities of contemporary African life making the consensual, non-party precedents of traditional African politics, now unusable, they make them indispensable'.[72] Wiredu does not seem to have estimated the distance between a past disfigured by the decisive onslaughts of a colonial encounter and the exigencies of the perplexing machinations of modernity on the one hand, and the new configuration of forces and problems in the postcolony on the other. The African mind is inevitably caught between those too frustrating and elusive sets of circumstances. To believe that a certain African historical reality may be summoned at will and completely is to underestimate the excruciating impact absorbed by the African self in relation to the decisive event of the colonial encounter. The event we must never fail to remind ourselves (no matter how attractive it is to forget or reduce it) should be the yardstick by which we attempt to retrieve whatever can be recalled from the past. The arguments rehearsed here form the basis of our critique of Wiredu's conception of decolonisation and also his understanding of political existence in contemporary Africa. And they are extremely crucial to the points to be established in the following chapter.

In the next section, the discussion on Wiredu will be extended by bringing him into conversation with Olusegun Oladipo. In doing so, we shall be able to focus on broader areas of the 'African predicament' and also the direction that this study subsequently takes.

Rationality and Self-Identity: A Critique

Africa's problems are getting increasingly complicated and even the best minds are often hard-put to proffer suitable solutions. However, that solutions are still being advanced is by itself commendable, but it is quite another matter how these solutions have affected and continue to affect African societies. The tremendous hegemonic power of Western civilisation no doubt has contributed to various forms of anomie in other less fortunate societies, in terms of the political, economic, technological and least of all, cultural difficulties which developing societies are experiencing.

Kwasi Wiredu and Olusegun Oladipo are two African philosophers who demonstrate admirable inventiveness in addressing African problems. Indeed, the methodologies with which they negotiate the widening chasm of African disintegration should provide worthy topics of debate. Nonetheless, one notices a certain flawed utopianist ethic that undercuts some aspects of their respective projects.

First of all, we should specify precisely what these projects constitute. For Wiredu, it is essential for the African philosopher to be 'critical, conceptual, and reconstructive'.[73] Even more importantly, Africans are advised to scrutinise influences from other cultures in 'the spirit of due reflection'.[74]

Oladipo on his own part counsels that 'it is not only conceptual understanding that we need to develop a critical attitude'[75] (sic) concerning the modern world. One should note the predominantly rationalist outlook that informs the views of Wiredu and Oladipo, a rationalism whose origins are found in eighteenth century Europe, when the thought of Voltaire, Rousseau and Diderot formed the dominant intellectual climate. Postmodernist thought has succeeded in challenging the adequacy of rationalism in apprehending and shaping the world.

It is not that something is innately wrong with the discursive origins of the rationalism they employ. Both Wiredu and Oladipo in the attempt to create an African identity suggest that multicultural dialogue is also required.[76] Both agree that the prerequisites of science and technology make it imperative to hold multicultural intercourse at several levels in order to advance the cause of 'human flourishing'.[77] In general, this attitude is commendable, but the deplorable conditions of the contemporary African world, in addition to the realities of the present global order (political and economic), make some of the pronouncements of Wiredu and Oladipo somewhat over-optimistic and, as such, inadequate for confronting Africa's numerous problems.

Oladipo affirms that:

> It does not require any philosophical acumen to see that reason is a crucial factor in the practice and realization...of self appraisal and openness.[78]

Indeed, the need for self-appraisal in order to arrive at an acceptable kind of self-identity is one that has troubled Africans since the time of the colonial encounter. The crisis of self-identity began when Europe commenced its so-called 'civilising mission' in Africa. As African social and political institutions, cosmologies and cultures, declined, the ways of the West gained rapid ascendancy. Since the turn of the nineteenth century, educated Africans from Monrovia, Freetown, Accra and Lagos have struggled to acquire the attributes of Western culture. Eurocentric racism ensured that the denigration of African traditional cultures has been widespread. However, the labour of colonial Africans to acquire the habits of modern European culture, assiduous as it was, received only limited acceptance and encouragement. In fact, sometimes it elicited the outright derision of the colonial overlords. In the words of Basil Davidson:

> It did them no good. The more they proved they knew, and the more artfully they argued their case for admission to equality of status, the less

they were listened to. Better by far, pestered officials were bound to think, the 'uncorrupted child of nature' than these wretchedly 'Europeanized' Negroes.[79]

This virulent flood of Eurocentric racism had telling consequences for the African's sense of self. Again Basil Davidson observes that colonised Africans were condemned to 'wander in some no-man's-land of their own until the trumpet of destiny, at some unthinkable time in the future, should swing wide the doors of civilization and let them in'.[80] It is because these problems still exist that scholars like Wiredu and Oladipo continue to tackle issues related to the question of African identity. The hegemonic nature of Western culture has definitely not helped matters, and Africa on its part has not been able to interrogate fruitfully, let alone subvert, the dominance of the Western/metropolitan culture in the global order. Both Wiredu and Oladipo apparently think that the dialogue between the West and Africa, and by extension, between the modern and the traditional, can take place on an equitable basis. They need to realise more distinctly the scope and nature of the problems mediating against mutual cultural understanding.

Not unexpectedly, within the broad and immensely diverse spectrum of the Western philosophical heritage are various canons of rationality. As noted, the eighteenth century rationalist outlook of Europe seems to have a strong influence on Wiredu and Oladipo. This is coming at a time when there is an acute suspicion of all candidates for 'truth' in the West, and when the postmodernist temper has instituted a rigorous questioning of all assumptions, both classical and modern.

In her paper 'Beginning to Theorise Post-modernism', Linda Hutcheon writes:

> It is no longer big news that master narratives of bourgeois liberalism are under attack. There is a long history of many such skeptical sieges to positivism and humanism and today's foot soldiers of theory—Foucault, Derrida, Habermas, Rorty, Baudrillard—follow in the footsteps of Nietzsche, Heidegger, Marx and Freud, to name but a few, in their challenges to the empiricist, rationalist, humanist assumptions of our cultural systems including those of science.[81]

Western opposition to traditional orders of knowledge and culture is getting increasingly widespread. Richard Rorty, for instance, has done some seminal work in attacking analytic philosophy. A particular metaphilosophical passage captures his view on traditional epistemology:

> We owe the notion of philosophy as a tribunal of pure reason, upholding or denying the claims of the rest of culture, to the eighteenth century especially to Kant, but this Kantian notion presupposed general assent to

Lockean notions of mental process and Cartesian notions of mental substance. In the nineteenth century, the notion of philosophy as a foundational discipline which 'grounds' knowledge claims was consolidated in the writings of neo-Kantians.[82]

The deconstruction of Western metaphysics (*eidos, arche, telos, and aletheia*) has surely become a significant trend in Western philosophy and this intellectual phenomenon is bound in the long run to affect philosophical discourse in cultures other than the West. But this knowledge does not appear to influence significantly the deliberations of Wiredu and Oladipo. This is just one aspect of the matter.

A significant part of the African philosophical enterprise is guided by 'a quest for freedom and development'.[83] Indeed, after the demise of colonialism on the continent an equally insidious form of oppression took its place. The failure of African political leadership is all too well known. Consequently, the quest for freedom has, by and large, remained truncated. Furthermore, the African future is usually decided in the disconcerting theatre of pseudo-politics, so intellectuals, journalists, artists, the rural and urban poor, together with other sectors of the underclass, can do very little to shape their own future. Intellectuals who have been able to penetrate the political terrain and the corridors of power have been largely ineffectual. The disenfranchisement of the majority of Africans, in real terms, is almost total. Claude Ake captures graphically the helplessness of the situation:

> The African who is slated for democracy is a rural dweller who lives in a society which is still predominantly communal. She is a subsistence farmer toiling for a precarious existence. She has virtually no access to safe drinking water, health services and sanitary facilities and she is illiterate or nearly so. What does democratization mean in this setting and for this person? There is no chance in her ignorance, her debilitating poverty and precarious existence. She is offered only a spurious choice which is framed by forces beyond her control often beyond her understanding and of little relevance to her needs.[84]

This state of disempowerment, as mentioned earlier, applies to most Africans. Criticism is a monopoly of the state in Africa, and any other criticism is often considered dissension, if not outright treason. The state also attempts to be the major arbiter over collective thought. Herein lies the over-optimism of Wiredu and Oladipo in not fully taking into cognisance the anomalous functions of the state in most African countries.[85]

Political leadership in Africa generally lacks vision and competence (since the postcolonial state basically inherits the terror and arbitrariness of the colonial state),[86] yet it is the primary architect of the people's fate. Most opposing

views—and they need to be oppositional to challenge creditably the dominant mediocrity and abuse of power for the even greater challenge of development—lack the required means and resources to make any significant headway in determining policies of state. Wiredu and Oladipo are not very forthcoming on this aspect of the African dilemma. This critique of authoritarianism is a key ingredient in the quest for freedom and development. In other
words, it is also important to evolve alternative modes of critical inquiry that
are necessary for her collective health. In many respects, this critique (of authoritarianism) has been so feeble that the international community has now
taken up some of the responsibility of providing this much-needed service
with all its neo-imperialist implications.

However, Wiredu and Oladipo are more forthcoming on the question of
African identity, as opposed to the critique of authoritarianism. Oladipo agrees
with Wiredu that there can be multicultural intercourse without the loss of
identity, as the Japanese have demonstrated. Their views on culture in the
formation of self-identity are reasonably balanced, until when one is confronted with the fact that the power to create approved cultural identities lies,
to a large extent, with oligarchic reactionaries in Africa. Unless this disturbing
equation is adequately contested and changed, debates about canons of rationality and cultural identities will be meaningless. However, the search for
suitable forms of rationality and self-identity is bound to remain an enduring
one, and various intellectuals are certain to offer different responses. The
Senghorian conception of 'the African personality'—Negritude—has been
severely criticised, but the current trends of nativist discourses have hardly
moved beyond the Senghorian signature. Indeed, the way both Wiredu and
Oladipo conceptualise and project their notions of identity do not capture
the range and intensity of debates surrounding the concept. Consequently,
'the new popularity of identity as an interpretative devise is also a result of the
exceptional plurality of meanings the term can harness.'[87] Of course, the temptations and pressures to project an identity that is formed along national,
racial, ethnic, regional and local lines are very powerful but we also need to be
aware that identity-making can end up being fascistic. Examples of how
identity-making can become radically evil include the activities of the Afrikaners
of South Africa in the years of the apartheid regime and of course the Nazis
of Germany. Gilroy argues for rethinking of the concept we become more
appreciative of the fact 'that identity-making has a history even though its
historical character is often systematically concealed.'[88] In view of the danger
posed to human security Gilroy alerts us to how identity-making can be destructive and also impede the quest for a cosmopolitan ethic. On this point,
he argues that 'identity forever sets one group apart from others who lack the

particular, chosen traits that become the basis of typology and comparative evaluation. No longer a site for the affirmation of subjectivity and autonomy, identity mutates. Its motion reveals a deep desire for mechanical solidarity, seriality, and hypersimilarity. The scope for individual agency dwindles and then disappears.'[89] Ultimately all these discourses, in spite of their obvious limitations, are necessary for the unending task of social, political, economic and cultural rejuvenation within the African continent, and the establishment and consolidation of a more humane civic culture in a continent where the authoritarian statist systems regard such matters to be their sole domain.

We shall now return to the issue of conceptual decolonisation with which we began this chapter from the perspective of a critique of Wiredu's views on rationality and self-identity.

Of Universals and Particulars

Kwasi Wiredu's latest volume of essays, *Cultural Universals and Particulars (1996)*, marks a considerable development since the publication of his first text, *Philosophy and an African Culture*, for a number of reasons. In this work Wiredu argues that the Akan mode of religious worship is different from the Judeo-Christian practice imposed by the missionaries of colonialism. As a result, Africans themselves have become enmeshed in the entanglements created by the imposition of alien categories and modes of conceptualisation. Pursuing this line of argument, Wiredu writes:

> It is a more striking fact that many contemporary African expositors of their own traditional systems of thought yield no ground to their Western colleagues in stressing the role of belief in the supernatural in African thinking. It is hard not to see this as evidence of the fact in some ways, Christian proselytization and Western education have been over-successful in Africa.[90]

Furthermore, Wiredu argues that the notion of a Supreme Being created out of nothing does not occur in traditional Akan thought and perhaps most traditional African systems of thought. It is all well and good to discover all this, but then how do we commence the task of conceptual decolonisation in this vital area in which several other variables have become implicated, without negative implications and consequences? Conceptual decolonisation undoubtedly forms a major thrust of Wiredu's recent philosophical deliberations. In addition, the manner in which Wiredu conflates religion with the rationalist outlook decidedly privileges the latter over the former. It should be noted that several aspects of religion confound and are in turn confounded by rigid rationalism. And once people decide on a mode of worship, an internal logic that oftentimes can only make sense within the frame of blind faith is instituted. Wiredu notes—and it is indeed true—that efforts have been made all over Africa to indigenise Christianity, and so one does not need to contend only with the original Judeo-Christian conception but also the indigenised forms of Christianity that one finds. In most parts of Africa, religion is a highly fractious affair in which, oftentimes, mere rational argument may not prevail. It is apparent enough that Wiredu is criticising the mode of worship imposed by early Christian missionaries, but he also needs to undertake a critique of what now obtains in post-coloniality, a more overtly complicated matter. In this instance also, reason alone is not a sufficient analytical tool, especially in cases where the most virulent forms of religious fundamentalism are to be found.[91]

However, Wiredu is on safer philosophical grounds when he debunks Cartesianism within the Akan context, saying:

> the category is inadmissible in this system of thought. Should the reader be curious at this stage as to whether mind too is quasi-material in the Akan way of thinking, the short answer is that mind is not thought of as an entity at all but rather simply as the capacity, supervenient upon brain states and process, to do various things. Hence the question whether mind is a spiritual or material or quasi-material entity does not arise.[92]

Wiredu has repeatedly addressed some of the practical aspects of his theories, notably those pertaining to conceptual decolonisation. In his essay entitled 'Custom and Morality: A Comparative Analysis of some African and Western Conceptions of Morals', Wiredu demonstrates in various ways how morality has come to be confused with custom and vice-versa. Polygamy, for instance, was attacked by Christian moralists as being unacceptable in African societies, even when custom validated it. In Wiredu's words, 'the Christian missionaries who came to Africa to 'save' our souls, perceiving the practice to be incompatible with their own norms of good conduct condemned it as immoral and worked assiduously to eradicate it.'[93] This in his view, and perhaps correctly so, has led to 'a kind of ethical schizophrenia in the consciousness of many of our people'.[94] Nonetheless, the mere realities of operating within a modern economy have made the practice of polygamy unsupportable, as he subsequently adds.

Similarly, the Christian missionaries preached that pre-marital sex was immoral conduct, whereas custom in traditional Akan society held that carnal knowledge among intending marriage partners was indeed legitimate. Christianity eroded this age-long custom and also conflated it with immorality. In this regard, Wiredu's main argument is that 'this notion of the dependence of morality on religion... does not even make sense in the Akan context'.[95] Here, his arguments are quite illuminating. But as I have argued earlier, the Christian

intrusion into the traditional Akan sphere of existence touches on many domains beginning with the radical violence of the colonial encounter itself, its
equally violent ethnosexual dimensions, the general sexual economy and its
multiple discourses and the transformations of categories of the private and
the public. These various domains of inquiry deserve greater attention.

In his essay, 'Formulating Modern Thought in African Languages', we get
a full glimpse of his ultimate theoretical intentions. Unambiguously he states:

> It would be a major first step toward the correct formulation of modern
> thought in African languages if we in Africa were to cultivate the habit of
> thinking in our own indigenous languages as much as possible when talk-
> ing in one metropolitan language or another about issues involving con-
> cepts such as 'God', 'Mind', 'Person', 'Soul', 'Spirit', 'Sentence', 'Existence'
> and about categorical distinctions such as 'the Physical and Spiritual', 'the
> Natural and the Supernatural', 'the Religious and the Secular', and 'the
> Mystical and Nonmystical'.[96]

In the same essay, Wiredu says categories relating to the 'mystical', spiritual'
and the 'supernatural' do not exist in Akan thought. This assertion is clearly
debatable, otherwise how else would the belief in witchcraft and paranormal
phenomena that is so prevalent in traditional societies be termed?[97] In fact,
not a single essay in *Cultural Universals and Particulars* refers to this situation.[98]
Consequently, Wiredu's description of traditional Akan rationality seems to
negate the possibility of dealing with anything remotely resembling the mytho-
logical, which, all things considered, fails to put the traditional culture of his
choice in its proper perspective.

Wiredu's theoretic agenda is thrown into sharper focus in his essay 'African
Philosophical Tradition', where he declares that 'the agenda for contemporary African philosophy must include the critical and reconstructive treatment
of the oral traditions and the exploitation of the literary and scientific resources of the modern world in pursuit of a synthesis'.[99] This seems to be a
fairly sensible, almost unavoidable, line of thought, considering the present
circumstances in Africa. The problem, however, lies in how one arrives at a
synthesis. Wiredu goes on to decry the fact that Christian theology, in addition
to Western education, has often prevented the educated African from thinking 'in terms of the categories of thought embedded in his own language in
theoretical matters.'[100] It is difficult to see how Wiredu himself is not implicated in all this. As such, arriving at a synthesis in the theoretical realm is not
quite as easy as Wiredu implies. He is staunch in his attempts to recuperate
fixed or perhaps even petrified cloisters of knowledge in traditional Akan
thought for the modern/post-colonial sensibility, but what must also be realised is that the theatre of knowledge in the contemporary Akan context or

indeed any other similar setting is often mediated by several sundry cognitive forces that are bound to make his attempts at total philosophical recall by and large futile. This is not to say that Wiredu's entire venture is hopeless; it only means that more circumspection is required in the delineation of limits.

In 'The Need for Conceptual Decolonisation in African Philosophy' Wiredu urges African philosophers to try to think out various philosophical concepts 'in your own African language and on the basis of the results, review the intelligibility of the associated problems or the plausibility of the apparent solutions that have tempted you when you have pondered them in some metropolitan language'.[101] As we have observed this is a recurrent injunction with Wiredu; furthermore, he provides some interesting examples of how this is to be done. In 'Post-Colonial African Philosophy' he cautions that it is 'a program that is easier prescribed than implemented, but to which there is no alternative'.[102] But the feasibility of this proposition is another matter entirely. In particular, Wiredu does not appear to be concerned with the knowledge/power nexus as so comprehensively treated in the Foucauldian corpus.

In terms of the world's linguistic and cultural capital, it is disheartening to know that half of the world's languages—which number about 6500—are threatened with imminent extinction. The factors that guarantee a language's survival include the economic power, military superiority and cultural prestige of the people who speak it.[103] Thus, powerful imperial underpinnings are responsible for the dominance of English in the global map of languages. In the present times, telecommunications technology and the Internet, coupled with America's new-found status as the only global superpower, has further strengthened the position of English as a world language. But what must also be recognised is that as the hegemony of English widens within the global sphere, non-native users of the language are also compelled to transform the texture of the language to suit local conditions. In other words, if English has been able to capture the world then it also means it has had to undergo several cultural and linguistic metamorphoses that invariably go with conquest. As for minority languages, it must be said that none exists in a vacuum. To be sure, modernisation and urbanisation have eroded several minority languages, but perhaps even more significantly, they have produced new linguistic variants that possess innate characteristics of their own. For instance, Yoruba as spoken in the urban centres is rapidly becoming different from the version(s) spoken in the provinces, where traditional mores still manage to hold sway.

Another way of questioning the issue of conceptual decolonisation as postulated by Wiredu is to note that Africa alone has almost two thousand languages and so one can imagine the sheer laboriousness involved in finding competent thinkers skilled in both metropolitan languages and indigenous African ones to carry out the task. One can be sure that the task would not be left to philosophers alone and, judging by what often happens in Africa, politicians and military despots are likely to dominate the debate. As it is, English as a dominant language must adapt to the historical consequences of colonisation, which includes subtle recolonisation by post-colonial subjects. It is a pity that these important perspectives are not reflected in Wiredu's work.

To summarise, Wiredu's advocacy of the non-party system in the political realm in Africa is unsettling. His argument is that the multi-party systems practised by the sophisticated democracies of the West are so unduly competitive that they make an unsuitable model for African political conditions. He also says that traditional African life was marked by a consensual character, and that Africans would do well to re-adopt the spirit of consensus in their political existence, as opposed to the cut-throat rivalry that characterises democracies in which majoritarianism is enforced. How such political utopianism could be re-established in present-day Africa is unimaginable. If the spirit of consensus ever existed at all in the political realm in Africa, it was during pre-colonial times and even this claim is indeed doubtful. But surely the realities of post-coloniality are so disruptive of the lure of traditionalism that naïve historical recall is impossible. If indeed we consider reverting to the old pre-colonial political order, then surely it would also make sense to reinforce pre-colonial geographical boundaries and its essentially itinerant territoriality[104] an obvious impossibility.

Notes

1. For various publications on the nature of this thorny problematic see Paulin Hountondji's *African Philosophy: Myth and Reality, Bloomington*, Indiana University Press, 1996 and *The Search for Meaning: Reflections on Philosophy, Culture and Democracy in Africa,* Athens, Ohio Center for International Studies, 2002; P. O. Bodunrin 'The Question of African Philosophy', R. A. Wright, ed., *African Philosophy: An Introduction 3rd ed.* Lanham: University of America Press, 1984; Kwame Gyekye, *Tradition and Modernity; Philosophical Reflections on the African Experience,* New York and Oxford: Oxford University Press, 1997; D. A. Masolo, *African Philosophy in Search of Identity, 1994*; V. Y. Mudimbe, *The Invention of Africa: Gnosis, Philosophy and the Order of Knowledge,* Bloomington: Indiana University Press, 1988, *Parables and Fable: Exegesis, Textuality, and Politics in Central Africa,* Madison: University of Wisconsin Press, 1991 and also *The Idea of Africa,* Bloomington: Indiana University Press, 1994; Oyekan Owomoyela, 'Africa and the Imperative of Philosophy: A Skeptical Reconsideration', *African Studies Review*, 30, 1; Olabiyi Yai, 'Theory and Practice in African Philosophy', *Second Order*, 2, 2, 1977.

2. This particular problematic has continued to elicit considerable attention from African philosophers. See for instance, Kwame Gyekye, *Tradition and Modernity: Philosophical Reflections on the African Experience*, 1997.

3. Olusegun Oladipo, *Philosophy and the African Experience,* Ibadan, Hope Publications, 1996, p. 70.

4. Kwasi Wiredu, *Conceptual Decolonisation in African Philosophy,* Ibadan, Hope Publications, 1995, p. 23.

5. Frantz Fanon, *The Wretched of the Earth,* Middlesex; Penguin Books, 1963, p. 20.

6. Kwasi Wiredu, *Conceptual Decolonisation in African Philosophy,* 1995, p. 14.

7. Homi K. Bhabha's theorizations regarding hybridity, mimicry and ambivalence are certainly relevant here. See his *Location of Culture,* London, Routledge, 1994.

8. Kwasi Wiredu, *Conceptual Decolonisation in African Philosophy,* 1995, p. 20.

9. It is important to note that Cheikh Anta Diop had advocated that African languages be used in formulating African thought as far back as 1954.

10. Kwasi Wiredu, 'The Concept of Truth in Akan Language' in P.O. Bodunrin, ed., *Philosophy in Africa: Trends and Perspectives,* Ile-Ife: University of Ife Press, 1985, p. 46.

11. Ibid.

12. Ibid.

13. This is a theoretical issue that has animated many debates in literary studies. A recent account of the current state of the debate can be found in Abiola Irele's book, *The African Imagination: Literature in Africa and the Black Diaspora*, New York: Oxford University Press, 2001.

14. Anthony K. Appiah's *In My Father's House: Africa in the Philosophy of Culture*, New York: Oxford University Press, 1992, is an eloquent meditation on the limits of discourses of nativism.

15. Anne McClintock, *Imperial Leather: Race, Gender and Sexuality in the Colonial Conquest*, New York and London, Routledge, 1995, p. 13.

16. Kwasi Wiredu, *Conceptual Decolonisation in African Philosophy,* 1995, p. 21.

17. See his interview with Olusegun Oladipo, *The Third Way in African Philosophy,* Olusegun Oladipo ed. Ibadan, Hope Publications, 2002, p. 337.

18. Again, the postmodernist critiques of universal canons of rationality by theorists such as Foucault, Derrida, Lacan, Lyotard and Baudrillard are certainly most instructive in this regard.

19. Kwasi Wiredu, 'The Akan Concept of Truth' in *Ibadan Journal of Humanistic Studies*, No.3, October 1983, p. 113.

20. Kwasi Wiredu, *Conceptual Decolonisation in African Philosophy,* 1995, p. 24.

21. Kwasi Wiredu, 'The Akan Concept of Mind', 1983, p. 113.

22. For an account of the difference between oral knowledges and knowledges produced advanced capitalist systems see, Jean-Francois Lyotard, *The Postmodern Condition: A Report on Knowledge*, trans. Geoff Bennington and Brian Massumi. Minneapolis: University of Minnesota Press, 1984

23. Kwasi Wiredu, 'The Akan Concept of Mind', 1983, p. 121.

24. Ibid. p. 128.

25. Kwasi Wiredu, *Conceptual Decolonisation in African Philosophy*, 1995, p. 44.

26. Ibid. p. 46.

27. Ibid.

28. Ibid. p. 48.

29. For a working list of publications that grapple with these various issues and discourses see, Dennis Altman, *Global Sex*, Chicago: Chicago University Press, 2001; Adam Ashforth, 'Weighing Manhood in Soweto', *CODESRIA Bulletin*, Nos. 3&4, 1999; George Bataille, *Eroticism, Death & Sexuality*, San Francisco: City Lights, 1986; T. K. Biaya, 'Eroticism and Sexuality in Africa', *CODESRIA Bulletin*, Nos. 3&4, 1999; Rosemary Hennessy, *Profit and Pleasure*, New York: Routledge, 2000; Anne McClintock, *Imperial Leather: Race, Gender and Sexuality and the Colonial Conquest*, New York: Routledge, 1995; Joane Nagel, Race, *Ethnicity and Sexuality: Intimate Intersections, Forbidden Frontiers*, New York: Oxford University Press, 2003; Martha Nussbaum, *Sex and Social Justice*, Oxford, Oxford University Press, 1999; Robert Young, *Colonial Desire: Hybridity in Theory, Culture and Race*, London and New York: Routledge, 1995; Jeffrey Weeks et al. eds., *Sexualities and Society*, Cambridge, Polity Press, 2003.

30. For an account of the violent, diverse and contradictory nature of the colonial encounter see John L. Comaroff and Jean Comaroff, *Of Revelation and Revolution: Christianity, Colonialism and Consciousness in South Africa*, Vol. 1, Chicago: Chicago University Press, 1991 and *Of Revelation and Revolution: The Dialectics of Modernity on a South African Frontier*, Vol. 2, Chicago: Chicago University Press, 1997.

31. Anne McClintock, *Imperial Leather: Race, Gender, Sexuality and the Colonial Conquest*, 1995, p. 44.

32. Joane Nagel, *Race, Ethnicity, and Sexuality: Intimate Intersections, Forbidden Frontiers*, New York: Oxford University Press, 2003, pp. 65-66.

33. Ibid. p. 68.

34. Anne McClintock, *Imperial Leather: Race, Gender and Sexuality in the Colonial Conquest*, 1995, p. 56.

35. Ibid. pp. 58-9.

36. Samir Amin, 1993, *Empire of Chaos*, New York, Monthly Review Press; and *Capitalism in the Age of Globalisation*, London and New York: Zed Books.

37. See Claude Ake, 1996, *Democracy and Development in Africa,* Ibadan, Spectrum Books and also Achille Mbembe, 2001, *On the Postcolony*, Berkeley and California: University of California Press.

38. Wole Soyinka's exact words on the partition of Africa by the colonial powers are, 'much of the division of Africa owed much more to a case of brandy and box of cigars than to any intrinsic claims of what the boundaries enclosed'. See his *The Burden of Memory: The Muse of Forgiveness,* New York: Oxford University Press, 1999, p. 40.

39. Claude Ake, 1996, *Democracy and Development in Africa*, p. 14.

40. See Mahmood Mamdani, 1996, *Citizen and Subject: Contemporary Africa and the Legacy of Late Capitalism* and also his 'Beyond Settler and Native as Political Identities: Overcoming the Political legacy of Colonialism' in P. I. Ozo-Eson and U. Ukiwo, eds., *Ideology and African Development,* 2001, Port Harcourt and Abuja: AFRIGOV and CASS.

41. Claude Ake, 1996, *Democracy and Development in Africa*, p. 14.

42. Ibid. p. 94.

43. See Achille Mbembe, 2001, *On the Postcolony,* Berkeley and California: University of California Press.

44. See Samuel P. Huntington, 1996, *The Clash of Civilizations and Remaking of World Order*, New York: Torchstone.

45. See Kwame Gyekye, 1997, *Tradition and Modernity: Philosophical Reflections on the African Experience,* New York: Oxford University Press.

46. Samuel P. Huntington, 1996, *The Clash of Civilisation and the Remaking of World Order,* p. 53.

47. Walden Bello, 2001, 'Global Capitalism: From Triumph to Crisis' in *International Socialist Review Issue* 19.

48. Ibid.

49. See Vision 2020 which is available on line at www.spacecom.af.mil/usspace / visbook.pdf.

50. Noam Chomsky, 2001, 'Militarizing Space to protect U.S. interests and investment' in *International Socialist Review Issue* 19. p. 11.

51. Ibid. p. 14.

52. Ibid.

53. John Pilger, 2001, 'The State is more powerful than ever' in *International Socialist Review Issue* 19.

54. Cited by John Pilger, 2001, 'The State is more powerful than ever', p. 15.

55. 'Peter Rachieff, 2001, 'Globalisation and Union democracy' in *International Socialist Review Issue* 19, p. 55.

56. Ibid. p. 58.

57. Harvey Wasserman, 2001, 'Deregulation: The Mantra of Corporate Globalization' in *International Socialist Review Issue* 19, p. 60.

58. Ken Danatier, 2001, 'People's Globalisation vs. Elite Globalisation' in *International Socialist Review Issue* 19, p. 60.

59. Achille Mbembe, 1999, 'At the Edge of the World: Boundaries, Territoriality and Sovereignty in Africa' in *CODESRIA Bulletin*, Numbers 3 & 4.

60. Michel Lowy, 2001, 'Davos and Porto Alegre: Two opposing plans for civilization' in *International Socialist Review Issue*, 19, p. 122.

61. Ibid.

62. Chinweizu, 1997, 'Black Redemption' in *Index on Censorship*, 2 p. 173.

63. Ibid. p. 181.

64. See Olusegun Oladipo, ed., 1998, *Remaking Africa: Challenges of the Twenty-First Century*, Ibadan: Hope Publications. In this volume, several scholars proffer a multiplicity of perspectives (interdisciplinary) by which Africa can develop.

65. Achille Mbembe, 2001, *On the Postcolony*, p. 241.

66. See Samuel P. Huntington, 1996, *The Clash of Civilizations and the Remaking of World Order*. To be sure, his anti-multicultural stance makes his text a bible for conservative orthodoxy while the 'politically correct' may find it repulsive.

67. See M. Duffield, 1998, '"Postmodern Conflict" Warlords, Post-Adjustment States and Private Protection' in *Civil Wars* 1, 1.

68. See Jean and John L. Comaroff, 2000, 'Naturing the Nation: Aliens, Apocalypse, and the Postcolonial State' in *HAGAR, International Social Science Review* Vol. 1.

69. See Achille Mbembe, 1999, 'At the Edge of the World: Boundaries Territoriality and Sovereignty in Africa' and also his 'An Essay on the Political Imagination in War time' in *CODESRIA Bulletin* 2, 3 & 4, 2000.

70. Ibid.

71. See Karl Maier, 2000, *This House has Fallen: Midnight in Nigeria*, New York: Public Affairs.

72. Ibid. p. 62.

73. Olusegun Oladipo, citing Wiredu in the 'Introduction' to *Conceptual Decolonisation in African Philosophy*, 1995, p. 1.

74. Kwasi Wiredu, *Conceptual Decolonisation in African Philosophy*, 1995, p. 21.

75. Olusegun Oladipo, 'Traditional African Philosophy: Its Significance for Contemporary Africa', in *African Notes*, Vol. XV, Nos. 1 & 2, 1991, p. 102.

76. Olusegun Oladipo, 'Reason, Identity and the African Quest' in *Africa Today*, Vol. 42, No.3, 1995, p. 31.

77. Ibid. p. 33.

78. Ibid. p. 32.

79. Basil Davidson, *The Black Man's Burden*, Ibadan: Spectrum Books, 1993, p. 45.

80. Ibid.

81. Linda Hutcheon, 'Beginning to Theorise Post-Modernism' in *Textual Practice*, Vol. 1, No. 1, Spring, 1987, p. 13.

82. Richard Rorty, *Philosophy and the Mirror of Nature*, Oxford, Basil Blackwell, 1983, p. 4.

83. Olusegun Oladipo, 'Reason, Identity and the African Quest' in *Africa Today*, 1995, p. 36.

84. Claude Ake, *Democratization of Disempowerment in Africa*, CASS Occasional Monograph, No. 1, Lagos: Malthouse Press Ltd., 1994, p. 20.

85. In the social sciences, several academics have conducted studies on the phenomena known as 'the collapse of the state', 'the exit of the state', and more recently what has been termed 'the terror of the state.' See the numerous research activities and publications of the Council for the Development of Social Research in Africa, (CODESRIA) for explanations of these phenomena.

86. On an interesting reconceptualisation of the postcolonial state in Africa see the article by John L. Comaroff, 'Reflections on the colonial state in South Africa and elsewhere: factions, fragments, facts and fictions' in Abebe Zegeye, ed., *Social Identities in the New South Africa*, Cape Town: Kwela Books, 2001.

87. Paul Gilroy, *Against Race: Imagining Political Culture Beyond the Color Line*, Cambridge, Harvard University Press, 2000, p. 98.

88. Ibid. p. 100.

89. Ibid. p. 104.

90. Kwasi Wiredu, *Cultural Universals and Particulars*, Bloomington and Indiana: Indiana University Press, 1996, p. 51.

91. See for instance, Michael Watts, 'Islamic Modernities? Citizenship, Civil Society, and Islamism in a Northern Nigerian City', in James Holston, ed., *Cities and Citizenship*, Durham, Duke University Press, 1999 which is an insight account of the Maitatsine riots that ravaged Kano city of Nigeria in 1980.

92. Ibid. p. 53.

93. Ibid. p. 69.

94. Ibid.

95. Ibid. p. 74.

96. Ibid. p. 93.

97. Nigerian philosopher Sophie Oluwole has written on the question of witchcraft in traditional African cultures, and how they possess their own ontological frames of

reference; see *Witchcraft, Reincarnation and the God-Head* (*Issues in African Philosophy*), Lagos: Excel Publishers, 1992.

98. For sophisticated studies of the phenomenon of witchcraft in Africa see the contributions by Wim van Binsbergen and Peter Geschiere. See in particular, W. M. J. van Binsbergen 'Witchcraft in modern Africa as virtualised boundary conditions of the kinship order', C. G. Bond and D. M. Giekawy, eds., *Witchcraft Dialogues: Anthropological and Philosophical Exchanges,* Athens: Ohio University Press, 2001 and Peter Geschiere, *The Modernity of Witchcraft: Politics and the Occult in Postcolonial Africa,* trans. Peter Geschiere and Janet Roitman, Charlottesville: University of Virginia Press, 1997.

99. Kwasi Wiredu, *Cultural Universals and Particulars*, p. 112.

100. Ibid. p. 118.

101. Ibid. p. 137.

102. Ibid. p. 153.

103. On this issue, see Gauri Viswanathan, ed., *Power, Politics, and Culture, Interviews with Edward W. Said,* New York: Vintage Books, 2001.

104. See Achille Mbembe, 'At the Edge of the World: Boundaries, Territoriality and Sovereignty in Africa', *Public Culture,* 30, 2000.

4

Articulation of a Mode: Wiredu on Marx

Kwasi Wiredu's interests and philosophical importance are certainly not limited to conceptual decolonisation alone. He has offered some useful insights on Marxism, mysticism, metaphysics and the general nature of the philosophical enterprise itself. Although his latter text, *Cultural Universals and Particulars* has a more Africa-centred orientation, his first book, *Philosophy and an African Culture* presents a wider range of discursive interests; a vigorous critique of Marxism, reflections on the phenomenon of ideology, analyses of truth and the philosophy of language among other preoccupations. It is interesting to see how Wiredu weaves together these different preoccupations and also to observe how some of them have endured while others have not.

Wiredu has always believed that traditional modes of thought and folk philosophies should be interpreted, clarified, analysed and quite simply subjected to critical evaluation and assimilation.[1] Also, at the very beginning of his philosophical reflections, he puts forth the crucial formulation that there is no reason why the African philosopher 'in his philosophical meditations [...] should not test formulations in those against intuitions in his own language.'[2] And rather than just talking about the possibilities for evolving modern traditions in African philosophy, African philosophers should actually begin to do it.[3] In carrying out this task, the African philosopher has few methodological approaches. First, he urged to 'acquaint himself with the different philosophies of the different cultures of the world, not to be encyclopaedic or eclectic, but with the aim of trying to see how far issues and concepts of universal relevance can be disentangled from the contingencies of culture.'[4] He also adds that 'the African philosopher has no choice but to conduct his philosophical inquiries in relation to the philosophical writings of other peoples, for his ancestors left him no heritage of philosophical writings.'[5] For Wiredu, the use of translations is a fundamental aspect of the contemporary African philosophical project. However, writing on the dilemmas of translation in the current age of neoliberalism, it has been noted: 'translations are [..] put 'out of joint.' However correct or legitimate they may be, and whatever right one may acknowledge them to have, they are all disadjusted, as it were unjust in the gap that affects them. This gap is within them, to be sure, because their meanings remain necessarily equivocal; next it is in the relation among them and thus their multiplicity, and finally or first of all in the irreducible inadequation to the other language and to the stroke of genius of the event that makes the law, to all the virtualities of the original.'[6] Wiredu does not contemplate the implications of this kind of indictment in his formulations of an approach to African philosophy. Perhaps the task at hand is simply too important and demanding to cater for such philosophical niceties. In relation to the kind of philosophical heritage at the disposal of the African philosopher, Wiredu identifies three main strands: 'a folk philosophy, a written traditional philosophy and a modern philosophy.'[7] This categorisation is very different from Achille Mbembe's formulation. Mbembe, on his own part, identifies two major counterproductive trends in modes of African philosophic writing; Marxism and what he terms the discourse of nativism.[8] According to him, African Marxist discourses have only led to dead-ends while the 'prose of nativism' has aided the continuing ghettoisation of African institutional and intellectual forms of production. But what Mbembe fails to do is to identify a way out of the impasse. We may disagree with Wiredu's methods but at least he never fails to offer often well-considered solutions. Wiredu's approach to questions of this sort is embedded in his general theoretical stance: 'It is a function, indeed a duty, of philosophy in any society to examine the intellectual foundations of its culture. For any such examination to be of any real use it should take the form of reasoned criticism and, where possible, reconstruction. No other way to philosophical progress is known than through criticism and adaptation.'[9]

The drive to attain progress is not limited to philosophical discourse alone. Entire communities and cultures must strive to improve upon their institutions and practices in order to remain relevant. Societies can lose the momentum of growth and 'various habits of thought and practice can become anachronistic within the context of the development of a given society; but an entire society too can become anachronistic within the context of the whole world if the ways of life within it are predominantly anachronistic. In the latter case, of course, there is no discarding society; what you do is to modernise it.'[10] The theme of modernisation occurs very frequently in Wiredu's corpus. He does not fully conceptualise it nor relate it to the various ideological histories it has encountered in the domains of social science where it became a fully fledged industry. Modernisation for him is based on an uncomplicated pragmatism, one that owes much to Deweyan thought.

This kind of posture, that is, the consistent critique of the retrogression inherent in tradition and its knack for the fossilisation of culture is directed at Leopold Sedar Senghor. On Senghor, he writes, 'it is almost as if he has been trying to exemplify in his own thought and discourse the lack of the analytical habit which he has attributed to the biology of the African. Most seriously of all, Senghor has celebrated the fact that our (traditional) mind is of a non-analytical bent; which is very unfortunate, seeing that this mental attribute is more of a limitation than anything else.'[11] Wiredu's main criticism of Senghor is one that is always levelled against the latter. Apart from that charge that Senghor essentialises the concept and ideologies of blackness, he is also charged with a certain defeatism that undermines struggles for liberation and decolonisation. However, Paul Gilroy has unearthed a more sympathetic context in which to read and situate Senghorian thought. In Gilroy's reading, an acceptable ideology of blackness emerges from Senghor's work. And in this way, Wiredu's critique loses much of its originality.

Senghor is cast as a traditionalist and tradition itself is the subject of a much broader critique. On some of the drawbacks of tradition Wiredu writes, 'it is as true in Africa as anywhere else that logical, mathematical, analytical, experimental procedures are essential in the quest for the knowledge of, and control over, nature and therefore, in any endeavour to improve the condition of man. Our traditional culture was somewhat wanting in this respect and this is largely responsible for the weaknesses of traditional technology, warfare, architecture, medicine etc.'[12] Sometimes, Wiredu carries his critique of tradition too far as when he advances the view that 'traditional medicine is terribly weak in diagnosis and weaker still in pharmacology.'[13] In recent times, a major part of Hountondji's project is to demonstrate that traditional knowledges are not only useful and viable but also the necessity to situate them in appropriate modern contexts.[14] Hountondji's latest gesture is curious since both himself and Wiredu are supposed to belong to the same philosophic tendency as classified by Bodunrin. However, Wiredu's attack on tradition is vitiated by his project of conceptual decolonisation which in order to work requires the recuperation of vital elements in traditional culture.

Wiredu's stance in relation to modernisation and tradition gets further complicated by his condemnation of certain aspects of urban life which smacks of a blend of postmodern environmentalism. First, he writes, 'it is quite clear to me that unrestricted industrial urbanisation is contrary to any humane culture; it is certainly contrary to our own.'[15] Also, 'one of the powerful strains on our extended family system is the very extensive poverty which oppresses our rural population. Owing to this, people working in the towns and cities are constantly burdened with the financial needs of rural relatives which they usually cannot entirely satisfy.'[16] Contemporary anthropological studies dealing with Africa have dwelt extensively on this phenomenon. The point is, in Africa, forms of sociality exist that can no longer be found in the North Atlantic civilisation. If this civilisation (the North Atlantic) is characterised by extreme individualism, African forms of social existence on the other hand tend towards the gregarious in which conceptions of generosity, corruption, gratitude, philanthropy, ethnicity and even justice take on different slightly forms from what obtains within the vastly different North Atlantic tradition.

Also problematic is Wiredu's reading of colonialism which is very similar to those of authors such as Ngugi wa Thiong'o, Walter Rodney or even Chinua Achebe. In this reading, the colonised is abused, brutalised, silenced and reconstructed against her/his own will. Colonialism causes the destruction of agency. On de-agentialisation, Wiredu states, 'any human arrangement is authoritarian if it entails any person being made to do or suffer something against his will, or if it leads to any person being hindered in the development of his own will.[17] However, theorists (for instance, John L. Comaroff and Jean Comaroff) have started to show that the colonised subject was not just a passive space awaiting the intrusion of euromodern reason and modes of consciousness. Bhabha formulated the notion of ambivalence to highlight the cultural reciprocities inherent in the entire colonial encounter and structure. This kind of reading of the colonial event has led to a rethinking of colonial theory. But Wiredu's reading of the colonial encounter is still caught within the old framework:

> The period of colonial struggle was [...] a period of cultural affirmation. It was necessary to restore in ourselves our previous confidence which had been so seriously eroded by colonialism. We are still, admittedly, even in post-colonial times, in an era of cultural self-affirmation.[18]

Thus, Wiredu dwells on the evident violence of the colonial encounter (as it affects primarily the colonised) without also acknowledging the possibilities and actualities on counter-violence of the part of the colonised or decolonising agent. This a lapse that much of contemporary postcolonial theory has been able to address convincingly.

Marxist theory and discourse generally provided many African intellectuals with a platform on which to conduct many sociopolitical struggles. In fact, for many African scholars, it served as the only ideological weapon. But not all scholars found Marxism acceptable. Wiredu was one of the scholars who had deep reservations about it. But he was not in doubt about the philosophical significance of Marx: 'I regard Karl Marx as one of the great philosophers.'[19] Derrida is even more forthcoming on the depth of this significance: 'It will always be a fault not to read and reread and discuss Marx-which is to say also a few others—and to go beyond scholarly 'reading' or 'discussion.' It will be more and more a fault, a failing of theoretical, philosophical, political responsibility.'[20] Again, he writes, 'the Marxist inheritance was—and still remains, and so it will remain—absolutely and thoroughly determinate. One need not be a Marxist or a communist in order to accept this obvious fact. We all live in a world, some would say a culture, that bears, at an incalculable depth, the mark of this inheritance, whether in a directly visible fashion or not.'[21]

Marxism during the era of the Cold War was the major ideological issue and in the present age of neoliberalism it continues to haunt (Derrida's precise phrase is hauntology) us with its multiple legacies. Wiredu's critique of Marx and Engels belongs to the epoch of the Cold War. But from it, we get a glimpse of not only his political orientation but also his philosophical predilections. For instance, at a point, he claims 'the food one eats, the hairstyle one adopts, the amount of money one has, the power one wields- all these and such circumstances are irrelevant from an epistemological point of view.'[22] But Foucauldian analyses have demonstrated that these seemingly marginal activities have a tremendous impact on knowledge/power configurations that we cannot simply ignore. More recently, Michel de Certeau has shown all these so-called inconsequential acts become significant as gestures of resistance for the benefit of the weak and politically powerless. In his words, 'the weak must continually turn to their own ends forces alien to them.'[23] On those specific acts of the weak, he writes, 'many everyday practices (talking, reading, moving about, shopping, cooking, etc.) are tactical in character. And so are, more generally, many 'ways of operating': victories of the 'weak' over the 'strong' (whether the strength be that of powerful people or the violence of things or of an imposed order, etc.), clever tricks, knowing how to get away with things, 'hunter's cunning,' manoeuvres, polymorphic simulations, joyful discoveries, poetic as well as warlike. The Greeks called these 'ways of operating' metis.[24] This reading gives an entirely different perspective on acts and themes of resistance as panoptical surveillance in the age of global neoliberalism becomes more totalitarian in nature or even outright fascistic.

As a philosopher versed in analytic philosophy, truth is a primary concern of Wiredu and this concern is incorporated into his analysis of Marxist philosophy. Hence, he identifies the following points, (1) 'the cognition of truth is recognised by Engels as the business of philosophy; (2) What is denied is absolute truth, not truth as such; (3) The belief, so finely expressed, in the progressive character of truth; (4) Engels speaks of this process of cognition as the 'development of science.' (5) That a consciousness of limitation is a necessary element in all acquired knowledge.[25] Wiredu explains that these various Marxian assertions on truth are no different from those of the logician, C. S. Peirce who had expounded them under a formulation he called 'fallibilism.' John Dewey also expounded them under the concept of 'pragmatism'.[26] So the point here is that some of the main Marxist propositions on truth have parallels in analytic philosophy. Nonetheless, he raises an unsettling question about Marxism and its relation to truth: 'How is it that a philosophy which advocates such an admirable doctrine as the humanistic conception of truth tends so often to lead in practice to the suppression of freedom of thought and expression? Is it by accident that this comes to be so? Or is it due to causes internal to the philosophy of Marx and Engels.'[27] Wiredu demonstrates strong reservations about what Ernest Wamba dia Wamba calls 'bureaucratic socialism.' Derrida on his part, urges us to distinguish between Marx as a philosopher and the innumerable specters of Marx. In other words, there is a difference between 'the dogma machine and the 'Marxist' ideological apparatuses (States, parties, cells, unions, and other places of doctrinal production)'[28] and the necessity to treat Marx as a great philosopher. We need to 'try to play Marx off against Marxism so as to neutralise, or at any rate muffle the political imperative in the untroubled exegesis of classified work.'[29] We also need to remember that 'he doesn't belong to the communists, to the Marxists, to the parties, he ought to figure within our great canon of [...] political philosophy.'[30]

Wiredu's reading of Marxism generally is quite damaging. First, he states, 'Engels himself, never perfectly consistent, already compromises his conception of truth with some concessions to absolute truth in *Anti-Duhring.*'[31] He then makes an even more damaging accusation that an authoritarianism lies at the heart of conception of philosophy propagated by Marx and Engels. On what he considers to be a deep-seated confusion in their work, he writes, 'Engels recognises the cognition of truth to be a legitimate business of philosophy and makes a number of excellent points about truth. As soon, however, as one tries to find out what he and Marx conceived philosophy to be like, one is faced with a deep obscurity. The problem resolves round what one may describe as Marx's conception of philosophy as ideology.'[32] Here, Wiredu makes the crucial distinction between Marx as a philosopher and the effects of his numerous spectralities and for this reason he offers his most important criticism of his general critique of Marxism. He also accuses Marx of instances of 'carelessness in the use of cardinal terms' which he says 'may be symptomatic of deep inadequacies of thought.'[33] This charge, which relates to Marx's conception of consciousness is indeed serious since it borders on the question of conceptual clarification as advanced by the canon of analytic philosophy. Wiredu argues that Marx and Engels are unclear about their employment of the concept of ideology: 'Marx and Engels are [...] on the horns of a dilemma. If all philosophical thinking is ideological, then their thinking is ideological and, by their hypothesis, false.'[34] Wiredu's insights are very important here: 'He and Engels simply assumed for themselves the privilege of exempting their own philosophizing from the ideological theory of ideas.'[35] Consequently, Marx commits a grave error 'in his conception of ideology and its bearing upon philosophy.'[36]

Another area Wiredu finds Marx and Engels wanting is moral philosophy. In other words, Marx 'confused moral philosophy with moralism and assumed rather than argued a moral standpoint.'[37] Furthermore, he had precious little to say on the nature of the relationship between philosophy and morality. Engels does better on this score as there is a treatment of morality in *Anti-Duhring*. Nonetheless, Engels is charged with giving 'no guidance on the conceptual problems that have perplexed moral philosophers.'[38] Henceforth, Wiredu becomes increasing dismissive of Marx, Marxism and its followers. First, he writes, 'the run-of the-mill Marxists, even less enamoured of philosophical accuracy than their masters, have made the ideological conception of philosophy a battle cry.'[39] And then he singles out 'scientific socialism' which he regards as being unclear in its elaboration and which he typifies as 'an amalgam of factual and evaluative elements blended together without regard to categorical stratification.'[40] In one of his most damaging assessments of Marxism, he declares: 'Ideology is the death of philosophy. To the extent to which Marxism, by its own internal incoherences, tends to be transformed into an ideology, to that extent Marxism is a science of the unscientific and a philosophy of the unphilosophic.'[41]

In sum, Wiredu's general attitude towards Marxism is one of condemnation. However, in the contemporary re-evaluations of Marxism a few discursive elements need to be clarified; the inclusion of the demarcation Cold War and post Cold War assessments of Marxism ought to be employed as an analytical yardstick and also the necessity to sift through the various specters and legacies of Marx as distinct from those of Marxism. This is the kind of reading that Derrida urges us to do and it is also one to which we shall now turn our attention.

Derrida asks us to distinguish between the legacies of Marx and the various spectralities of Marxism. To this distinction we might add another crucial one: analyses of Marxism before and after the fall of the former Soviet Union. Wiredu's critique is based on the pre-Soviet debacle whilst Derrida's draws some of its reflections on the post-Soviet fall. In these two different critiques, we must be careful to always strive to isolate the theoretical elements and insights that bypass short-lived discursive trends and political interests which often tend to vitiate the more profound effects of the works of Karl Marx and those that do not.

The debacle of the former Soviet Union and the apparent hegemony of neoliberal ideology have generated discourses associated with the 'ends' of discourse. But Derrida points out that there is nothing new in the contemporary discourses of endism which are in fact anachronistic when compared to the earlier versions of the same discursive orientation that emerged in the 1950s and which in a vital sense owed a great deal to a certain spirit of Marx: 'the eschatological themes of the 'end of history,' of the 'end of Marxism,' of the 'end of philosophy,' of the 'ends of man,' of the 'last man' and so forth were, in the 1950s, that is, forty years ago our daily bread. We had this bread of apocalypse in our mouths naturally, already, just as naturally as that which I nicknamed after the fact, in 1980, the 'apocalyptic tone in philosophy.'[42] In a way, the contemporary discourses of endism that draw from the spirit of neoliberal triumphalism, without acknowledging it, are greatly indebted to Marxism and the more constructive critiques of it. Deconstruction, in part, emerged from the necessity to critique the various forms of statist Stalinism, the numerous socio-economic failings of Soviet bureaucracy and the political repression in Hungary. In other words, it emerged partly from the need to organise critiques for degraded forms of socialism.

In speaking about the inheritance of Marx, Derrida also reflects on the injunction associated with it. The task of reflecting on this inheritance and the injunction to which it gives rise is demanding: ... ' one must filter, sift, criticise, one must sort out several different possibles that inhabit the same injunction. And inhabit it in a contradictory fashion around a secret. If the readability of a legacy were given, natural, transparent, univocal, if it did not call for and at the same time defy interpretation, we would never have anything to inherit from it.'[43] Derrida's employment of terms and phrases such as 'inheritance,' 'injunction,' and the 'spectrality of the specter' in relation to the legacies of Marx has to do with the question of the genius of Marx: 'Whether evil or not, a genius operates, it always resists and defies after the fashion of a spectral thing. The animated work becomes that thing, the Thing that, like an elusive specter, engineers [s'ingenie] a habitation without proper inhabiting, call it a haunting, of both memory and translation.'[44]

A work of genius, a masterpiece in addition to giving rise to spectralities also generates legions of imitators and followers. Of the Marxists who came after Marx, Wiredu writes: 'I find that Marxists are especially prone to confuse factual with ideological issues. In point in fact the great majority of those who call themselves Marxists do not share the ideology of Marx.'[45] In order to transcend the violence and confusion of Marxists who misread Marx, we need 'to play Marx off against Marxism so as to neutralise, or at any rate muffle the political imperative in the untroubled exegesis of a classified work.'[46] The work of re-reading Marx, of re-establishing his philosophical value and importance is a task that needs to be performed in universities, conferences, colloquia and also in less intellectual sites and fora.

Within the contemporary cultural moment, new configurations have arisen that were not present during Marx's day. Indeed, 'a set of transformations of all sorts (in particular, techno-scientific-economic-media) exceeds both the traditional givens of the Marxist discourse and those of the liberal discourse opposed to it.'[47] Also:

> Electoral representativity or parliamentary life is not only distorted, as was always the case, by a great number of socio-economic mechanisms, but it is exercised with more and more difficulty in a public space profoundly upset by techno-tele-media apparatuses and by new rhythms of information and communication, by the devices and the speed of forces represented by the latter, but also and consequently by the new modes of appropriation they put to work, by the new structure of the event and of its spectrality that they produce.[48]

Here, the instructive point is that the new information technologies have radically transformed the possibilities of the event and the modes of its production, reception and also interpretation. But there is a far more radical change that has occurred and which signals a profound crisis of global capitalism and the neoliberal ideology that underpins it: 'For what must be cried out, at a time when some have the audacity to neo-evangelise in the name of the ideal of liberal democracy that has finally realised itself as the ideal of human history: never have violence, inequality, exclusion, famine, and thus economic oppression affected as many human beings in the history of the earth and of humanity'.[49] Also, 'never have so many men, women, and children been subjugated, starved, or exterminated on the earth.'[50]

So Derrida identifies a few new factors that need to be included in the critique of Marxism in the contemporary moment namely the phenomenon of spectralisation caused by techno-science and digitalisation, the weakening of the practice of liberal democracy and also the crises and multiple contradictions inherent in global capitalism. One might as well add another element into the present configuration which is the rise of political Islam as an alternative ideology, its subsequent fervent politicisation and its reconstruction into an ideology of terror.[51]

Wiredu's reading of Marx focuses on the conceptual infelicities in the latter's theorisations of notions such as 'ideology,' 'consciousness', and 'truth'. Wiredu also criticises Marx's project of moral philosophy or in fact the lack of it. On the whole, his reading isn't complimentary. Indeed, it amounts to a dismissal of Marx in spite of the attempt to read him without the obfuscations of innumerable legacies.

Notes

1. Kwasi Wiredu, *Philosophy and an African Culture*, Cambridge, Cambridge University Press, 1980, p. x.

2. Ibid. p. xi

3. Paulin Hountondji also stresses this view in his *African Philosophy: Myth and Reality*, 1983.

4. Kwasi Wiredu, *Philosophy and an African Culture*, p. 31.

5. Ibid. p. 48.

6. Jacques Derrida, *Specters of Marx: the State of the Debt, the Work of Mourning, and the New International*, trans. Peggy Kamuf, New York and London, Routledge, 1994, p.19.

7. Kwasi Wiredu, *Philosophy and an African Culture*, p. 46.

8. Achille Mbembe, 'African Modes of Self-Writing', *Public Culture*, 2002, Vol. 14, No. 2.

9. Ibid. p. 20.

10. Ibid. p. 1.

11. Ibid. p. 12.

12. Ibid.

13. Ibid.

14. See Paulin Hountondji, *Les saviors endogènes*, Dakar, CODESRIA, 1994.

15. Kwasi Wiredu, *Philosophy and an African Culture*, p. 22.

16. Ibid.

17. Ibid. p. 2.

18. Ibid. p. 59.

19. Ibid. p. 63.

20. Jacques Derrida, *Specters of Marx: the State of the Debt, the Work of Mourning, and the New International*, p. 13.

21. Ibid.

22. Kwasi Wiredu, *Philosophy and an African Culture*, p. 66.

23. Michel de Certeau, *The Practice of Everyday Life*, Berkeley: University of California Press, 1984, p. xix.

24. Ibid.

25. Kwasi Wiredu, *Philosophy and an African Culture*, pp. 64-65.

26. Ibid. p. 67.

27. Ibid. p. 68.

28. Jacques Derrida, *Specters of Marx: the State of the Debt, the Work of Mourning, and the New International*, p. 13.

29. Ibid. p. 31.

30. Ibid. p. 32.

31. Kwasi Wiredu, *Philosophy and an African Culture*, p. 68.

32. Ibid. p. 70.

33. Ibid. p. 74.

34. Ibid. p. 76.

35. Ibid. p. 77.

36. Ibid. p. 81.

37. Ibid. p. 79.

38. Ibid. p. 80.

39. Ibid. p. 82.

40. Ibid. p. 85.

41. Ibid. p. 87.

42. Jacques Derrida, *Specters of Marx: the State of the Debt, the Work of Mourning, and the New International*, pp. 14-15.

43. Ibid. p. 16.

44. Ibid. p. 18.

45. Kwasi Wiredu, *Philosophy and an African Culture*, p. 94.

46. Jacques Derrida, *Specters of Marx: the State of the Debt, the Work of Mourning, and the New International*, p. 31.

47. Ibid. p. 70.

48. Ibid. p. 79.

49. Ibid. p. 85.

50. Ibid.

51. See Mahmood Mamdani, *Good Muslim, Bad Muslim*, New York, Pantheon Books, 2004.

5

Wiredu and the Boundaries of Thought

Philosophy, Politics and Post-Coloniality

Kwasi Wiredu postulates that a 'major first step' for African philosophy would be 'the correct formulation of modern thought in African languages'.[1] 'Modern thought' in this context can be taken to mean mainly Euro-American philosophy. In carrying out Wiredu's project of decolonisation, we are compelled to look at concepts such as 'God', 'Mind', 'Person', 'Soul', 'Spirit', 'Sentence', 'Proposition', 'Truth', 'Fact', 'Substance', 'Existence', and categorical distinctions such as 'the Physical and Spiritual' 'the Natural and the Supernatural', 'the Religious' and 'the Secular', and 'the Mystical and the Nonmystical".[2] But new developments in Western philosophy necessitate caution in going about this enterprise, for instance, the questioning of traditional binarisms, both philosophical and cultural.

The main argument here is that one must take into account the Western deconstruction of traditional philosophical concepts, so as not to fall prey to the pitfalls that attend them. Wiredu does not do this. As regards the deconstruction of Western philosophy, Richard Rorty writes in *Philosophy and the Mirror of Nature*:

> The aim of the book is to undermine the reader's confidence in 'the mind' as something about which one should have a 'philosophical' view, in 'knowledge' as something about which there ought to be a 'theory' and which has 'foundations' and in 'philosophy' as it has been conceived since Kant.[3]

Jacques Derrida, on his own part, writes:

> That philosophy died yesterday, since Hegel or Marx, Nietzsche or

Heidegger—and philosophy should wander toward the meaning of its death—or that it has always lived knowing itself to be dying (as is silently confessed in the shadow of the very discourse which declared *philosophia perennis*); that philosophy died one day within history, or that it has always fed on its own agony, on the violent way it opens history by opposing itself to non-philosophy, which is its past and its concern, its death and well spring; that beyond the death, or dying nature, of philosophy, perhaps even because of it, thought still has a future, or even, as is said today, is still entirely to come because of what philosophy has held in store; or more strangely still, that the future itself has a future—all these are unanswerable questions: By right of birth, and for one time at least these are problems put to philosophy as problems philosophy cannot resolve.[4]

It is obvious that Wiredu does not take those vital questionings of Western philosophy into consideration when conducting his project of conceptual decolonisation in African philosophy. This omission vitiates his project. If we agree that conceptual decolonisation is necessary in African philosophy, we are also forced to agree that deconstruction is a worthwhile goal in Western philosophy.

It can be argued thus, because the concepts we are also dealing within African philosophy such as 'Mind' and 'Truth' have a long philosophical history, of which deconstruction also is a part. In essence, conceptual decolonisation in African philosophy would be an incomplete project if it fails to recognise this fact. However, Wiredu does not demonstrate this in his writings. The post-structuralist interrogations of the notion of epistemology as having a foundation, and the idea of philosophy as an architectonic discipline, should be vital ingredients in any project of decolonisation. If we accept this strategy, we can be sure that the project of conceptual decolonisation would become more rigorous.

There are indeed similar elements in deconstruction and decolonisation, since they are both concerned with the subversion of particular epistemologies. Wiredu needs to widen the scope of his project to make it more viable and productive. If we fail to incorporate the deconstruction of Western philosophy in the project of conceptual decolonisation, we are likely to end up repeating the excesses of Euro-American philosophy, excesses that pertain to imperialism, racism and sexism. As it is now, Wiredu has not undertaken a painstaking examination of imperialism, racism and sexism and as such it can be argued that his writings are not adequately gender sensitive.

Even in the realm of language, we require a reading in recent analytic philosophy to understand the problems posed by language. Wiredu does not do this. For instance, Rorty distinguishes between what he calls 'pure' philosophy of language from 'impure' philosophy of language. He states that 'pure' philosophy of language tries to 'produce a clear and intuitively satisfying picture of the way in which notions like 'truth', 'meaning', 'necessity', and 'name' fit together.[5] On the other hand, 'impure' philosophy of language is tainted with Kantian foundationalism, that is, the attempt to view philosophy as a natural discipline that investigates the validity of the rest of culture. Rorty informs us that Donald Davidson's work represents what he has defined as 'pure' philosophy of language.

Before we go any further we might as well clarify more distinctly what Rorty terms 'pure' philosophy of language. 'Pure' philosophy of language in Davidsonian semantics does not attempt to conflate matters of meaning and reference with epistemological preoccupations. To do so would be reverting to the old Kantian *problematique* of adopting epistemology as constituting a permanent framework for knowledge-claims. Rorty supports Davidson's claim that one need not infiltrate philosophy of language with 'some adventitious philosophical puritanism.'[6] Instead, the primary concern should be to discover how language works and how we can come to possess 'an understanding of the inferential relations between sentences'.[7] In Rorty's view, 'Davidson's work can best be seen as carrying through Quine's dissolution of the distinction between questions of meaning and questions of fact.'[8]

At the other end of the spectrum that is 'impure' philosophy of language can be found in the likes of Putnam and Dummett, who in several ways represent the views of the schools of Vienna and Oxford. Philosophers such as those just mentioned see philosophy as concerned with the analyses of meanings. This preoccupation for them represents the central tendency of philosophy. Rorty observes that:

> Dummett sees philosophy of language as foundational because he sees epistemological issues now, at last, being formulated correctly as issues within the theory of meaning.[9]

Of course Rorty disagrees with this view for the simple reason that Dummett has failed to see that he is rehashing an old, philosophical *problematique* that need not necessarily dominate contemporary philosophical considerations. Rorty, in a not too dissimilar vein, argues that Putnam and Dummett thought they had discovered a more appropriate way of dealing with the relation between realism and idealism. The entire project of trying to analyse how words 'hook up' to the world in Rorty's view is a mistaken one, and both Putnam and Dummett (and Wiredu, need one add?) are guilty of this charge. On the contrary, one should view philosophy as 'a cultural genre, a voice in the conversation of mankind'.[10] Rorty also writes that:

> If we press Quine's and Davidson's criticisms of the language-fact and
> scheme-content distinctions far enough, we no longer have dialectical room
> to state an issue concerning 'how language hooks onto the world', be-
> tween the 'realist' and the 'idealist' (or the 'pragmatist').[11]

The logical implications of this assertion should be apparent enough. It means
that the old philosophical *problematique*, as fostered by those who in Rorty's
view practise 'impure' philosophy of language, would be rendered pointless.
This conclusion obviously agrees with the entire thesis of *Philosophy and the
Mirror of Nature*, which as we have seen is to demonstrate how philosophy
over centuries has become saddled with obsolete questions that impede the
course of cultural and philosophical discourse.

Rorty then turns to Quine, whose canonical paper, 'Two Dogmas of
Empiricism', has heightened the tempo of debate in philosophy of language.
Rorty declares:

> The first dogma enshrined what Quine called 'essentialism'-the notion that
> one could distinguish between what people were talking about and what
> they were saying about it by discovering the essence of the object being
> discussed.[12]

He also states:

> The second dogma held that such a translation could always be found,
> and that such analytic statements could always be formulated because to
> determine the meaning of any referring expression one need only dis-
> cover which reports in a 'neutral observation language' would confirm,
> and disconfirm, a statement asserting the existence of the referent in ques-
> tion.[13]

Having redefined the essential thrust of Quine's paper, Rorty then goes ahead
to disagree with him. His main criticism is that Quine does not face up to the
implications of his arguments. The fact that Quine wants a naturalised version
of epistemology does not agree with Rorty's picture of a de-epistemologised
philosophy of language. The inclusion of Sellars in this part of our discussion
is most certainly instructive. Sellars attacks the myth of the given, while Quine
rejects the analytic/synthetic and necessary/contingent distinctions. In this
regard, Leon Pompa notes:

> Rorty's aim is not merely to defend their claims but to show neither
> philosopher has been able wholly to free himself of the notion of privileged
> representation. As a result, theories have come forward in contemporary
> philosophy of mind and philosophy of language which, while attempting
> Sellar's and Quine's claims, are nevertheless simply new attempts to carry
> out the tasks of philosophy in accordance with the conception which
> Rorty rejects.[14]

On the other hand, Rorty in the domain of philosophy of language finds Davidsonian semantics exemplary, and this is because, he says, Davidson makes no attempt to conjoin epistemological issues with those relating to philosophy of language.

At this juncture, it would certainly be of help to find out why Rorty finds Davidson's work interesting. In this regard a cursory examination of Davidson's equally stimulating paper, 'Truth and Meaning', would serve our purpose. Davidson reminds us that there is a clear distinction between meaning and reference and goes on to state the difficulties involved in formulating a theory of meaning. In affirming his position on the matter, he states:

> My objection to meanings in the theory of meaning is not that they are abstract or that their identity conditions are obscure but they have no demonstrated use.[15]

Rorty, as is to be expected, supports this view. Davidson has no grand illusions about what a theory of meaning should be in the foundational connotations of the term. Instead, for him a theory of meaning is largely empirical and is concerned with the functional processes within a natural language. Davidson also recognises the problematic nature of natural languages, which he describes as being 'too confused and amorphous to permit the direct application of formal methods'.[16] He also adds that the task of a theory of meaning should not be to reform or change but rather to attempt to understand how a language works.[17] Linguists have been able to demonstrate how complex natural languages can be and hence the difficulties involved in putting together a truly acceptable theory of meaning. Davidson states that he finds Tarski's notion of truth plausible because it is not motivated by 'some adventitious philosophical puritanism'[18] a phrase that Rorty frequently borrows. But more importantly, Rorty repeatedly argues that the same 'adventitious philosophical Puritanism' that Davidson finds absent in Tarski's conception of truth is also absent in Davidsonian semantics.

Most philosophers are always looking for what Rorty terms 'the touchstone of truth'.[19] Yet many philosophers are unable to deal with the conclusion of philosophers such as Quine, Kuhn and Feyerabend, which is that all candidates for truth are 'theory-laden'. Rorty writes that:

> The philosopher had been portrayed since the beginnings of the 'linguistic turn' as a man who knew about concepts by knowing about the meanings of words, and whose work therefore transcended the empirical.[20]

He then shows us the perplexities involved when meanings and conceptual schemes become subject to change, as ably demonstrated by Feyerabend. If we are to hold on to what Feyerabend calls 'meaning invariance', it would logically imply that conceptual schemes and, more importantly, meanings do not change. Still pursuing that line of argument, Rorty writes:

> For 'meaning invariance' was simply the 'linguistic' way of stating the Kantian claim that inquiry, to be rational, had to be conducted within a permanent framework knowable a priori, a scheme which both restricted possible empirical content and explained what it was rational to do with any empirical content which came along.[21]

Rorty therefore urges us to view our conceptual schemes as the sum total of the opinions that dominate our current cultural concerns. If we do so, philosophers need not despair about not having conceptual frameworks with which to scrutinise our methods of inquiry. Conceptual schemes need to be related to specific cultural epochs as opposed to being transformed into non-historical points of reference for the rest of culture. Rorty, in more ways than one, admits his admiration for philosophers such as Kuhn and Feyerabend who hold views similar to his own. On the other hand, he refutes Frege's 'intentionalist' theory of reference. On this issue, he states:

> I think, then that the quest for a theory of reference represents a confusion between the hopeless 'semantic' quest for a general theory of what people are 'really talking about' and the equally hopeless 'epistemological' quest for a way of refuting the skeptic and underwriting our claim to be talking about nonfictions.[22]

Theories of reference for Rorty, to put it rather mildly, serve no useful purpose, and he makes several attempts to promote this view.

Let us now conclude this part of our discussion by restating some of the assertions Rorty makes in relation to the philosophy of language. To understand a language all we need to do is to study the components of sentences instead of trying to establish how words are related to the world. A more edifying enterprise would be to adopt Davidsonian semantics, which is not only a de-epistemologised and hence 'pure' philosophy of language, but which would also render pointless 'philosophically interesting questions about meaning and reference'.[23]

This vital area in the philosophy of language is absent in Wiredu's writings, as are many invaluable deconstructionist insights in philosophical discourse. Wiredu's project of conceptual decolonisation compels us to face problems pertaining to the philosophy of language, since he urges African philosophers to examine various philosophical concepts 'in your own African language'.[24] Obviously, this crucial aspect of his project necessitates a thorough examination of current practice in the philosophy of language that he fails to undertake. This shortcoming, one would contend, undermines a large part of his project.

Another aspect of his project that requires drastic rethinking is that which pertains to politics. In arguing for a non-party consensual political arrangement, Wiredu states that:

political associations will be avenues for channelling all desirable pluralisms, but they will be without the Hobbesian proclivities of political parties, as they are known under majoritarian politics. And second, without the constraints of membership in parties relentlessly dedicated to wrestling power or retaining it, representatives will be more likely to be actuated by the objective merits of given proposals than by ulterior considerations. In such an environment willingness to compromise, and with it the prospects of consensus, will be enhanced.[25]

Wiredu therefore concludes that:

far from the complexities of contemporary African life making the consensual, non-party precedents of traditional African politics now unusable, they make them indispensable.[26]

Nonetheless, it could be argued that the above conclusion does not portray the entire picture regarding contemporary African politics, and that the political realities of contemporary Africa make Wiredu's propositions in this respect unviable.[27]

The process of globalisation is something we must not fail to discuss at this juncture even though scholars often mention its slipperiness as a concept. Let us note how a couple of African scholars have attempted to situate it. Concerning globalisation, Claude Ake states:

It is about structural differentiation and functional specialization in the world economy. It is about incremental interdependence, the growing spread and intensity of interactions among nations and about the nation state coming under pressure from transnational phenomena, and so on. The process is complex, ambiguous and contradictory.[28]

According to S.B. Diagne and H. Ossebi, under globalisation:

cultural stakes thus become the strategic place for an increasingly visible rivalry between economic powers: standardization of life style and consumption patterns reveal this process of cultural homogenization strongly and abundantly broadcast by the media whose technology is increasingly sophisticated (intercontinental satellites, 'information highways', cable, etc).[29]

So as Ake notes, the process of globalisation is characterised by 'the nation-state coming, under pressure from transnational phenomena'. Wiredu says nothing on how developing nations can circumvent its awesome power, a situation necessary to confront in the re-ordering of our political existence in

Africa. Again, Claude Ake presents a more accurate picture of the African political dilemma:

> The African elite marginalized the African role in the development of Africa by their politics. The legacy of colonial politics, the clash of two exclusive claims to power had started the problem. But the African elite which succeeded the colonial regime compounded it by deciding to inherit the colonial system rather than transforming it in accordance with the democratic aspirations of the nationalist movement. Invariably, they fell out with their followers and became repressive. Repression bred more hostility which invited more repression in a vicious spiral which rendered politics Hobbesian.[30]

It would be naïve to believe that the solution to African political conundrums lies in the adoption of Wiredu's ill-defined consensual politics, given the disorienting realities of post-coloniality generally and the conditions of political existence in Africa. Rather, it may lie as Basil Davidson avers:

> In devolving executive powers to a multiplicity of locally representative bodies. It would be found in reestablishing 'vital inner links' within the fabric of society. Democratic participation would have to be 'mass participation'. And 'mass participation', patiently evolved and applied would be able to produce its own version of a strong state: the kind of state, in other words, that would be able to promote and protect civil society.[31]

Thus the African political situation necessitates that we apply pragmatism in forging a viable political ethos as opposed to succumbing to the romantic lure of tradition. Tradition can be a hindrance for cultural growth and diversity and there are well-reasoned arguments on this point.[32] The realities of the modern nation state preclude a reversion to pre-colonial political arrangements, with the dynamics of the process of globalisation making such a reversion even more problematic. These are vital issues Wiredu fails to address. To forge a vision for the political future of the African continent entails a thorough understanding of contemporary African realities. This, more than anything else, would be an adequate guide towards making appropriate formulations for the attainment of good governance in Africa.

Let us now commence the discussion of post-coloniality. But before we go on, it is important to note that Wiredu in his essay entitled 'The Need for Conceptual Decolonisation in African Philosophy' states:

> By conceptual decolonisation I mean two complementary things. On the negative side, I mean avoiding or reversing through a critical conceptual self-awareness the unexamined assimilation in our thought (that is, in the thought of contemporary African philosophers) of conceptual frameworks

embedded in the foreign philosophical traditions that have had an impact on African life and thought. And on the positive side, I mean exploiting as much as is judicious the resources of our own indigenous conceptual schemes in our philosophical meditations on even the most technical problems of contemporary philosophy.[33]

Wiredu needs to interrogate the question of post-coloniality in fuller dimensions. It is necessary to know how he problematises and appreciates the postcolonial condition. In this regard, essays such as 'Post-colonial African Philosophy' and the one quoted above indicate that he has not given sufficient thought to the issue, even though there is more than sufficient material. Since conceptual clarification is crucial to Wiredu's philosophy, it is important to know what he understands to be the 'post-colonial'. Stuart Hall, for instance, informs us:

> What 'post-colonial' certainly is not is one of those periodisations based on epochal 'stages' when everything is reversed at the same moment, all the old relations disappear forever and entirely new ones come to replace them.[34]

Instead, Hall argues that the post-colonial is marked by:

> hybridity, syncretism, multi-dimensional temporalities, the double inscriptions of colonial and metropolitan times, the two way cultural traffic characteristic of contact zones of the cities of the 'colonised' long before they have become the characteristic tropes of the cities of the 'colonising', the forms of translation and transculturation which have characterised the 'colonial relation' from its earliest stages, the disavowals and in-betweenness, the here and theres...[35]

What Hall demonstrates is that Wiredu's project of conceptual decolonisation does not take into consideration the perplexities of post-coloniality. If hybridity and syncretism are some of the hallmarks of the post-colonial condition, then Wiredu's project fails to demonstrate a corresponding sophistication.

However, Third World theorists have been able to construct theories that depict with much greater awareness the post-colonial condition which has also been inscribed into the global system. Alterity, for instance, has been 'constituted as distribution of places and spaces where each place is not only the site of substantive becomings but also of multiple hybridities and agencies'.[36] Third World theorists need to evolve more befitting theories for our present condition, 'since the philosophies we have do not seem to describe our reality very well'.[37] We need to examine the characteristics of globalisation more closely, which are:

> the increasingly apparent autonomy and simultaneously, interdependence and intersection of local, regional, national and international flows, forces

and interests, and the real pain of such dislocations and relocations. In other words, there is...the increasing internationalisation of the circuits of mobility of capital, information, manufacturing and service, commodities, cultural practices, populations and labour.[38]

In doing this, we would be able to understand the global system much better and our place within it.

Anthony Appiah appears to be subtler in negotiating the postcolonial condition. For instance, in his book *In My Father's House* Appiah argues that 'ideological decolonisation is bound to fail if it neglects either endogenous 'tradition' or exogenous 'western ideas', and that many African (and African American) intellectuals have failed to find a middle way'.[39] In electing to construct identities for ourselves we have to bear in mind that not only 'race but also categories of class, gender and sexuality'[40] come into play. On the issue of traditional languages, Appiah posits that to find a larger international community, most of them would have to be translated, something that hardly occurs in Africa with the possible exception of Swahili.[41] He goes on to mention that 'we cannot ignore, for example...the practical difficulties of developing a modern educational system in a language in which more of the manuals and textbooks have be written'.[42] These are real problems pertaining to conceptual decolonisation which we shall have to deal with at one stage or the other.

In My Father's House has generated a lot of controversy since its publication. Odia Ofeimun, a Nigerian writer, has written a rather damaging critique of it. Nkiru Nzegwu's essay, 'Questions of Identity and Inheritance: A Critical Review of Kwame Anthony Appiah's *In My Father's House*, (1996)' is a particularly damaging feminist critique of the book). Ofeimun wrongly states that Appiah does not envision 'a racialised conception of one's identity' because according to Appiah such a conception is 'retrogressive, especially as it becomes self-isolating in societies where blacks are in a minority'.[43] Ofeimun also goes on to say 'Appiah states that there is no race'.[44] Finally, he argues that for Appiah, 'the differences between African cultures are so fundamental that Soyinka's Yoruba metaphysics suggests cultural imperialism over his own Ashanti people'.[45]

First of all, Appiah does not argue that a racialised conception of identity is retrogressive. Instead he states that Africans do not have a common race.[46] To prove this, he cites Hountondji:

> The Beninois philosopher Paulin Hountondji has dubbed this view that Africa is culturally homogeneous-the belief that there is some central body of folk philosophy that is shared by black Africans quite generally 'unanimism'.[47]

I think the matter of Appiah on race needs to be further clarified. To be sure, he states:

> The truth is that there are no races: there is nothing in the world that can do all we ask race to do for us. As we have seen the biologist's notion has only limited uses, and the notion that Du Bois required, and that underlies the more hateful racisms of the modern era, refers to nothing in the world at all.[48]

What Appiah wants us to do is to see that the terminologies of race which are numerous and highly unstable are also historically constructed. He is exploring theoretical possibilities apart from the signifier 'race' as a way of constituting other modes of identity. In this regard, he argues:

> To a person unencumbered with the baggage of the history of the idea of race, it would surely seem strange that the independence of one nation of black men and women should resonate more with black people than with other oppressed people; strange too that it should be the whiteness of the oppressors-'the white man'-as opposed, say, to their imperialism.[49]

The signifier 'race', Appiah informs us, has moved from being a biological concept to being a socio-historical one, and this makes its fixity rather problematic. These clarifications, to be sure, are quite important.

Put in more concrete terms, he argues that a pan-African 'unanimist' identity is nothing more than the obverse side of Eurocentric racism and is ultimately an affirmation of it. Valentine Mudimbe on his part notes that: 'Africans were not identical, their social organisations are not equal, nor necessarily similar, and finally their traditions do not merely reflect each other and are not the same.'[50]

Appiah's critique of African unanimism is contained in the following passage:

> Compare Evans-Pritchard's famous Zande oracles, with their simple questions and straightforward answers, with the fabulous richness of Yoruba oracles, whose interpretation requires great skill in the hermeneutics of the complex corpus of verses of Ifa; or our own Asante monarchy, a confederation in which the king is first among equals, his elders and paramount chiefs guiding him in counsel, with the more absolute power of Mutesa the First in nineteenth-century Buganda; or the enclosed horizons of a traditional Hausa wife, forever barred from contact with men other than her husband, with the open space of the women traders of Southern Nigeria; or the art of Benin—its massive bronzes—with the tiny elegant gold-weight figures of the Akan. Face the warrior horsemen of the Fulani jihads with Shaka Zulu's impis; taste the bland foods of Botswana after

the spices of Fanti cooking; try understanding Kikuyu or Yoruba or Fulfulde with a Twi dictionary. ... Whatever Africans share, we do not have a common traditional culture, common languages, a common religious or conceptual vocabulary. ... we do not even belong to a common race; and since this is so, unanimism is not entitled to what is, in my view, its fundamental presupposition.[51]

Appiah then argues with regard to Soyinka's metaphysics that 'the African World' Soyinka counterposes in his fiction of Africa is one against which we revolt...because it presupposes a false account of the proper relationships between private "metaphysical" authenticity and ideology; a false account between literature, on the one hand, and the African world, on the other'.[52]

Appiah's text should prove useful for any decolonising operation because of the manner in which it conceptualises the postcolonial condition. The fact that it is able to deal fruitfully and comprehensively with post-coloniality and post-modernism is an advancement on Wiredu's work. Appiah writes:

In philosophy, postmodernism is the rejection of the mainstream consensus from Descartes through Kant to logical positivism and foundationalism (there is one route to knowledge which is exclusivism in epistemology) and of metaphysical realism (there is one truth, which is exclusivism in ontology), each underwritten by a unitary notion of reason; it thus celebrates figures as Nietzsche (no metaphysical realist) and Dewey (no foundationalist).[53]

We are also told that 'postmodern culture is global'[54] which is a fairly accurate assessment. On the other hand:

Postcoloniality is the condition of what we might ungenerously call a comprador intelligentsia of a relatively small, Western-style, Western-trained, group of writers and thinkers who mediate the trade in cultural commodities of world capitalism at the periphery. In the West they are known through the Africa they offer; their compatriots know them both through the West they present to Africa and through an Africa they have invented for the world, for each other, and for Africa.[55]

It is curious to note that Wiredu, who has written on 'post-colonial African philosophy', says nothing on this crucial issue.

Another problematic aspect of Wiredu's project of conceptual decolonisation is the one that says we ought to go about it with 'due reflection'. But Wiredu does not mention the canons of rationality we are supposed to employ.[56] In other words, one is forced to pose the question:

Whose rationality is it? with acknowledging the multiplicity of rationalities, with enquiring into the specific articulations by which the inherited discourses of rationality have been accomplished, even while remaining with the broad terrain of modern rationality.[57]

Let us now attempt to rehearse some of the arguments put forward so far. First of all, we looked at the issue of philosophy of language. If we shall be translating modern Western thought into indigenous African languages, we have to confront some of the epistemological problems that attend the question of translation. Using the work of Rorty, we demonstrated the difficulties that arise when we try to construct a non-historical theory of meaning and reference. Undeniably, a significant part of this study is post-structuralist and as such it is partial to the writings of 'post analytical' philosophers such as Richard Rorty, where deconstruction comes to figure as a handy cover-term for everything that points beyond the 'old dispensation of reason, knowledge and truth, and Derrida comes to play the role of the arch-debunker, a latter day sophist who dances rings around the earnest philosophical seekers-after-truth'.[58]

Since post-structuralist thought has been fundamental in questioning the hegemonic systems of thought in Western philosophy, it is my view that aspects of it can be incorporated into projects of decolonisation which seek to contest the aftermath of colonialism and the ongoing onslaught of imperialism. My argument here is that there is the need to look into the more progressive aspects of Western thought, those that subvert phallocentrism, racism and imperialism. To a large extent, Appiah has been able to do this, thereby transcending the customary nativism of decolonising operations.

On Quine and Translation Theory

It is important to know what translation theory Wiredu is employing, because it is central to his project of decolonisation. Translation is a complex process that requires a conscious theoretical position. If one is to translate philosophical concepts from one language to another, one must define the conceptual framework one is employing. A number of works explain the difficulties of translation and translation theory. It should be helpful to examine some of the debates in the field of translation theory.

Willard van Quine's thesis of indeterminacy of translation is crucial to the debate in recent philosophy of language. Quine's position is that no translation is exempt from the problem of indeterminacy, and the problem of how meaning is construed and transferred from one linguistic context to another. Drawing on Quine's indeterminacy of translation thesis, George Steiner has noted:

> The theory of translation, so largely literary and ad hoc, ought not to be
> held to account for having failed to solve problems of meaning, of relations

between words and the composition of the world to which logic and metaphysics continue to give provisional, frequently contradictory answers.[59] Steiner also believes that a theory of language:

> is either an intentionally sharpened, hermeutically oriented way of designating a working model of all meaningful exchanges, of the totality of semantic communication (including Jakobson's intersemiotic translation or 'transmutation'). Or it is a subsection of such a model with specific reference to interlingual exchanges, to the emission and reception of significant messages between different languages.[60]

These are vital issues theories of translation will have to address. But we are never notified of which of these paradigms Wiredu is availing himself with. These issues cannot be overlooked because as Spivak argues, 'the politics of translation takes on a massive life of its own if you see language as the process of meaning-construction'.[61]

In *Word and Object* W. van Quine makes philosophical pronouncements that are somewhat similar to those of Ludwig Wittgenstein in his *Philosophical Investigations* regarding the question of indeterminacy. For Quine, more or less every interlinguistic transfer is subject to the rule of indeterminacy. In his words:

> There can be no doubt that rival systems of analytical hypotheses can fit the totality of speech behaviour to perfection, and can fit the totality of dispositions to speech behaviour as well, and still specify mutually incompatible translations of countless sentences insusceptible of independent control.[62]

This is so given the very complex nature of language itself and the innumerable linguistic determinants that make every language unique. We should however note that the current debates concerning the thesis of indeterminacy of translation are numerous and that there is no widely accepted understanding of it. A concise apprehension of the thesis is perhaps desirable at this point:

> The thesis is that divergent translation manuals can be set up between natural languages such that they are compatible with empirical facts but nevertheless diverge radically from each other in what sentences they prescribe as translations of sentences in the foreign language. Each manual works individually, but they cannot be used in alternation: the fusion of two of these manuals does not in general constitute a manual that is compatible with all enquiries.[63]

It is important to bear in mind that the thesis of indeterminacy of translation is somehow different from the indeterminacy of reference thesis, even though they share some similarities. A great deal in Quine's work protests against 'the uncritical appeal to meanings and analyticity that characterised the logical positivists'.[64] If metaphysics had made the essence of things its central project, analytical philosophy as formulated by G.E. Moore and after was concerned with the meanings of words. Ultimately, Quine's indeterminacy of translation thesis has been a damaging critique of familiar philosophical semantic concepts such as 'meaning', 'synonymy', 'analyticity', 'intention', and 'belief'. As such 'the indeterminacy thesis says something to the effect that our notion of meaning is irremediably confused'.[65] But Quine himself has formulated the thesis differently on various occasions.

Quine's *Word and Object* and subsequent writings formulate his indeterminacy thesis by presenting the methodological options available to a radical translator and goes on to debunk those very options. In other words, there are no facts to determine the suitability of two or more incompatible translation frameworks. Quine puts it in this manner:

> Manuals for translation of one language into another can be set up in divergent ways, all compatible with the totality of speech disposition, yet incompatible with one another. In countless places they will diverge in giving, as their respective translations of a sentence of one language, sentences of the other language which stand to each other in no plausible sort of equivalence however loose.[66]

Quine's indeterminacy thesis is a result of what has been termed his behaviouristic conception of language and also his rejection of the analytic/synthetic distinction.

For a translation to be acceptable several variables have to be taken into account, which include 'conservation of phrase structure, frequency of use, emotional connotation, cumbersomeness of pronunciation, etc.'.[67] The following passage illustrates some of the difficulties involved in translation:

> a manual may conserve truth conditions yet be incorrect as a translation manual in the ordinary sense. So if the incompatibility of Quine's rival manuals consists only in that their fusion would be an incorrect translation manual in the sense of the word, this does not imply that they are incompatible in the relevant way, i.e. that their fusion does not conserve truth conditions.[68]

Alongside Quine's work on translation theory, many other works have been produced that draw heavily on modern linguistics. By virtue of some of these works we know for instance that:

> A translation model should consider the overall textual components, how sentences are interlinked and how they depend on one another in a stretch of text to convey the intended meaning.[69]

Translation is also 'a complex dichotomous and cumulative process which involves a host of activities drawing upon other disciplines related to language, writing, linguistics and culture'.[70] Finally, 'translation can be defined as a continuous decision-making process which is affected by the degree of indeterminacy a source language text might present'.[71]

Defining Limits of the Postcolonial Condition

We noted earlier that Wiredu does not situate his treatment of the postcolonial within a distinct framework. When viewed from this perspective, Wiredu's scheme of conceptual decolonisation appears not to have grappled with certain problematics in postcolonial discourse. He needs to look at issues related to class, gender, ethnicity, postmodernism and post-coloniality with a self-reflexive, updated vocabulary to become truly relevant within the globalisation process, a process which he fails to discuss adequately.

We earlier observed that most current Third World philosophies cannot describe or adequately deal with our present realities. However, theorists like Stuart Hall, Paul Gilroy, Dick Hebridge and, more importantly, Anthony Appiah, have been able to produce sufficiently theoretically sophisticated work in which Third World problems are addressed with a globally oriented vocabulary.

On the issue of politics, Wiredu's nativism is even more pronounced. How is it possible to revert to a consensual system of governance without re-establishing the old pre-colonial geographical boundaries and without the numerous ethnic conflicts that are bound to result? Wiredu fails to demonstrate how this could be achieved, while what is required is a thorough acquaintance with African political problems, that is, their origins from colonial times to the post liberation epoch. From this foundation Africans must muster the political will to develop the democratic ethos as well as protect civil liberties. Mere nativism is not sufficient.

When compared to Ngugi wa Thiong'o's, Wiredu's decolonisation project is far less comprehensive and less radical, because he does not take into consideration global tendencies regarding the post-colonial condition. Appiah also goes further than Wiredu in engaging with the registers of the postmodern/post-colonial condition. All these factors contribute to the delineation of the limits of Wiredu's project of conceptual decolonisation.

The next chapter examines other issues we have to confront when discussing decolonisation, more specifically, issues that pertain to knowledge production in Africa.

Notes

1. Kwasi Wiredu, *Cultural Universals and Particulars,* Bloomington and Indiana: Indiana University Press, 1996, p. 93.

2. Ibid.

3. Richard Rorty, *Philosophy and the Mirror of Nature,* Oxford: Basil Blackwell, 1983, p. 7.

4. Jacques Derrida, *Writing and Difference* trans. A. Bass, Chicago: Chicago University Press, 1978, p. 79.

5. Richard Rorty, *Philosophy and the Mirror of Nature,* 1983, p. 259.

6. Ibid.

7. Ibid. p. 260.

8. Ibid. p. 261.

9. Ibid. p. 263.

10. Ibid. p. 264.

11. Ibid. p. 265.

12. Ibid. p. 268.

13. Ibid.

14. L. Pompa, 'Philosophy Without Epistemology' in *Inquiry: An Interdisciplinary Journal of Philosophy and Social Sciences,* Vol. 24, No. 3, October 1981, p. 363.

15. Donald Davidson, 'Truth and Meaning' in F. Rosenberg and C. Travis, eds., *Readings in Philosophy of Language,* New Jersey: Prentice Hall Inc., 1971, p. 453.

16. Ibid. p. 458.

17. Ibid. p. 460.

18. Ibid.

19. Richard Rorty, *Philosophy and the Mirror of Nature* 1983, p. 269.

20. Ibid. p. 272.

21. Ibid.

22. Ibid. p. 293.

23. Ibid. p. 299.

24. Kwasi Wiredu, *Cultural Universals and Particulars,* 1996, p. 137.

25. Kwasi Wiredu, *Conceptual Decolonisation in African Philosophy,* 1995, p. 61.

26. Ibid. p. 62.

27. For a more plausible account of the political condition(s) in Africa, see Mahmood Mamdani, *Citizen and Subject: Contemporary Africa and the Legacy of Late Colonialism,* New Jersey: Princeton University Press, 1996 and his *When Victims Become Killers: Colonialism, Nativism, and the Genocide in Rwanda,* New Jersey: Princeton University Press, 2001; Peter Ekeh, 'Colonialism and the Two Publics in Africa: A Theoretical

Statement', *Comparative Studies in Society and History: An International Quarterly,* Vol. 17, 1975; and Achille Mbembe, *On the Postcolony,* Berkeley: University of California Press, 2001

28. Claude Ake, *The Marginalization of Africa,* CASS Monograph No. 6, Lagos: Malthouse Press Ltd, 1996, p. 14.

29. S.B. Diagne and H. Ossebi, *The Cultural Question in Africa,* Dakar: CODESRIA Working Paper, 3/96 p. 27.

30. Claude Ake, *The Marginalization of Africa,* 1996, p. 14.

31. Basil Davidson, *The Black Man's Burden,* Ibadan: Spectrum Books Ltd., 1993, pp. 294-5.

32. See Paul Gilroy, *Against Race: Imagining Political Culture Beyond the Color Line,* 2000, p. 84

33. Kwasi Wiredu, *Cultural Universals and Particulars,* 1996, p. 136.

34. Stuart Hall, 'When was 'the post-colonial'? Thinking at the Limit' in I. Chambers and L. Curti, eds., *The Post-colonial Question,* London and New York: Routledge, 1996, p. 247.

35. Ibid. p. 251.

36. Lawrence Grossberg, 'The Space of Culture, the Power of Space' in I. Chambers and L. Curti, eds., *The Post-colonial Question,* London and New York: Routledge, 1996, p. 182.

37. Ibid. p. 171.

38. Ibid. p. 170.

39. Anthony Appiah, *In My Father's House,* New York: Oxford University Press Inc., 1992, p. x.

40. Marie Helene Laforest, 'Black Cultures in Difference' in I. Chambers and L. Curti, eds., *The Post-colonial Question,* London and New York: Routledge, 1996, p. 118.

41. Anthony Appiah, *In My Father's House,* 1992, p. 4.

42. Ibid.

43. Odia Ofeimun, 'African Many Mansions', Review of A. Appiah's *In My Father's House* in *ANA Review,* Nov. 1995, p. 15.

44. Ibid.

45. Ibid.

46. Anthony Appiah, *In My Father's House,* 1992, p. 26.

47. Ibid. p. 24.

48. Ibid. p. 45.

49. Ibid.

50. Valentine Mudimbe, *The Invention of Africa: Gnosis, Philosophy and the Order of Knowledge,* Bloomington/Indianapolis: Indiana University Press, 1988, p. 20.

51. Kwame Anthony Appiah, *In My Father's House: Africa in the Philosophy of Culture*, London: Methuen, 1992.

52. Ibid. p. 80.

53. Ibid. p. 147.

54. Ibid. p. 144.

55. Ibid. p. 149.

56. See Sanya Osha 'A New Direction in African Philosophy', review of K. Wiredu's 'Conceptual Decolonisation in African Philosophy' in *Journal of Philosophy and Development*, Vol. 2, Nos. 1 & 2 Jan. 1996, Ogun State University Ago-Iwoye, pp. 136-9.

57. Lawrence Grossberg, 'The Space of Culture, the Power of Space' in *The Post-colonial Question*, 1996, p. 171.

58. David Morley, 'EurAm, modernity, reason and alterity: or postmodernism, the highest stage of cultural imperialism' in *Stuart Hall: Critical Dialogues in Cultural Studies,* eds. D. Morley and K. Chen, London and New York: Routledge, 1996 p. 334.

59. George Steiner, *After Babel: Aspects of Language and Translation*, London: Oxford University Press, 1975, p. 277.

60. Ibid. p. 275.

61. Gayatri Spivak, *Outside in the Teaching Machine,* New York and London: Routledge, 1993, p. 179.

62. W. van Quine, *Word and Object,* Cambridge: MIT Press, 1960, p. 72.

63. Nick Bostrom, 'Understanding Quine's Theses of Indeterminacy', unpublished MA thesis, LSC and Stockholm University, July 1995. Also available online www.hedweb.com/nickb

64. Ibid. p. 2.

65. Ibid. p. 2.

66. W. van Quine, *Word and Object,* p. 27.

67. Ibid. p. 5.

68. Ibid. p. 5.

69. Ali Darwish, 'The Translation Process: A View of Mind', paper written for the postgraduate students of the Diploma in Translation and Interpreting at Victoria College, Melbourne, Australia, 1989, http://www.surf.net.au/writescope/translation/mindview.html

70. Ibid. p. 2.

71. Ibid. p. 9.

6

Africa as Text

This chapter examines the environment for knowledge generation in Africa and issues relating to textuality on the continent. It is necessary to undertake this task to apprehend some other impediments to the various forms of decolonisation, conceptual/ ideological/epistemological. Furthermore, it should prove an apt extension of some of the discussions broached so far in this study. The processes of disinstitutionalisation taking place in contemporary Africa are well known. In addition, knowledge generating mechanisms are also affected by the general phenomenon of structural decay. In this instance, I attempt to recount the dissolution of productive infrastructure on the one hand, and also indicate 'resistant' (Afrocentricism) forms of textuality and also alternative textual products (Appiah and Soyinka) that manage to resonate within a transnational space. Thus this chapter counterposes conditions of death/decay with celebratory, Nitzschean *jouissance*.

Thought in a Post-Colonial Context

Colonialism has always brought drastic changes to societies so unfortunate as to have experienced it. For good or for ill, the far-reaching transformations within those societies are indeed enormous for reasons that should be obvious enough. The impact of colonialism in all its various ramifications-political, economic, structural and socio-cultural-constitute in almost all cases, a drastic change in the perceptions of both the colonised and the coloniser. Yet it is all too easy to gloss over those disruptive transformations by the parties involved. The worlds of both the colonised and the coloniser resume their 'normal' courses in ways that are often oblivious of the acute disruptions that are the logical consequences of the colonial encounter. A tortuous process of masking and unmasking begins in which the changing faces of reality become inevitably undecipherable. This indecipherability can be observed at several levels. First, at the level of narrating the collective history of a people and the points at which necessary connections with that history ought to be established and maintained. Second, at the level of scrutinising the face of imperialism or perhaps neo-colonialism for what it is.

It is important to note the difficulty of this situation so that the questions of agency and autonomy of the decolonising subject can remain in focus. The decolonising agent must seek to describe an independence that is truly based on terms of autonomy and which are devoid of the encroaching forces of alienation both internal and external. Third, the agent must seek to define a structurality in which social relations and institutions are balanced on an equation that not only promotes growth but also maintains stability. These are some of the primary tasks that face a society intent on embarking on the arduous process of decolonisation.

Thought in a post-colonial context is always somewhat ambivalent.[1] It is the consequences of this ambivalence that we shall be treating here, that is, the crippling sense of hesitation that confronts the decolonising agent, the uncertain paternalism of the colonising agent, and the resultant breakdown of structural divisions in thought and society as a whole. This debacle is not only evident in contemporary African thought and social structures but also in the intellection and social formations of peoples of African descent in the diaspora.

Wole Soyinka in his Nobel prize lecture (1986) entitled 'This Past Must Address its Present' reminds us that Friedrich Hegel said that the African had not yet reached the stage where he 'attained that realization of any objective existence'.[2] In Hegel therefore, Eurocentric racism evidently found a formidable intellectual basis.

For the African about to embark on the study of Western philosophy and culture, there are usually Eurocentric impediments hurled in his way. Olusegun Oladipo confirms this position when he reveals that his 'first encounter with Russell's book turned out to be a failure'[3] for this reason. Hence, the African student of philosophy is invariably confronted with the thesis that 'African philosophy could not be philosophy in the 'real sense', except it comes as an extension, or better still, a copy of Western philosophy'.[4]

Apart from the forceful seizure of African territories which came with colonialism, there was also an overwhelming syndrome of psychological dependence, an occurrence that evidently affected the intellectual outlook of the newly decolonised peoples. Mannoni in his study of the psychological undercurrents of colonialism, *Prospero and Caliban*, has much to say on this debilitating syndrome of dependence and psychological transformations wrought by the colonial encounter. Preliterate societies had their own stable cosmological systems before the advent of colonialism. Theirs was a world filled with myths, rituals, gods and of course superstitions which provided the basis for some arrangement of the psychosocial order. Needless to say, in varying degrees, colonialism changed the coherences of tribal cultures. According to Mannoni, the symbol of the white man, in several instances, became invested with the psychological support systems withdrawn from the old fallen gods. Thus with this transference of psychological loyalties, a strange syndrome of dependence began.

Wiredu has written that Christianity is one of the most prevalent ways through which colonised peoples 'are afflicted with the colonial mentality'.[5] The ability to circumvent this pervasive mentality would depend on the extent to which they are able to employ 'due reflection'. However, as we noted in the previous chapter, he is less than precise about how this is to be executed. It isn't only the African who manifests the dependence syndrome. The paternalism of Eurocentricism also constitutes an equally pressing problem.

So it may be argued that Eurocentricism has a certain sense of superiority which it is as yet unable to relinquish completely. It is this attitude that has in turn provoked what may be regarded as 'an Afrocentric paradigm'.[6] Appiah argues that Afrocentric discourse is infiltrated by the same ethnocentricism which it attacks in Eurocentricism and that there is a deliberate selectivity in its tendencies and foundations which has resulted in its 'essentially reactive structure.[7]

Afrocentricism: The Discourse and the Debates

We might as well look, if only briefly, at the project of Afrocentricity itself. Although is usually assumed that Afrocentricity seeks to establish the African origins of some aspects of global culture it is primarily a theory of African agency. In the popular imagination, it is believed that it looks towards ancient Egypt (Kemet) (and also places such as Nubia, Axum and Meroe) in establishing those origins, which undoubtedly contributed immensely to the development of the civilisation of Ancient Greece. Cheikh Anta Diop,[8] the Senegalese intellectual, is regarded as one of the major inspirational figures of the Afrocentric movement, and scholars like Molefi Kete Asante, Yosef Ben-Jochannan, Ibrahim Sundiata and Maulana Karenga have continued to keep Afrocentric discourse alive. Chancellor Williams' *The Destruction of the Black*

Civilization and George James' *Stolen Legacy* are important texts in Afrocentric discourse. Appiah argues that a considerable part of the Afrocentric discourse engendered 'misogyny and homophobia' and has helped in fostering 'a cultural brew as noxious as any currently available in popular culture'.[9] Orlando Patterson, a Jamaican-born sociologist in Harvard in the 1970s criticised Afrocentricism as a movement that eulogises 'pageants, pyramids and princes.'[10] Critics such as Arthur Schlesinger and Dinesh D'Souza regard it as 'the historical groundwork for Black separatism.'[11]

Afrocentricism has been described, among other things, as a movement and an attitude. For Africanists, it is deployed 'to topple the perceived 'Eurocentricism' of the pedagogical status quo'.[12] Afrocentricists are of the view that Eurocentricism is entrenched not only in corporations and churches but also in the academy, the supposed bastion of impartial intellection and progressive ideas, to those who believe in multiculturalism. Just as Afrocentricism is on the ascendancy, there are at the same time intellectual reactions to it. Martin Bernal's *Black Athena: The Afroasiatic Roots of Classical Civilization* (1987) argues for the African roots of the Hellenic civilisation, and this work provoked renewed interest in Egyptology and classics. Scholars such as Mary Lefkowitz[13] have in turn argued against the core thesis of Bernal's work, and she 'has become doyenne of those who wish to see her as the end of liberal 'relativism' in the academy, including many on the Right who see her as the opening wedge in a crusade to cleanse the temples of learning of creeping multiculturalism'.[14] In 1994, a collection of articles were published in a volume, *Alternatives to Afrocentrism* and it had contributions by Lefkowitz, Gerald Early, Stanley Crouch, Wilson Moses and Frank Yurco. These anti-afrocentricists usually have the backing of well funded institutions such as the Bradley and Olin Foundations which have provided support for Lefkowitz onslaughts against Afrocentricism.

The challenges to Afrocentricism notwithstanding: 'Afrocentricity creates an ideology of hope, telling the reader who s/he is, what s/he can know and what s/he must do, and what true history is from an African perspective'.[15] Molefi Kete Asante, a foremost theorist of Afrocentricity, explains:

> Afrocentricity can stand its ground among any ideology or religion: Marxism, Islam, Christianity, Buddhism, or Judaism. Your Afrocentricity will emerge in the presence of these other ideologies because it is from you. It is a truth even though it may not be their truth.[16]

In his critique of Asante's book James Palermo writes '*Afrocentricity* reveals the story of an oppressed people whose history has been fabricated, whose language has been devalued, whose names have derived from an alien culture and who are today suffering the severe economic exploitation of a capitalist/racist society.'[17] Palermo's critique marks a different trajectory from Lefkowitz's. Palermo's main argument is that *Afrocentricity* reinforces the conditions of alienation for most African-Americans. But what we must bear in mind is that Afrocentricity proposes a critique of domination and hegemony, and challenges 'the imposition of Eurocentricism as universal without attempting to claim such universality for itself.'[18]

However, in spite of its transracial and transcultural intentions, Afrocentricity needs to carry out a more incisive critique of the differences, in terms of economic status, and the dislocations brought on by capitalism within the African-American populace. This is a legitimate argument against the ideology. Furthermore, Afrocentricity has to respond to the information revolution. In other words, the next phase of the struggle is to ensure 'the virtualization of the Black experience.'[19]

Mary Lefkowitz's attack on Afrocentricism should also not be taken lightly. She claims:

> Afrocentrists are not content with establishing a special relationship to the ancient Greeks. Instead, they seek to remove the ancient Greeks from the important role they have previously played in history, and to assign to the African civilization of Egypt the credit for the Greeks' achievement.[20]

Martin Bernal, who espouses the Afrocentric viewpoint, disagrees. He maintains that:

> Mary Lefkowitz's...claim...can easily be explained in terms of her eagerness to separate Greece from Egypt and the desire to use her knowledge of language to intimidate the Afrocentrists. It does not cast doubt on Mary Lefkowitz's knowledge of Greek and Latin. On the other hand, while she knows these languages, she does not know much about linguistics and she has virtually no understanding of language contact, which is the relevant field when looking at the relations between Egypt and Greece.[21]

Lefkowitz makes other objections to Afrocentric discourse. For instance, she claims that Afrocentrists ignore chronology and that 'their historical methodology allows them to alter the course of history to meet their own specific needs'.[22] Furthermore, she posits that the Afrocentric myth is not only inaccurate but is also basically unAfrican, because it is the product of Eurocentric, not African, culture. The basis of Afrocentricism is both unscientific and false. Another opinion Lefkowitz expresses on a prominent Afrocentric theorist, Cheikh Anta Diop, is that:

> Diop's historicism is not so liberating as it first may seem, because it requires adherents to confine their thinking to rigid ethnic categories that

have little demonstrable connection with practical reality.[23]

In the final analysis she advocates what she calls 'a wider cosmopolitanism' as opposed to the insularity of ethnocentrism.

But Bernal accuses Lefkowitz of the same deliberate selectivity she charges Afrocentrists. According to him, 'she selects her evidence rejecting data that does not support her arguments'.[24] In addition, he faults Lefkowitz's competence to proffer a credible critique of Afrocentric discourse, which in effect means that the debate is not yet over. Academics continue to participate actively in the Afrocentric discourse. In the contemporary moment, the debates around Afrocentricism are often reduced to squabbles over the social construction of race in America and the debates around multiculturalism. The racial underpinnings become quite evident in Lefkowitz's remark that 'if you go by the American 'one drop rule', the Egyptians would be black.'[25]

We must not fail to disregard the powerful resistance of Eurocentricism to the cultural antecedents of non-African peoples. This resistance, to be sure, has a long history. Basil Davidson amply demonstrates this when he writes that 'the whole white establishment...multiplied its sneers and contempt for literate Africans, 'useless visionaries, detestable clerks' as one colonial governor called them in speaking the mind of other colonial governors'.[26] What we are talking about is the profound ethnocentricism of Western culture, in other words, its racism. This single factor may decide the extent to which non-Africans may be admitted into the Western archive and deemed worthy inheritors of the fruits of Western civilisation.

There is indeed an 'impasse' regarding discursive practices in a post-colonial condition. The condition of post-coloniality either encourages a wholesale adoption of Western culture or a violently reactive response that becomes virtually impossible to sustain beyond certain limits. There is also evidently a potent determinism in these two responses that are more or less direct offshoots of the colonialist discourse. To get around this all-too-probable determinism, other responses have been advanced. Oladipo, for instance, has argued in his paper 'Traditional African Philosophy: Its Significance for Contemporary Africa' for a critical engagement with our indigenous traditions, but that to do so, we require 'some conceptual understanding'[27] to determine our place within a highly technologised modern framework. This, certainly, cannot be end of the story. However, he states that:

> Our participation in a universal cultural dialogue can be significant only if it is based on a firm foundation of concepts, theories and ideas which we have developed by ourselves in the attempt to come to terms with the African reality in its various socio-historical dimensions.[28]

There is nonetheless an equally pressing practical aspect to the matter. The generally repressive character of African political institutions and systems has gone a long way in shaping not only what is possible within the realms of thought but also the peoples' capacities to think by, for example, its restriction and corruption of the language of the public sphere.

In most African countries, the 'University Idea'[29] has clearly derailed, leading to a mass exodus of Africa's best brains to more agreeable shores, usually Europe and the United States. But before we proceed, let us consider another response that tries to undermine the determinism of colonialist discourse. To revert to the physical environment of Africa itself, where thought must also take place, is something we must do at this juncture as opposed to focusing on only the academic environment of Europe and America, where the institutional infrastructure for thought is considerably more developed. The inexorable rate of decline at many levels within the African continent is indeed awesome. This scenario of decline in its broadest sense is picturesquely captured by an assessment of the Nigerian situation:

> Nigeria has many fine lawyers, but the judiciary is tinted by trials settled with bribes. It has fine academics, but universities are tarnished by the trade in diplomas. It has respected chiefs, but the nobility has been mocked by the sales of chieftaincy titles. In many ways, the institution that has suffered the most under this military government is the military itself. 'Military men are not soldiers anymore', is a common Nigeria observation.[30]

A central argument is that thought, rather than being on the ascendancy—especially in regions within the African continent plagued by war, military rule, and socio-economic stagnation—is in rapid decline. Nothing betrays this fact more than the mass exodus of African intellectuals to Europe and America, where they are likely to be subsumed by Western hegemony. Another form of discursive determinism may result from this situation, one that we can hardly begin to predict in relation to its pathology and theoretical tendencies.

Most African governments do all they can to stifle opposition and alternatives that are not in line with their objectives. This is very injurious to the development of intellection, civil liberties and finally democracy. So it can be said that the disqualification of all manner of opposition within officialdom has become, to all intents and purposes, institutional. In consequence, the institutional environment for the development of thought in the troubled regions of Africa is lacking. Even in traditional African societies, this was not exactly the case. There were elaborate systems of checks and balances that regulated traditional societies like the ancient kingdoms of Ghana, Kanem-

Bornu and Oyo. Furthermore, it was never raised to the level of government policy to extinguish manifestations of scholarship as is being done in several parts of contemporary Africa. A lot of institutional anomalies have to be addressed to improve the level of debate in contemporary African societies. Only when this is achieved will one be able to hope for better chances of collective development.

Euro-America certainly has a role to play in all this. Euro-America has got to do away with its entrenched paternalism, its ethnocentricism and racism, and its unshakable sense of superiority before 'the conversation of mankind' can truly take place. Similarly, the equally disturbing ethnocentricism of extreme Afrocentricity will not generate the kind of reflections necessary for the development of African peoples and peoples of African descent. The disturbing part of this Afrocentricity is its almost systemic selectivity regarding world history and its characteristic fascination for the very monologism it professes to refute. It has not really succeeded in getting around it. As Appiah puts it:

> The proper response to Eurocentricism is surely not a reactive Afrocentricism, but a new understanding that humanizes all of us by learning to think beyond race.[31]

Perhaps it is of this understanding that Rorty speaks when he talks about the commencement of 'the conversation of mankind'. The crucial question at this juncture is how far are both Euro-America and Africa able to agree with the principles enshrined in this conversation of mankind? Euro-America definitely has a lot to do in terms of overcoming the psychological complexes engendered by its sense of superiority. Africa, for its part, has to develop the structures necessary for its development and not just survival (in the sense that it has proved it can survive under almost any condition).

The contention, then, is that Africa is unable as of yet to reconcile itself to its past and its full potential when viewed through the lenses of post-coloniality. Also, there exists a disorienting ambivalence of thought and a confusion as to theoretical alternatives, and this is also reflected at the practical level.[32] There is a widespread structural malformation that leads to acute institutional failure and, finally, thought on real development on the part of most African governments is also rare.

Any project of conceptual decolonisation that fails to take into account these important variables is bound to be restrictive and insufficiently viable. Wiredu has not undertaken a thorough examination of authoritarianism in Africa, which needs not only to be critiqued, but also needs to be contested. In doing this, it will then be possible to discern some of the limits of conceptual decolonisation and perhaps also the possibilities to overcome them. In the next section we examine another vital area absent in Wiredu's project, that is the question of textuality.

Thought and Writing: Two Views on African Textual Practice

There continues to exist an extremely problematic chasm that African thinkers are compelled to negotiate in the terrain of African intellectual discourse. This chasm is the division that lies between a preliterate culture and a condition of post-modern textuality. As a result, chimerical discursive interventions have been made since the very beginnings of the colonial encounter to camouflage the deep wound inflicted on the progressive African consciousness by the seemingly irreversible march of Western-inspired modernity. This wound upon the modern African consciousness forms one of the overriding thrusts of this section, which also seeks to address how the distance between orality and textuality has eroded most well-intentioned efforts at conceptual elucidation. (I have argued elsewhere that Wiredu does not explore the distance between textuality and orality adequately).[33]

The project of modernisation in Africa is not only an ambitious one but also an extremely confusing one as well. The root of this difficulty must be sought in the event of colonialism itself. Expectedly, colonialism has left in its train a bitter legacy, a loss of orientation that the emancipated nations of Africa are as yet unable to overcome. Basil Davidson captures the destructiveness of colonialism when he writes:

> the whole great European project in Africa stretching over more than a hundred years, can only seem a vast obstacle thrust across every reasonable avenue of African progress out of preliterate and prescientific societies into the modern world... It taught that nothing useful could develop without a ruthless severing from Africa's roots and a slavish acceptance of models drawn entirely from different histories.[34]

Even more distressing is the fact that many African ideologies found it necessary until recently to accept 'their necessary self-alienation from Africa's roots',[35] as they were obviously unable to surmount the overwhelming 'tide of Europeanisation'. Regrettably, this almost unquestioning acceptance of the 'necessary self alienation' has not placed the beleaguered African continent within a suitable context of modernisation. Instead, the continent continues to suffer other forms of alienation, both internal and external, and those who apparently seem to endure the worst deprivation in this respect are in fact the literate Africans.

From the advent of colonialism to the present post-colonial period, the African text in relation to the event of imperialism has taken two basically distinct orientations, which are the pre-colonial or the crudely Afrocentric.

The Negritudist agenda is a direct reaction to the colonial encounter just as the impassioned ideological replies to it. Negritude as an ideology sought to integrate a collective African persona, a persona that has now, for the most part, generated a lot of bitter debate. Subsequently, a new level of ideological contestation was attained. All along, thought and writing were fused together to constitute meaning. It never fully occurred to African thinkers of the colonial era to consider the act of writing as a new birth in the evolution of the modern African consciousness, that is, the rise of a novel discursive awareness.

However, there are a few cases when African thinkers have been able to contemplate fruitfully the implications of the distance between orality and textuality. Perhaps one needs to elaborate. There have been a few African intellectuals who have been able to apprehend textuality by itself and for itself. This apprehension/contemplation was able to reveal to them that the scribal endeavour has its own inner mechanisms, its own determinate history, project and future that cannot simply be taken for granted. When taken in those terms, textuality becomes a less nebulous object and project. The struggle to acquire a scribal culture, coming from a pre-scientific background, has to begin within the very boundaries of textuality and not just within the presence of thought or the living manifestation of speech.

As noted earlier, some African theorists have pointed towards the same direction (textuality as properly constituted, that is, by itself and for itself) either by word or deed. Abiola Irele in his inaugural lecture, 'In Praise of Alienation' argues that:

> Western civilization, at least in its contemporary manifestations and circumstance, provides the paradigm of modernity to which we aspire.[36]

He later talks of 'the cultural hold which Europe has secured upon us-of the alienation which it has imposed upon us as a historical fate'.[37]

The point is that Africa has not been able to grapple effectively with this fate. Irele's sentiments are not new within the field of African ideologising. In fact, the history of such sentiments dates much further back. Basil Davidson writes this of West Africans of the early part of the twentieth century:

> They formed learned societies. They presided over race courses. They founded musical circles, debating clubs, charitable exercises. Above all, they started newspapers – several dozen in British West Africa alone – and wrote them with the fire and fury of a true literary vocation. They promoted more constitutions that stayed on paper. They elaborated federal projects that met the same fate. Nothing abashed, they showed themselves masters of British law and science. They read voraciously. They knew everything.[38]

But in the end, Davidson concludes:

> It did them no good. The more they proved they knew, and the more artfully they argued their case for admission to equality of status, the less they were listened to.[39]

Today, the discourse of raciology as Gilroy terms still dominates socio-political life in the West.

Another problem that deserves attention is that of conflating Western and African modes of intellectual culture and interests. This problem is often reflected in the constitution of African texts. But because traditional cultural mores still hold sway, the decolonised subject is confronted with the problem of constituting the appropriate authorial identity. Anthony Appiah, in a now-famous essay entitled 'Soyinka and the Philosophy of Culture', asserts:

> There is a profound difference between the projects of contemporary European and African writers: a difference I shall summarize, for the sake of a slogan as the difference between the search for the self and the search for a culture.[40]

In this instance, then, Appiah notes some of the implications of this crucial distinction, one that both Africans and Europeans have not yet adequately interrogated. True, there are several lines of division when comparing European and African traditions of textuality, but there is also that facile readiness to view the entire textual practices of mankind as one continuous, undifferentiated whole, that the project of textuality is motivated by one homogeneous impulse. This attitude certainly has its harmful effects, namely that it basically precludes the development of appropriate strategies, objectives and priorities that would in turn influence the development of African textual practices. Again Appiah captures the dilemma of the African intellectual:

> If the European intellectual, though comfortable inside his culture and its traditions, has an image of himself as outsider, the African intellectual is an uncomfortable outsider, seeking to develop his culture in directions that will give him a role.[41]

Alongside this problem is also the crisis of self-identity—which is even more pronounced in a post-colonial milieu—and the attendant pressures for traditional African societies to adopt modern frames of reference dictated along Western lines.[42]

Before proceeding, we should mention some problems Davidson has listed as facing the African intellectual since the time of the colonial encounter. African intellectuals have for a very long time been condemned to 'wander, in some no-man's-land of their own until the trumpet of destiny, at some unthinkable time in the future, should swing wide the doors of civilization and let them in'.[43] In other words, the African intellectual is, first of all, alienated from his own roots, and then effectively denied access to most of the segments of post-modern civilisation as conceived by the industrialised world. Appiah shows how Soyinka with all his customary brilliance is also a victim of this dilemma or, more precisely, alienation. His final verdict on the renowned theorist of culture is that:

> Soyinka is... enmeshed in Europe's myth of Africa. Because he cannot see either Christianity or Islam as endogenous (even in their more syncretic forms) he is left to reflect on African traditional religions and they have always seemed from Europe's point of view to be a much of a muchness.[44]

So Soyinka for all his much-vaunted sense of Africanness becomes in the final analysis ensnared by the dearth of options occasioned by the decisiveness of the European colonial enterprise. Appiah fully recognises 'the most horrifyingly deterministic assumptions'[45] involved in constructing a 'metaphysical or mythic unity' about an African experience. It is assumptions such as these that create other perplexing conundrums within the African textual field. We have simply not discarded completely the mindset that a preliterate/oral background forces upon us. Even the most sophisticated textualists among us are not immune, as we will observe in due course. Appiah identifies and theorises a condition that exemplifies the postcolonial in Soyinka, a condition that gets increasingly complex with the globalisation of culture and postcoloniality itself.[46] Appiah's reading of Soyinka reconfigures what has been termed as vernacular cosmopolitanism, a term which seeks to explain the cultural, religious, social and economic insertion of 'marginals' within global circuits of circulation and production.[47] Appiah accuses Soyinka of unanimism since he homogenises African experiences and scenarios. But a critic has found shortcomings in Appiah's critique of Soyinka's perhaps most famous play; 'in order to get to his postinterpretative rejection of Soyinka's account of a unitary metaphysics, Appiah does not linger enough on the play. He is thus unable to tease out a fuller lesson from the dramatist struggle.'[48] This point is quite valid but it does not completely absolve Soyinka of a problematic cosmopolitanism on the one hand, and a tortuous mode of postcoloniality on the other. In milder terms, Africa's first winner of the Nobel prize for literature is possessed of a truly cosmopolitan temper which when inscribed between the currents of the humanities and social sciences in Africa is shot through with vernacular tropes.

Let us examine the conditions inherent in his vernacularist cosmopolitanism. Soyinka was educated in Nigeria and Leeds in the United Kingdom where he studied under a Shakespearean scholar. After this mix of educational backgrounds he commenced a period of practical training in the theatres of London during the late fifties when dramatic experimentation was at its height in the United Kingdom and voices such as Samuel Beckett, Eugene Ionesco, Harold Pinter, Edward Bond and Arnold Wesker were beginning to make an impact. In this vital period of cultural ferment, Soyinka's background as a Nigerian came to include elements from a crucial moment in Western drama and this accounts for a strident and unending eclecticism in his vast corpus which encompasses the genres of drama, poetry, novelistic discourse, music and even film.

However, Soyinka is also an advocate of traditional African religions as demonstrated by his espousal of the cult of Ogun, the Yoruba god of war and iron.[49] Now this angle complicates his obviously propulsive cosmopolitanism and opens the way for interrogations of a doubly problematic nativism. Problematic because his espousal of a strand of nativism cannot be read in literal terms since it is anchored on a dialectic that incorporates complications of power, agency and subjectivity. Soyinka's promotion of the cult of Ogun, in this sense, can also be construed as a gesture of decolonisation, a reaffirmation of (de)colonised(ing) subjectivity in the face violent disputations of imperial power.

This problematic assemblage of the ingredients of culture and consciousness is carried over to his creative life and engagements. Soyinka is the translator of D. O. Fagunwa's *Ogboju Ode Ninu Igbo Irunmale* which is entitled in English, *The Forest of a Thousand Daemons: A Hunter's Saga* (1968). D. O. Fagunwa (1903–63)[50] is an important Yoruba novelist who wrote a number of creatively formidable works that went on to influence Wole Soyinka, Amos Tutuola and Wale Ogunyemi among others.[51] He trained as a school teacher in colonial Nigeria and wrote his novels in Yoruba. He adopted the Christian faith and his stories which draw a considerable proportion of their material from Yoruba mythology and cosmology in the final analysis project a Christian ethos. Such is the way in which his life and work were marked and reconfigured by the event of colonisation. His inflection by the event of colonisation is in some ways fundamentally different from the trajectories of history and consciousness that shaped the course of Soyinka's life and work and yet the former was able to influence considerably the latter. Soyinka writes in English and has become a highly visible academic within the North Atlantic context thereby enjoying the benefits and institutional power that accrues from that location. D. O. Fagunwa hardly left the shores of his native Nigeria and also had considerably less institutional support. This scenario, it is hoped, evokes some of the ways in which the event of colonisation and also the processes of decolonisation take shape on the grounds of agency and subjectivity.

Wiredu has no doubt contributed immensely to African philosophical discourse. Yet one notices some major shortcomings in his thought that this study has addressed.

Wiredu privileges the written text over the oral text, yet he is translating from an oral culture to a written one. But he does not interrogate between the two kinds of texts and the problems involved. Moreover, he does not undertake a hermeneutical interpretation of oral concepts. Instead, he has undertaken cross-cultural interrogations of oral concepts. However, crosscultural interrogations cannot transfer the essence of one culture to another.

The next part of this chapter focuses on the context of knowledge production, since it is connected to any genuine effort at conceptual decolonisation.

Institutions, Contexts and Histories of Knowledge Production

In her book *Outside in the Teaching Machine* (1993) Gayatri Spivak focuses our attention on 'the difference and the relationship between academic and revolutionary' practices in the interest of social change.[52] She also stresses the necessity of bringing this difference to what she calls a 'productive crisis'. She reminds us in addition that our descriptions of the university as a site of knowledge production have to be fluid and mobile. Spivak's views present a picture of what role universities ought to be playing within an ever-changing global context.

But Abiola Irele on his own part addresses the specificities of knowledge production within the African context and the role of the university within these parameters. To effect the reconstruction of Africa, the universities have a major role to play. Irele then asserts that:

> the universities have been major casualties of economic depression that has been ravaging Africa in the past two decades; almost without exception, African universities are today in a shambles. The present damage can be measured against the hopes inspired by the steady development of higher education in Africa all through the sixties, and its potential as a key factor of economic and social development. The consequences of the precipitous decline of our universities, the effect upon our future prospects, are yet to be fully grasped, but it is plain that one of the most urgent tasks in Africa today is the restoration of the universities to something of their earlier position. This, incidentally, affords an opportunity for a return to the debates of the late fifties and early sixties concerning the role and function in the African context.[53]

Irele's description of the state of universities in Africa is a direct and disturbing contrast to what obtains in the Western world. So instead of universities developing, as they should, into a locus for the exchange and development of knowledge and ideas, their ability to perform their traditional functions has been sapped. They are neither focused on themselves nor are able to negotiate the problems and challenges of their external space.

Philosophers are now preoccupied with how to merge their public and professional roles. In the American public sphere there has been an increased politicisation of culture and a redefinition of the public role of the intellectual in a bid to elicit a more holistic involvement from her. The African-American philosopher Cornel West is one intellectual engaged in this pursuit. In his book *Keeping Faith,*[54] he makes a strong case for black intellectuals to engage in the public sphere as vigorously as possible. This is only an instance of the intellectual contending with his external space.

But Irele's portrayal of the typical African university does not predict such an occurrence in the near future. We must bear in mind that the university is not only a place where learners and teachers interact. In the traditional sense the university 'is also a place for the communication and circulation of thought, by means of personal intercourse.'[55]

However, the production and circulation of ideas are mediated by many variables depending on social, historical and economic context. For instance, Edward Said in his book *Representations of the Intellectual* describes how the social conditions prevailing in the post-Fordist context make increasing demands on the public role of the intellectual. Said notes that in the modern world 'the emergence of journalism, advertising, instant celebrity, and a sphere of constant circulation in which all ideas are marketable',[56] place new constraints on the intellectual and the production of ideas.

The French philosopher and sociologist Pierre Bourdieu has proffered some interesting theoretical constructs on the social production of reason. It has been said that:

> Bourdieu's philosophical status is useful in raising fruitful questions concerning the current institutional limits of philosophy and how those limits might be overcome to revitalise this discipline through a more robust alliance with the social sciences and the practical social world.[57]

Furthermore, it has been noted that:

> Bourdieu goes much further than either Austin or Wittgenstein in providing the theoretical tools and empirical methods for a systematic analysis of the social forces, structures and contexts that actually shape linguistic meaning.[58]

Bourdieu demonstrates how the institutionalisation and circulation of knowledge is far from being objective and why we must expand our epistemological vocabulary to include diverse national epistemic histories and socio-cultural contexts in the appreciation and critiques of discourses. Bourdieu observes that:

> a large number of translations can only be understood if they are placed in the complex network of international exchanges between holders of dominant academic posts, the exchanges of imitations, honorary doctorates, etc.[59]

For Bourdieu the production of social knowledge is never wholly scientific, and his critique of the underlying social conditions for the production of knowledge compels us to constantly examine the circumstances, contexts, histories and institutions for knowledge production.

If conceptual decolonisation is a worthy theoretical and practical pursuit, then it is necessary to understand and critique the factors that determine the production and institutionalisation of social reason and meaning. The capacity to carry out this important function prescribes the limits and effectiveness of conceptual decolonisation.

Richard Rorty in numerous writings has stressed the necessity to adopt a pragmatist approach to expressions of logocentricism, philosophical truth, objectivity, science and culture. This sort of approach in its anti-logocentric formulation provides a desirable option to confront philosophical totalitarianism. In his words:

> anything that philosophy can do to free up our imagination a little is all to the political good, for the freer the imagination of the present the likelier it is that future social practices will be different from past practices.[60]

Rorty's anti-essentialist critique of philosophy is one that compels us to re-examine our entrenched preconceptions about epistemology and metaphysics. His view is that 'the picture of philosophy as pioneer is part of a logocentric conception of intellectual work with which we fans of Derrida should have no truck'.[61]

Rorty's ideas on education owe much to Dewey's conception of the twin processes of socialisation and individualisation. The aim of education in the view of both philosophers is to accomplish freedom in the private realm and also in the field of social action. Education should ultimately create social reason through the instrumentality of consensus. Finally, education at its tertiary stage ought to induce experiments for self-recreation. For Rorty education is 'a matter of inciting doubt and stimulating imagination, thereby challenging the prevailing consensus'.[62]

The Text in Africa

The final segment of this chapter continues the exploration of social realities connected with decolonisation. The conditions for knowledge generation in

Africa play a crucial role in determining whether or not the continent is able to subvert the hegemonic structures of imperialism. In this regard, Philip C. Altbach argues:

> First, the unequal distribution of intellectual products results from a complex set of factors including historical events, economic relationship, language, literacy and the nature of educational systems. Second, industrialized nations have benefited from their control of the means for distribution of knowledge and have at times used their superiority to the disadvantage of developing countries. Third, patterns of national development, the direction and rate of scientific growth, and the quality of cultural life are related to issues of intellectual productivity and independence.[63]

In the Third World, the ruling elites 'have often used the colonial language to protect their own privileged position'.[64] This is another point Wiredu does not address properly. There is the need to undertake a rigorous questioning of African forms of authoritarianism, so that more democratic means of mass enlightenment may also evolve. In this light, decolonisation has two vital strategies or components: external (the struggle against foreign imperialism) and internal (the struggle against reactionary ruling elites).

It is also necessary to examine the politics of publishing to understand more of the obstacles that face decolonisation as a project. Most publishers prefer to publish in the dominant metropolitan languages such as English and French 'since communication seldom runs directly between one developing country and another but is mediated through advanced nations'.[65] As such, 'a complex web of economic and intellectual relationships and traditions makes it difficult to stop publishing in European languages'.[66] One cannot but agree with this assessment. To be sure, all these delimiting social realities are issues Wiredu does not explore in any appreciable detail. Consequently, they limit the possibilities of his project of conceptual decolonisation. Altbach's disturbing conclusions about intellectual productivity in the Third World ought to be of considerable intellectual and practical interest:

> Low reader density, great distances between settlement, and poor transportation facilities make book distribution in developing countries particularly difficult. Just as developing countries themselves are at the periphery of the world's knowledge system, regions outside of capital cities, especially rural areas, which are often completely without access to books, periodicals or newspapers, are at the periphery of knowledge systems within these nations.[67]

Such a scenario must be a crucial equation in any project of decolonisation.

Notes

1. See Homi K. Bhabha, *Location of Culture*, London: Routledge, 1994.

2. F. Hegel cited by Wole Soyinka in 'Nobel Lecture 1986: This Past Must Address its Present' in A Maja-Pearce, ed., *Wole Soyinka: An Appraisal*, Oxford: Heinemann, 1994, p. 14.

3. Olusegun Oladipo, *The Idea of African Philosophy*, 1991, p. 2.

4. Ibid.

5. Kwasi Wiredu, *Conceptual Decolonisation in African Philosophy*, 1995, p. 19.

6. Anthony Appiah, 'Europe Upside Down' in *Sapina Newsletter. A Bulletin of the Society for African Philosophy in North America*, Vol. V, January-June, No. 1, 1993, p. 1.

7. Ibid. p. 5.

8. See Cheikh Anta Diop, *The African Origin of Civilisation: Myth or Reality*, trans. Mercer Cook, New York: Lawrence Hill Books, 1954 and his *Civilization or Barbarism: An Authentic Anthropology*, trans. Yaa-Lengi Meema Ngemi, New York: Lawrence Hill Books, 1981.

9. Ibid. p. 2.

10. See Ibrahim Sundiata, 'Afrocentricism: The Argument We're Really Having' in *DISSONANCE*, September 30, 1996. Also availabe online http://way.net/dissonance/sundiata.html/

11. Ibid.

12. Ibid.

13. See Mary Lefkowitz, *Not Out of Africa: How Afrocentricism Became an Excuse to Teach Myth as History*, New York: New Republic and Basic Books, 1996. http://www.pc.maricopa.edu/departments/ss/phi101/supplementary/more/Not_out_of_Africa.htm

14. Ibrahim Sundiata, 'Afrocentricism: The Argument We're Really Having'.

15. James Palermo, 'Reading Asante's Myth of Afrocentricity: An Ideological Critique', Philosophy of Education, 1997, http://x.ed.uiuc.edu/EPS/PES-Yearbook/97_docs/palermo.html

16. Molefi Kete Asante, *Afrocentricity*, Trenton: Africa World Press, 1988, p. viii.

17. James Palermo, 'Reading Asante's Myth of Afrocentricity: An Ideological Critique', *Philosophy of Education*, 1997, http://www.ed.uiuc.edu/EPS/PES-Yearbook/97_docs/palermo.html

18. Molefi Kete Asante, 'Multiculturalism and the Academy', *Academe: Bulletin of the American University Professors*, May/June 1996. http://www.pc.maricopa.edu/departments/ss/phi101/supplementary/more/Molefi_Kete_Asante.htm

19. Abdul Alkalimat, 'eBlack: A 21st Century Challenge', http://www.eblackstudies.net/ebblack.html

20. Mary Lefkowitz, *Not Out of Africa: How Afrocentricism Became an Excuse to Teach Myth as History,* New York: New Republic and Basic Books, 1996. http://www.pc.maricopa.edu/departments/ss/phi101/ supplementary/more/Not_out_of_Africa. Htm

21. Martin Bernal, 'Review of *Not Out of Africa* by Mary Lefkowitz' gopher://gopher.lib.virginia.edu/00/alpha/ bmcr/v96/96-4-5.

22. Mary Lefkowitz, *Not Out of Africa,* op. cit.

23. Ibid.

24. Martin Bernal, 'Review of *Not Out of Africa* by Mary Lefkowitz', op. cit.

25. Ibrahim Sundiata, 'Afrocentricism: The Argument We're Really Having'.

26. Basil Davidson, *The Black Man's Burden,* 1993, p. 43.

27. Olusegun Oladipo, 'Traditional African Philosophy: Its Significance for Contemporary Africa' in *African Notes,* Vol. XV, Nos. 1 & 2, 1991, p. 102.

28. Ibid.

29. Wole Soyinka has declared in several public forums that Nigerian universities should be shut down for two years for extensive restructuring.

30. Editorial in *Democracy and Development, a South African Journal,* December, 1994, p. 49.

31. Anthony Appiah, 'Europe Upside Down', 1993, p. 8.

32. On this point see Claude Ake, *Democracy and Development,* Ibadan: Spectrum Books, 2001.

33. See Sanya Osha, 'A New Direction in African Philosophy' in *Journal of Philosophy and Development,* 1996, pp. 136-9.

34. Basil Davidson, *The Black Man's Burden,* 1993, p. 42.

35. Ibid. p. 50.

36. Abiola Irele, *In Praise of Alienation,* 1987, p. 9.

37. Ibid.

38. Basil Davidson, *The Black Man's Burden,* 1993, p. 45.

39. Ibid.

40. Anthony Appiah, 'Soyinka and the Philosophy of Culture' in P.O. Bodunrin, ed., *Philosophy in Africa: Trends and Perspectives,* Ile-Ife: University of Ife Press, 1985, p. 251.

41. Ibid. p. 252.

42. For a philosophical reflection on this problem, see D. A. Masolo, *African Philosophy in Search of Identity,* Bloomington: Indiana University Press, 1994.

43. Basil Davidson, *The Black Man's Burden,* 1993, p. 47.

44. Anthony Appiah, 'Myth, Literature and the African World' in A. Maja-Pearce, ed., *Wole Soyinka: An Appraisal,* 1994, p. 111.

45. Ibid. p. 112.

46. On this theme, see Arjun Appadurai, *Modernity at Large: Cultural Dimensions of Globalization,* Minneapolis: University of Minnesota Press, 1996.

47. See Mamadou Diouf, 'The Senegalese Murid Trade Diaspora and the Making of a Vernacular Cosmopolitanism', in Carol A. Breckenridge et al. eds., *Cosmopolitanism* Durham: Duke University Press, 2002.

48. Olakunle George, *Relocating Agency: Modernity and African Letters,* New York: State University of New York Press, 2003, p. 168.

49. See his *Myth, Literature and an African World,* Cambridge: Cambridge University Press, 1976.

50. D. O. Fagunwa's published works include, *Igbo Olodumare* (The Forest of God), *Irinkerindo Ninu Elegbeje* (Wanderings in the Forest of a Thousand and Four Hundred), *Ireke Onibudo* (The Sweet One with a Secure Ground), and *Adiitu Olodumare* (God's Conundrum).

51. See Olakunle George, *Relocating Agency: Modernity and African Letters,* New York: State University of New York Press, 2003; Omolara Ogundipe-Leslie, 'The Poetics of Fiction by Yoruba Writers: The Case of Ogboju Ode Ninu Igbo Irunmale by D. O. Fagunwa', *Odu,* 16, July 1977; Afolabi Olabimtan, 'Religion as a Theme in Fagunwa's Novels', *Odu,* 11, January 1975; and Abiola Irele, *The African Experience in Literature and Ideology,* Bloomington: Indiana University Press, 1990.

52. Gayatri Spivak, *Outside in the Teaching Machine,* Routledge: New York and London, 1993, p. 53.

53. Abiola Irele, 'Toward Reconstruction in Africa', unpublished conference paper, 1998, p. 11.

54. See Cornel West, *Keeping Faith,* Princeton University Press, 1993.

55. John Henry Newman, 'The Idea of a University', *The Harvard Classics,* New York: P.F. Collier & Son Corporation, 1969, p. 31.

56. Edward Said, *Representations of the Intellectual,* New York: Vintage Books, 1996, p.19.

57. Pierre Bourdieu, 'The Social Conditions of the International Circulation of Ideas', *Bourdieu: A Critical Reader,* Richard Shusterman, ed., Oxford: Blackwell, 1999, pp. 1-2.

58. Ibid. p. 4.

59. Ibid. p. 223.

60. Richard Rorty, *Philosophy and Social Hope*, Harmondsworth: Penguin Books Ltd., 1999, p. 3.

61. Ibid. p. 3.

62. Ibid. p. 18.

63. Philip G. Altbach, 'Literary Colonialism: Books in the Third World' in Bill Ashcroft et al., eds., *The Post-colonial Studies Reader,* London and New York: Routledge, 1996, p. 485.

64. Ibid.

65. Ibid. p. 487.

66. Ibid.

67. Ibid. p. 489.

7

Theorising the Postcolony:
Parricide, Belonging, Exile

In this chapter, I continue the exploration of existential conditions and the theoretical preoccupations occurring in postcolonial Africa in order to indicate the various connections between theory and praxis and also the politics and trajectories of decolonisation within the context of the millennial moment. By inscribing the discourse of decolonisation into processes of contemporary globalisation we would be able to discern just how much its trajectories have been reconfigured and how much its complexion has been transformed by the new pressures and tendencies. I begin by examining the work of a recent theorist of African studies—Achille Mbembe—and end by reflecting on the work of an earlier scholar—V. Y. Mudimbe through the contributions of an Africanist and an anthropologist, W. M. J. van Binsbergen—to attempt to indicate the new variables in the discourse and politics of decolonisation and to indicate new and interesting forms of textuality, liminality and exilic existence (Mudimbe). Mbembe's work has generated considerable debate in theoretical circles and his positionality as an academic of transnational mobility forces us to reflect further on questions of subjectivity and discourse. The same consideration can be applied to Mudimbe as well. Binsbergen on the other hand, re-reads Mudimbe and foregrounds his often problematic multidisciplinarity in ways that generate questions pertaining to academic integrity, race, exile and belonging which are conditions that face the average commodified African intellectual.

Whatever reservations some might have about Mbembe's work, he has been quite inventive about laying the foundations for alternative textual and theoretical practices in Africa. It is often said that much of his work lacks socio-scientific merit. But he has tried to explain the technical novelties that inform his work: 'I argue that the reality with which I have been concerned with throughout the book exists only as a set of sequences and connections that extend themselves only to dissolve. It is a reality made up of superstitions, narratives and fictions that claim to be true in the very act through which they produce the false, while at the same time giving rise to both terror, hilarity and astonishment.'[1] On what he perceives to be the term postcolony he says it 'indicates his desire to take very seriously the intrinsic qualities and power of 'contemporaneousness' while firmly keeping in mind the fact that the present itself is a concatenation of multiple temporalities. Because of the entanglement of these multiple temporalities, Africa is evolving in multiple overlapping directions simultaneously.'[2]

Since the publication of his influential essay, 'Provisional Notes on the Postcolony' (1992), Achille Mbembe has demonstrated he is a theorist to watch. Indeed, Mbembe has succeeded in finding an interesting niche for himself within the field of African Studies by creating a particular mode of discourse that combines the fashionable but effective traditions of social science together with the humanities.

He served as the Executive Secretary of CODESRIA, the largest social science research institute in Africa for four years (1996–2000), yet he has been able to invent a kind of theorising that demonstrates the various purposes for which the grandest traditions of the humanities could be employed in debating, portraying and reconstituting the topics on, and relating to Africa. Contemporary social science practices in Africa have tended to be overly positivistic in a way that one only foresees dead-ends and missed opportunities.

On the Postcolony, Mbembe's first major book to be published in English definitely forces us to reconsider the strategies of textual construction for portraying Africa from the colonial moment to the present times. Postcolonial Africa is a subject that had become rather uninteresting because of its endless and predictable litany of political failures, economic crises and in some cases cultural stasis. Thus to contemplate a continent in seemingly endless decline had also become in academic terms, an exercise in contemplating the boredom of a long drawn-out dead-end. The difficulty from a theoretical and discursive standpoint lies in being able to dwell upon this gorge of ennui and create interesting pictures about the disturbing histories and contemporary realities of Africa. *On the Postcolony,* is a sustained meditation on this crucial *problematique.*

So many negatives have been ascribed and are still being ascribed to Africa. Africa is the mad, unreasonable and dark other by which the West states its claims of difference. Africa is the sub-human (infrahumanity) void waiting to be penetrated, conquered and reinvented by Western gaze, reason and technology. Africa is the continent that if left to itself continually collapses into madness, misery and destruction. Africa, in spite of the voluptuousness of untamed nature, eats itself. This is the Africa that steadily assaults the senses and human reason. Yet in spite of this deplorable state of affairs one gets encouraged when Mbembe reminds us that 'all struggles have become struggles of representation.'[3]

The first major task Mbembe sets for himself is examining the validity and weaknesses of some academic disciplines in their constructs of Africa. For instance, in relation to the literature of political science and development economics he writes, 'it becomes clear these disciplines have undermined the very possibility of understanding African economic and political facts. In spite of the countless critiques made of theories of social evolutionism and ideologies of development and modernisation, the academic output of these disciplines continues, almost entirely, in total thrall to these two teleogies.'[4] Even more distressingly, academic output in Africa seems to be 'wrapped in a cloak of impenetrability [...] the black hole of reason, the pit where its powerlessness rests unveiled.'[5] This apparent state of unreason and powerlessness within the African existential sphere is often equated with chaos which is also extended into and evident in the academic realm as Mbembe points out. Hence, the rather harsh judgement: 'the literature lapses into repetition, plagiarism; dogmatic assertions, cavalier interpretations and shallow rehashes become the order of the day.'[6]

If the above judgement relates to the African academic output, Mbembe has equally caustic remarks about Western rationality and by extension, universalism:

> The uncompromising nature of the Western self and its active negation of anything not itself had the counter effect of reducing African discourse to a simple polemical reaffirmation of black humanity. However, both the asserted denial and the reaffirmation of that humanity now look like the two sterile sides of the same coin.[7]

It was through Africa's eventual contact with the slave trade and subsequently colonialism that 'Africans came face to face with the opaque and murky domain of power, a domain inhabited by obscure drives and that everywhere and always makes animality and bestiality its essential components, plunging human beings into a never-ending process of brutalization.'[8]

Within the context of the poverty of research in Africa and the long established traditions of Western ethnocentrism Mbembe inscribes a mode of discourse that announces somewhat a priori, its own paradigmatic status in terms of existing explanatory models and discourses about his ways of 'inventing' and talking about Africa. He concludes his analysis of social scientific academic production in Africa by stating, 'I have tried to 'write Africa', not as a fiction, but in the harshness of its destiny, its power, and its eccentricities, without laying claim to speak in the name of anyone at all.'[9] Mbembe's reflections on the state of academic discourse on Africa seek to differentiate his own discourse from existing critical formations.

An effective way Mbembe stamps his own distinctive discursive signature is by his extensive analysis of the origins and force of the commandement which are to be found in what he terms the colonial rationality. This rationality has its roots in violence as it is evident in the way colonial authority legitimised its foundations, its operations and its self-perpetuating logic. Hegel's master/slave dichotomy provides the epistemic framework for the structural principles behind the inequalities of the colonial relationship:

> ... the native subjected to power and to the colonial state could in no way be another 'myself'. As an animal, he/she was even totally alien to me. His/her manner of seeing the world, his/her manner of being, was not mine. In him/her, it was impossible to discern any power of transcendence. Encapsulated in himself or herself, he/she was a bundle of drives but not of capacities. In such circumstances, the only possible relationship with him/her was one of violence and domination.[10]

Thus the commandement as an instrument of social organization can be regarded as part of what J. L. Comaroff and Jean Comaroff have termed 'the colonisation of consciousness' and has its origins and its elaboration in the colonial event itself. *On the Postcolony* traces its various trajectories through the postcolonial moment and also into the present moment of contemporary globalisation. It establishes that the postcolonial state in Africa is an extension of the colonial state with all the attendant processes of brutalisation: violence, force and domination.

In practical and theoretical terms, the dialectic of the commandement which is essentially founded on violence as a strategic instrument could not be reversed with the demise of the colonial state. One of Mbembe's central arguments is that its roots extend beyond the actual event of colonisation and all its various definitions and transformations into the postcolonial moment. As postcolonial subjects, we are products of the commandement and the illogic of its violences and we need to carry out painstaking examinations of all our human institutions and habits of consciousness to free ourselves of its tyrannical influence. This is a necessity since Mbembe argues that 'neither colonial commandement nor the postcolonial state was able to bring about the total dismantling, still less the disappearance, of every corporation and all lower-order legitimacies bringing people and communities together at the local level'.[11] As such, it means the forms of consciousness established and projected by the colonial order are still in force. To achieve greater levels of clarity, we must revisit those forms.

Mbembe explores the nexus—in terms of ruptures, continuities and mutual cancelling-out—between the colonial order and the postcolonial state and unearths a problem we will have to address for a long time to come:

> The general practice of power has followed directly from the colonial political culture and has perpetuated the most despotic aspects of ancestral traditions, themselves reinvented for the occasion. This is the reason why the postcolonial potentate was hostile to public debate, and paid little heed to the distinction between what was justified and what was arbitrary.[12]

The postcolonial state in contemporary Africa is very peculiar indeed. Having its raison d'être in the instrumentalisation of force as a condition of existence, it has reconfigured the postcolonial moment in a way that it has become difficult for it to ponder its own processes of atomisation. Thus Mbembe writes, 'the state has become a vast machine creating and regulating inequalities'.[13]

Not unexpectedly, this continuous distribution of inequalities has led to increases in the methods by which violence as a foundational and as an existential principle is recycled within the larger society. Mbembe in a separate article, 'An Essay on the Political Imagination in Wartime' explores this phenomenon of violence as a foundational principle of social norms and practices at great length. In it, he writes there is 'an unparalleled increase in private agents' ability to operate over broad areas [...] by violent attempts to immobilise and spatially fix whole categories of people, particularly by waging wars.'[14] Several graphic passages in Mbembe's corpus illustrate this view of war as a violent feature of postcolonial life. For instance:

> Where war is still avoided, chaos is descending, the implosion taking the form of general social breakdown. This breakdown feeds on a culture of raiding and booty [...]. The result is worsening civil dissension, the ever more frequent resort to ethnically, regionally, or religiously bared mobilization, and the giddying rise in the chances of violent death.[15]

What Mbembe terms implosion is fast becoming the general state of affairs. Both the political and economic realms are characterised by forms pertaining to 'flight, evasion, dissimilation, subterfuge, devison, a whole range of forms of indiscipline and disobedience'.[16] To be sure, implosion takes on a variety of forms and so does its levels of operationalisation.

What we have just noted is how implosion occurs at the local level of conflict-making in its widest sense. At the global level, its foundations and structural dimensions are even more daunting than at the local level because it assumes a stifling air of impersonality and also of impenetrability. Mbembe observes:

> In the countries of Africa with economic potential, the general configuration of the market, the industrial base, the structure of relations between the bureaucracy and local business circles and the nature of respective alliances with multinational firms ruled out any possibility either of gaining access to new technologies and new distribution networks or of accumulating any substantial manufacturing know-how or developing an entrepreneurial dynamic that could have helped to respond creatively to the constraints of the world market, as of elsewhere.[17]

With the end of the Cold War and the subsequent integration of Eastern Europe into the global system, Africa continues to succumb to forces of disintegration such that it reinforces the reality of its own isolation in the strictest sense. Its alienation ensures that it cannot speak to the world or with the language of the world. Whenever possible, the language of the world that trickles down to it is invariably stunted, incomplete and degraded.

Mbembe depicts a picture of Africa and all its numerous brutalities. A state of affairs that shows the various forms entropy can assume. We encounter different manifestations of criminalisation in its statist, economic and social forms. We also encounter the informalisation of economies and its in-built mechanisms for pauperisation and immiserisation. In another essay, Mbembe suggests another model for reading the African predicament in contemporary times that 'is characterized by a multiplicity of organizing principles, networks, and institutions' which bypass 'the trinitarian model of state, market, and civil society.'[18] However, in spite of the processes of brutalisation and disinstitutionalisation occurring in many parts of Africa, Mbembe is still able to offer a note of hope and with a tendency of social activism, 'With or without international creditors, Africa must face up to the challenge of competitiveness of its economies on the world level.'[19]

Mbembe examines how Africa's exclusion from the centres and forms of international economic activity has created and entrenched new subversive kinds of socio-political organisation. Here, he examines what he terms the 'multiple forms of private indirect government'. The emergence of new 'technologies of domination' in Africa, Mbembe argues, has further caused a greater diminution of the role of the state in the public realm. This very particular form of dissolution of the state is the result of adverse international and local economic factors as well as the vacuum left in the wake of the self-inflicted 'defeat of the state' itself. Mbembe notes that 'the continent is turning inward on itself in a very serious way'.[20] The vacuum created by the dissolution of the state and the way that vacuum is being addressed in collective terms is explained in the following manner:

> The upshot is an increase in resources and labour devoted to war, a rise in the number of disputes settled by violence, a growth of banditry, and numerous forms of privatisation of lawful violence. Contrary to the assertions of a rather sloppy literature, however, such phenomena are not automatically indicators of chaos. It is important to see in them, also, struggles aimed at establishing new forms of legitimate domination and gradually restructuring formulas of authority built on other foundations.[21]

These struggles for the legitimisation of new bases of authority definitely have a strong medieval element enshrined in them. Most Africans are caught within a number of unstable cosmologies as a result of these competing technologies of domination. What do concepts such as 'civil society', 'democracy', 'public good', 'law and order' mean in a context submerged in flux, apparent randomness and violent change? One of the major contributions of Mbembe lies in suggesting that those concepts and the languages associated with them in their classical taxonomies mean very little to contemporary Africa which is caught up in internal processes that transform, transcend and evidently subvert them. In a similar vein, he argues that 'the future of the state will be settled, as has happened previously in the world, at the point where the three factors of war, coercion and capital (formal or informal, material or symbolic) meet.'[22] In essence, Africa may be doomed to experience its own Dark Ages so many centuries after they first appeared on the stage of world history.

African societies are entering a period of statelessness in which 'functions supposed to be public, and obligations that flow from sovereignty, are increasingly performed by private operators for private ends. Soldiers and policemen live off the inhabitants; officials supposed to perform administrative tasks sell the public service required and pocket what they get.'[23] This situation also obtains in the sprawling slums of Brazil where those shanties have had to evolve their own regulatory mechanisms. Just to add to Mbembe's insights, Nigerians in urban centres have become engulfed by violent struggles and changes over place, space, name and belonging. What is an exclusive residential district and what is not? Where does the slum take over and where does it break off? What is civic mindedness and what is the seductive honour of the bandit? What rules are to be established within the ambit of the underground economy and whose responsibility is it to do so? These questions and numerous related ones are thrown up in different contexts, sectors and discourses and with hyphenated and mutilated lexicons. Like children we are learning to speak a language everyone claims to know with a purely individuated insight but without a general grammar. The crux of the matter is how do we survive what Mbembe terms 'tonton-macoutism'? Again, Mbembe suggests a bold and at the same time controversial point of departure in discursive terms by affirming that 'tonton—macoutization' has become a generalised condition of existence in Africa. Violence and coercion are what determine the fate of individuals in postcolonial Africa. As a partial conclusion, Mbembe submits that 'what we are witnessing in Africa is clearly the establishment of a different political economy and the invention of new systems of coercion and exploitation.'[24]

The edifying part in all this is that the struggle over these new forms of domination is not in the hands of bandits and corrupt bureaucrats alone. As Mbembe points out, 'most of the religious and healing movements proliferating in Africa today constitute visible, if ambiguous, sites where new normative systems, new common languages, and the constitution of new authorities are being negotiated.'[25]

Mbembe defines his famous understanding of the postcolony in the following manner:

> The notion 'postcolony' identifies specifically a given historical trajectory—that of societies recently emerging from the experience of colonisation and the violence which the colonial relationship involves. To be sure, the postcolony is chaotically pluralistic; it has nonetheless an internal coherence. It is a specific system of signs, a particular way of fabricating simulacra or reforming stereotypes.[26]

The postcolony, just as the colonial order, is established and sustained by a 'regime of violence'. Mbembe posits that 'in the postcolony, the commandement seeks to institutionalise itself, to achieve legitimation and hegemony (*recherché hégémonique*), in the form of a fetish.'[27] Even more, 'the postcolony is, par excellence, a hallow pretense, a regime of unreality (*régime du simulacra*).'[28]

The widespread prebendalisation of African postcolonial societies has resulted in the mutual zombification of the dominant and dominated classes. No one within the postcolony is free from its innate grotesqueness, its freewheeling violences and its abilities for rampant fetishisation. Also, 'the postcolony is a world of anxious virility, a world hostile to continence, frugality, sobriety.'[29] Ensconced within themes of power and coercion is the leitmotif of sexual politics which is in itself shot through with the reality of violence.

As a foretaste of the strong sexual current, Mbembe writes, 'to exercise authority is above all, to tire out the bodies of those under it, to disempower them not so much as to increase their productivity as to ensure the maximum docility. To exercise authority is, furthermore, for the male ruler, to demonstrate publicly a certain delight in eating and drinking well, and again in Labou Tansi's words, to pass most of his time in 'pumping grease and rust into the backsides of young girls'.[30]

In this fabulous postcolonial world, symbols and persons of authority are also transformed in objects of ridicule. Mbembe has observed that the postcolony maintains 'an economy of death'. And one major way to escape from the tyranny of this death is to arm and nourish oneself with the power of humour. This is something Milan Kundera understands so well having survived the realities of totalitarianism in former Czechoslovakia. Laughter is a way of forgetting, it is also a way of easing pain. In the postcolony, death, sex, birth, power, pain, filth and incontinence are merged in a seamless and at the same random economy of violence. The dominant could suddenly turn out to be victim and vice versa. According to Mbembe:

> This fact accounts for the baroque character of the postcolony: its unusual and grotesque art of representation, its taste for the theatrical, and its violent pursuit of wrongdoing to the point of shamelessness.[31]

Extending his discourse on the postcolony Mbembe notes:

> The postcolonial polity can only produce 'fables' and stupefy its 'subjects', bringing on delirium when the discourse of power penetrates its targets and drives them into realms of fantasy and hallucination.[32]

So within the postcolony, the force, violence, disfigurations and political outgrowths of the commandement are still very much evident. Its unabashed authoritarian character is where the dominant forces of the postcolony find both their political and epistemic justification. In a revealing passage, Mbembe comments on the economy that links the postcolonial body with the dictates and presence of power:

> In the postcolony, an intimate tyranny links the rulers with the ruled—just as obscenity is only another aspect of munificence, and vulgarity a normal condition of state power. If subjection appears more intense then it might be, this is because the subjects of the commandement have internalised authoritarian epistemology to the point where they reproduce it themselves in all the minor circumstances of life—social networks, cults and secret societies, culinary practices, leisure activities, modes of consumption, styles of dress, rhetorical devises, and the whole political economy of the body.[33]

In addition, Mbembe analyses the epistemological relationship between the visible and the occult and the role of the image within this framework and the criteria for the ascription of value to things and persons. Here, he unearths an interesting *problematique* in seeing the interconnectedness between what is seen, heard and not seen in a context of social want, denial and scarcity. These disparate elements are fused together by a general economy that owes much to African theories of evil or the paranormal. So as he puts it, 'by summoning up the world of shade in a context where there was no forced correspondence between what was seen, heard or said—or between what was and what was not, what was apparent and what partook of the spectre and the phantom—one was appealing to a particular ontology of violence and the phantom.'[34]

This theoretical postulate is reinforced by numerous practical occurrences in everyday life where general societal breakdown is marked by sudden reversals and upturnings of socially accepted norms, where the real becomes the unusual and where the unreal is treated as the accepted norm. In this way, phantasmagoric elements play upon and expand our understanding of the marvellous without necessarily liberating us from its often disorienting force. In practical terms, 'there is overloading of language, overloading of public transport, overloading of living accommodations, beginning with tightly packed homes. Everything leads to excess here.'[35]

The fear of survival, scarcity, famine, violence and practically everything is central to this pervasive degradation just as all classes of persons are affected from the victim to the victimiser. To prove this point, Mbembe writes 'if money is the supreme means of enjoyment, devouring the flesh and organs, and drinking the blood of others, are clear demonstrations of how the loci of power are also loci of danger, alienation, and slow death.'[36] It is interesting to note that in exploring the logics (or illogicalities) by which relationships that go into the constitution of the marvellous are assembled, Mbembe uses a copious amount of newspaper cartoons to project even more sharply the effects all these have in everyday life.

Indeed, Mbembe's analyses of what he terms the spirit of violence is quite extensive. We are reminded of how colonialism itself and the constitution of the African consciousness in Western discourse were events that had violence as their founding principles. Also, black sexuality and attributes foisted upon it by Eurocentric biases and the lingering effects of the commandement in its postcolonial colouring were shrouded by a spirit of violence. Mbembe, here, explores the phallus and its elaborate demonisation, its disorienting symbolisms, and its transformation into an object of menace, fear and arbitrariness. Beyond this demonology is the process of colonisation of which Mbembe writes, 'a miraculous act, the act of colonizing is one of the most complete expressions of the form of arbitrariness that is the arbitrariness of desire and whim. The pure terror of desire and whim—that is its concept.'[37] However, the reign of desire and whim continues after its arbitrary constructions of the mentalities of the slave and also the master. In other words, the postcolony thrives on an epistemology that does unhidden violence to the consciousness well after the end of the event of colonisation.

Africans in the postcolony are compelled to confront the forms of death and violences that dominate their cosmologies. According to Mbembe the African ought to ask himself/herself, 'who are you in the world?' to which the answer is 'I am an ex-slave'. He has also taken pains to establish that there is no difference between the slave and a native. Thus, the native's continuous struggle against 'the grammar of animality' to which history has condemned him/her. His/hers is also a struggle against the aesthetics of vulgarity and/or obscenity in its starkest form.

Achille Mbembe accomplishes the aesthetisation of vulgarity in relation to the African predicament but he also succeeds in maintaining the poise of a philosopher. No doubt, a difficult task to achieve in view of the predominant and corrupting dynamics of vulgarity and its permeation of life, thought and discourse in Africa. How can we avoid getting submerged by the mire as we stand contemplating its tremendous force? Mbembe's discourses are stylised products of force that perhaps only the African postcolony is capable of producing. They survive the forces of violence through their very own transformative will, through their own deliberate mode of aesthetisation and principles of construction.

In so doing, the text as an instrument of understanding, interpretation and communication comes to encompass all its various possibilities—it is both oral and aural, written and implicit, it has visual and sensory attributes and it is also fabulous and factual. Mbembe appropriates this definition of the text and makes it his own.

On the Postcolony is a polyphonous elaboration of the new forms of death and violence emerging within the African postcolony. It also a brave exploration of the theoretical possibilities available for constructing, reconstructing and eventually transcending multifaceted disconcerting scenarios of the postcolonial moment. Through this text, we are able to learn about new ways of speaking about our continental embarrassments and miseries from a positionality that turns us out of ourselves, that lays out much broader trajectories for our subjectification and finally that inscribes our existence in a much wider field of human experience.

In the next section, I will examine an intersection between a powerful African philosophical configuration and an equally impressive anthropological discourse in order to bring into sharper relief questions of subjectivity, belonging and discursive formations in African studies as they relate in a number of ways to the African postcolony.

The Hardline

The notion of parricide is very important to the production of knowledge, new discursive formations and to employ a concept of Deleuze and Guattari's, the production of production. In theoretical discourse, parricide is not a destructive notion because it includes elements of performativity, circulation and enhancement. Jacques Derrida, a former student of Michel Foucault deconstructs in a devastating manner the latter's *Madness and Civilization* concentrating on mainly three pages of the text. Derrida begins his famous critique by stating that the disciple's consciousness is an unhappy one when faced with the ego of the master. But Derrida's critique transcends the repressive consciousness of the disciple to attain difference, discourse and realisation. So in this sense, parricide becomes a force of production not only in the history of ideas but also in the history of human civilisation. Louis Althusser in an act of unintended parricide attempts to rewrite the texts of Marx and the history of Marxism. His act is a largely sympathetic one because he intends to transform the violence of omission into the violence of inclusion. Intellectual history is littered with similar exercises. Deleuze and Guattari in an attempt to liberate individual agency and chart a new libidinal economy, expose the repressiveness of Freudism. Parricide is always at the centre of the production of production.

Employing the concept of parricide, I will examine some of the work of the Dutch Africanist anthropologist and scholar, Wim van Binsbergen and the effects it produces in the field of African studies. Binsbergen's work is important in the field for many reasons and the choice of his work is informed by the productive fields of the academic discourse it highlights. Thus any serious discussion of his work is bound to lead to other conditions of possibility, parricidal ones included. Furthermore, Binsbergen by his close reading of V. Y. Mudimbe reveals interesting potential formations for the field of African studies and important issues concerning subjectivity, anthropologising orders of knowledge, exile and belonging.

For our purposes, two main strategies are adopted. First, this is a reading of Binsbergen's work and also a reading of Mudimbe to demonstrate how flows, continuities and ruptures are employed as productive discursive forces and how the deterritorialised and alienated African consciousness can profit from these disjunctive flows, continuities and ruptures.

Wim van Binsbergen's interventions, I would claim, deghettoise the field of African studies since ghettoisation has always been the bane of the field,[38] his work barring any racial prejudices, are efforts of incorporation within the global discursive economy. Needless to say, the deghettoisation of the field is an act of liberation and an invitation to production, at a more postmodern level given Africa's customary peripheralisation.

The organisation of discourse at several levels is due to a desire to be free. Without discourse, life and production become impossible. Relatedly, the body must possess functioning organs in order to aid processes of production. What is the nature of the body of Africa? What are her organs and how do they function? To answer this question we shall have to revisit the event of the Atlantic slave trade, the colonial situation and the structures of neocolonialism and imperialism. The perspectivisation of these major events of African history and African collective experiences would reveal the nature of the African body in a number of senses. Deleuze and Guattari conceptualise the relationship between power, production and the body:

> the desiring-machines attempt to break into the body without organs, and the body without organs repels them, since it experiences them as an overall persecution apparatus.[39]

These observations alert us to the operations of power, capital and other forms of oppression that structure and delimit existence. The task would be to project a productive consciousness into the 'overall persecution apparatus' so as to reduce and undermine its totalitarian tendencies. In other words, to make the production of production our sole preoccupation in spite of the inexonerable temptations towards totalitarianism. This recontextualisation of the law of the production of production only seeks to explain how rudimentary processes are further inscribed into other complex processes. Discourse only becomes aware of its limits in relation to other discourses. Similarly, the law of the production of production is thus defined:

> every machine functions as a break in the flow in relation to the machine to which it is connected, but at the same time is also a flow itself, or the production of a flow, in relation to the machine connected to it.[40]

And where does Binsbergen fit into all this? It is in discovering new discursive flows within the field of African studies that transform a condition of lack, aberration and deterritorialisation[41] (violence as alienation) into opportunities for dialogical intervention and recontextualisation. Human situations and seemingly predetermined categories are meant to be transcended by acts that reinscribe the element of contingency at the heart of history and events.[42]

Wim van Binsbergen's academic career has been a most interesting one which delineates trajectories of cosmopolitanism, hybridity, difference and recolonisation (in the positive sense). He began as an anthropologist and ended up as a philosopher of culture or rather a specialist of interculturality. These various disciplinary trajectories taken in a strict professional context have also been profoundly shaped by a personal history in which he has had to confront under difficult circumstances, questions pertaining to objectivity in the social sciences and research methodologies and also the role of personal consciousness on the conditions of truth. These personal and professional constellations reveal so much about questions of identity, situationality and commitment in an age of late capitalism. In a revealing passage, Binsbergen discloses the peculiar professional and personal transformations that have occurred in his life:

> In the town of Francistown, Botswana, from 1988, under circumstances which I have discussed at length elsewhere—the usual fieldwork become so insupportable to me that I had to throw overboard all professional considerations I became not only the patient of local diviner-priests (sangomas), but at the end of a long therapy course ended up as one of them, and thus as a believer in the local collective representations. At the time I primarily justified this as a political deed, for me as a white man in an area which had been disrupted by white monopoly capitalism. Now more than then I realize that it was also and primarily an epistemological position taking-a revolt against the professional hypocrisy in which the hegemonic perspective of anthropology reveals itself. It was a position taking which in fact expelled me from cultural anthropology (although I did so by my own choice) and which created the conditions for the step which I finally made when occupying my present chair in intercultural philosophy.[43]

He continues:

> becoming an intercultural philosopher means a further step: one that amounts to integrating that deed in a systematic, reflective and intersubjective framework, in order to augment the anecdotal, autobiographical 'just so' account with theoretical analysis, and to explore the social relevance of an individual experience.[44]

These two passages describe the peculiar professional and personal contexts just mentioned. They reveal also how both postmodernity and premodernity are deeply structured by borderless limits, far-flung spiritual homes and forms of community that reduce and transcend our traditional conceptions of locale and belonging. It is also interesting to observe how Binsbergen applies this conceptual as well as discursive perspective in his analysis of Mudimbe's project. In doing so, we are afforded interpretative perspectives that unravel both the strengths and weaknesses of the project.

Mudimbe's career has been no less interesting. A holder of a doctorate in linguistics, his scholarship has been marked by a high level of interdisciplinarity. It has also been influenced by a broad backdrop of North Atlantic intellectual traditions that have also obviously influenced his life. Mudimbe being a highly commodified scholar within the American academy, is re-read by Binsbergen to trace the effects of his positionality on the prioritisation of interests and structuration of his various discourses. Oftentimes, Binsbergen's insights on Mudimbe demonstrate how the infrastructure of consciousness, processes of identity formation and actualities of localisation motivate and delimit what is said, how it is said and the effects that emanate from the intermingling of these factors and processes. The lesson being we must not underestimate or too eager to name and describe the technologies of dispersal and the dynamics of authenticity or rather, the politics of identity that are at work all the time.

Two of Mudimbe's texts, *The Invention of Africa* and *The Idea of Africa* (even though he has also ground-breaking works such as *Parables and Fables* (1991), account for his distinguished standing within the field of African studies in general and African philosophy in particular. But it is through Mudimbe's *Tales of Faith* that Binsbergen discovers the full implications of the former's discursive preoccupations. In other words, it is through a reading of the text that the impressive architecture of a text such as *The Invention of Africa* unfolds under less formal and anecdotal circumstances.

At this juncture it is necessary to cast into bolder relief the original ideas of Mudimbe and the paths through which Binsbergen has granted us a rediscovery of them in their unfolding and undoubtedly engaging complexity. This conceptual nexus seeks to do two things—first, to restate the formidable dimensions of Mudimbe's project and its uniqueness within the domain of African studies and second, to demonstrate how Binsbergen's reading of it not only casts the latter's project as a possible alternative but also reveals some of the limits of the former's oeuvre. In so doing, we shall see how travellers and subjects in both metropolitan and peripheral cultures describe various destinies that sometimes connect with or sometimes cross out each other in ways in which the meanings and implications of belonging, locality and the politics of identity become considerably more complex.

V. Y. Mudimbe: Some discursive geographies

In the introduction to *The Invention of Africa* Mudimbe states that his text is 'a sort of archaeology of African gnosis as a system of knowledge in which major philosophical questions recently have arisen'.[45] It is also 'a critical synthesis of the complex questions about knowledge and power in and on Africa'.[46]

The last remark immediately reveals the Foucauldian/Saidian character of Mudimbe's programme. Africa within the European archive had been portrayed as a grim locus of Hobbesian strife and entropy. It had no arts, letters and civilisation as variously recounted by prominent philosophers such as Kant, Hegel and Hume. Thus it became an object for elaborate Eurocentric demonology.

But European postures and attitudinisation towards Africa did not end with demonology alone. Mudimbe writes that 'three complementary hypothesis and actions emerge: the domination of physical space, the reformation of natives' minds, and the integration of local economic histories into the Western perspective'.[47] However Western colonial policies only led to the peripheralisation and underdevelopment (skeletonisation) of the dependencies in addition to increasing alienation from the dominant structures of the global economy. The colonial/postcolonial situation also destroyed the internal coherence and stability of the dependencies in a way that 'a dichotomizing system has emerged, and with it a great number of current paradigmatic oppositions have developed: traditional versus modern; oral versus written and printed; agrarian and customary communities versus urban and industrialised civilization; subsistence economies versus highly productive economies'.[48]

At a less theoretical level, Mudimbe also lists well known African problems such as 'demographic imbalance, extraordinarily high birth rates, progressive disintegration of the classic family structure, illiteracy, severe social and economic disparities, dictatorial regimes functioning under the cathartic name of democracy, the breakdown of religious traditions, the constitution of syncretic churches, etc'.[49]

Mention also must be made of how Mudimbe inscribes this graphic canvas of entropy within the larger abstract canvas of Foucauldian art criticism. We are left to ponder the meaning of light and shade, the structures and poses of the human body as appropriated by technologies of power and inscription. Through this description we see the dark phantomless African body as appropriated and reinvented through the long established traditions of European artistic and technological imagination. The results are a libinal economy that situated and reconstructed the African body within a flow that could only be described as an economy of unreason. Having been ascribed a status well below European humanity (infrahumanity), the same Europeans directed the instruments of science and rationality towards not only the complete subjugation (and normalisation) of the African body but also African lands (pacification). The Atlantic slave trade and colonisation were the two key events (and also strategies) that were employed to achieve these ends. Mudimbe describes the methods by which European intellection sought to appropriate the African mind, body and land:

> Evolution, conquest and difference become signs of a theological, bio-
> logical, and anthropological destiny, and assign to things and beings both
> their natural slots and social mission. Theorists of capitalism, such as
> Benjamin Kidd and Karl Pearson in England, Paul Leroy-Beaulieu in France,
> Friedrich Naumann and Friedrich von Bernhard in Germany, as well as
> philosophers, comment upon two main complimentary paradigms. These
> are the inherent superiority of the white race, and, as already made explicit
> in Hegel's *Philosophy of Right,* the necessity for European economies and
> structures to expand to 'virgin areas' of the world.[50]

Thus the entire spectrum of European cultural practices was deployed for
the task of the total subjugation of less powerful peoples. Mudimbe's analysis
not only depicts this it also demonstrates the place and task of each academic
speciality in the subjugation and the re-invention of the African subject but
also the entire repertoire of subjectivity. In this way, the organless African
body was open to the most relentless Eurocentric technologies of power. In
making these important disciplinary distinctions Mudimbe accomplishes an
uncommonly sophisticated analysis of the colonising structure of the Western
disciplinary anthropologisation of the other which lies at the heart of a broader
general academic project. Furthermore, these distinctions highlight the value
of archaeological demonstrations as a searchlight for showing up the micro-
physics of power and how it reaches deep into even the most insignificant of
structures, for example, practices of everyday life. Indeed, a crucial part of
Mudimbe's project is to point out that anthropology which had been desig-
nated to scrutinise objects and subjects that were regarded as inferior, backward and underdeveloped was also marshalled to explore ways by which
uncivilised peoples can be inserted into modern civilisation.[51]

For Mudimbe, the theories of Lévi-Strauss and Foucault uncover a crucial
conceptual difficulty within the intellectual socius which is that 'we lack a theory
that could solve the dialectic tension between creative discourses and the epistemological field which makes them possible, on the one hand, and Lévi-
Strauss's unconscious that sustains discourses and accounts for their organization, on the other.'[52]

After the European intellectual reconstruction of the African infrastructure of consciousness had been accomplished an emergent class of African
intellectuals rose to deconstruct the Eurocentric inventions. They included theorists and thinkers such as W. E. Abraham, O. Bimwenyi, F. Eboussi Boulaga
Paulin Hountondji, T. Obenga, T. Okere, J. O. Sodipo, I. Sow, M. Towa,
Kwasi Wiredu and a host of others.[53] Again, Mudimbe reiterates the importance of Foucauldian theories on the pervasive power/knowledge nexus for

the deconstruction of Western constructs, perspectivisations and reinventions of Africa. His conclusion is that 'the African postulation would seem situated, metaphorically, between Nietzsche's predicament and Foucault's enterprise'.[54] Also in tracing the archaeology of African responses to hegemonic Eurocentric stereotypes Mudimbe states that 'in these enterprises one notes a remarkable mediation between the rigor of a philosophical exercise and the fantasies of a political insurrection'.[55]

Mudimbe names three crucial figures from Western culture that were central to the construction of Eurocentric stereotypes regarding Africa and colonial dependencies generally:

> The explorer, at the end of the fifteenth century was looking for a sea-route to India. Later on, he concerned himself with mapping out the continent and, in the nineteenth century, compiling information and organizing complex bodies of knowledge, including medicine, geography, and anthropology. The soldier constituted the most visible figure of the expansion of European jurisdiction. He built castles and forts on the coasts, was in charge of trading posts, participated in the slave trade, and, in the nineteenth century, implemented colonial power. Finally, there was the missionary, whose objective has been, throughout the enterprise, the most consistent: to expand 'the absoluteness of Christianity' and its virtues.[56]

Mudimbe stresses the point that the missionary as a representative of Christendom and also the Colonial Empire was very crucial to the destruction and subsequent transformation of traditional African societies and their various infrastructures of consciousness. In other words, the tasks of the missionary went in several directions which included spiritual, moral and educative responsibilities. Construed from this perspective, it becomes understandable why colonialism has had such a transformative impact on precolonial societies. The transformation of those pre-colonial societies assumed a serious intellectual form when missionaries began to problematise the relationship between Western culture—read also Christianity—and those traditional societies on the one hand, and the full implications of their duties as agents of moral and social transformation, on the other.

The nature of this problematisation is revealed in the work of the Belgian missionary, Placide F. Tempels who is known primarily as the author of *Bantu Philosophy*. Mudimbe describes the text thus:

> Rather than as a philosophical treatise [...] *Bantu Philosophy* could be understood simultaneously as an indication of religious insight, the expression of cultural doubt about the supposed backwardness of Africans, and a political manifesto for a new policy for a new policy of promoting 'civilisation' and Christianity.[57]

However, the overriding thrust of missionary discourse regarding precolonial societies tended to view those societies as paganistic, savage and uncivilised. As such, they were derided in the most unsparing terms. Christianity as conceived within the context of the same missionary discourse was associated with reason, history and power which were also reconstituted as the primary media by which the savagery of pre-colonial societies could be eradicated.

Nonetheless, Christianity in its undiluted Europeanised version was never completely transplanted in African soil and consciousness. Consequently, 'Tempels absolutely doubted the classical process of conversion: he was not sure in the least that assimilation constituted the best way, and he hated the 'evolués', whom he considered as bad copies of Europeans'.[58] The reality of this ambiguous transplantation of Christianity within African soil is captured in the following passage:

> If European Catholicism seems to be aging dangerously, the dynamism of its African counterpart belongs either to a holy nightmare or, if one prefers, to an incredible miracle: monasteries are being built; new religious movements, both activist and charismatic, are appearing and organizing themselves successfully.[59]

In other words, what followed was a process of Africanisation, indigenisation, naturalisation and adaptation of European Christianity. The African experience of slavery, exploitation and colonisation is also understood within a revised/reversed Judeo-Christian context; that just like the Jews, Africans were God's chosen people.

In spite of this African response to Christianity, the African subject still continued to be a target of Eurocentric anthropological projects, the major hypothesis being 'that Africans must evolve from their frozen state to the dynamism of Western civilization.'[60]

Mudimbe then begins to explore the reactions of European thinkers to this pervasive Eurocentric racism towards the African subject. Jean-Paul Sartre is credited with transforming Negritude into a major political event. Sartre argues that the Negro 'creates an anti-racist racism. He does not at all wish to dominate the world: he wishes the abolition of racial privileges wherever they are found.'[61]

However, in spite of this intervention on behalf of Negritude as a philosophy of consciousness by Sartre, it has not been well received by the generality of African intellectuals especially within the Anglophone divide. And one of the most consistent critics of Negritude is Wole Soyinka as we had noted in the earlier part of this study. Oftentimes Soyinka centres his critique of Negritude around the figure of Léopold Sédar Senghor, its chief exponent. He writes, 'Leopold Sédar Senghor was a priest—but a failed one'.[62]

As we know, Negritude in its Senghorian conception is for Soyinka an ideology of romantic simplicism lacking any real revolutionary or transformative properties. To discover or create the revolutionary potentials of Negritude, Soyinka argues that we look for them in the work of Jacques Roumain, Etienne Lero and René Depestre who 'represented the non-negotiable sector of the province of Negritude'[63] and not in Senghor, Damas and Aimé Césaire. But is Soyinka's reading of the Senghorian conception of Negritude complete? Mudimbe's account gives a different interpretation which enriches the debate. Indeed Sartre demonstrates that Negritude was not only a purely literary tendency but also an ideological construct that espouses evident revolutionary properties. This contextualisation of Negritude in which the formulations of Sartre embellish and amplify those of Senghor is largely due to Mudimbe's reading.

Mudimbe for his part urges us to view Negritude as an outcome of the alienation caused by colonialism.[64] It is also an African ideology of otherness constructed to challenge and subvert the racist Eurocentric claims pertaining the African subject. In Mudimbe's words 'negritude becomes the intellectual and emotional sign of opposition to the ideology of white superiority.'[65]

Through Mudimbe's reading of the Senghorian conception of negritude, the various previously unfully explored dimensions of the philosophy are thrown into bolder relief. In fact, it contains an inverted form of Hegelianism with all the same philosophical currents of totalisation. According to Mudimbe:

> Negritude and Marxist humanism are, according to Senghor, only stages in a dynamic dialectic process towards a universal civilization. Interpreting hypotheses of Pierre Teilhard de Chardin, Senghor bases his ideas of a universal civilization upon laws of evolution. He believes that the movement from microentities to more complex ones and finally consciousness expresses a natural law. This would imply at least three major theses: the principle of development of all human beings, the principle of harmony in development of God's existence as a natural necessity. Senghor thinks that some basic African values are well expressed in this perspective; namely the idea of community, the principle of harmony between evolving humans and changing nature, and finally, the vision of a unitary universe.[66]

The inclusion of the Marxist humanist element in the ideology of Negritude immediately creates other nuances that Soyinka's account fails to reveal. This makes Soyinka's reading quite suspect even though he has maintained a long standing and problematic ideological engagement with the Senghorian version of Negritude. Mudimbe's account on the other hand establishes within a much broader conceptual canvas the various contexts—geographical, literary, philosophical, ideological and personal—from which Negritude as a philosophy of consciousness emerged and the numerous discursive elements that went into its construction. And then in demarcating the lines of Senghor's ideological pursuits, Mudimbe establishes connections with Edward Blyden's own preoccupations which developed in another era.[67] Again, this demonstrates that we have to look beneath the surface in any description of Senghor's project.

Let us now return to the theme of parricide. Every new major philosopher rewrites and/or subverts the preceding one. Gramsci and Althusser in their various ways rewrite Marx. Althusser writes of his project:

> What I essentially tried to do was to make Marx's theoretical texts intelligible in themselves and for us as readers, because they were often obscure and contradictory, if not deficient in respect of certain key points.[68]

Derrida reads Rousseau's *Confessions* and constructs a theory of the sexual 'supplement' which he interprets as a metaphor of castration. Rewriting, recontexualisaiton, counter-interpretation and supplementarity are all variables of parricide within the epistemological field. Events from the African context also bear this out.

Tshiamalenga argues that 'Temples constructed a philosophy but did not reconstruct Bantu philosophy'.[69] Kagame addresses the theoretical limitations of Temple's project. Tshiamalenga in turn points out the shortcomings of Kagame's programme. In this way, conceptual rigour gradually evolves. Hountondji on his own part does not subvert merely a philosophical figure, instead he directs his attack on the entire school and project of ethno-philosophy. These various critiques and projects mark a crucial turning-point in African philosophical discourse.

Mudimbe writes that 'the history of knowledge in Africa and about Africa appears deformed and disjointed, and the explanation lies in its own origin and development.'[70] In concluding, Mudimbe offers an important formulation:

> The conceptual framework of African thinking has been both a mirror and a consequence of the experience of European hegemony; that is, in Gramsci's terms, the dominance of one social bloc over another, not simply by means of force or wealth, but by a social authority whose ultimate sanction a profound cultural supremacy.[71]

Undoubtedly, Mudimbe uses texts, discourses myths, fables and repressed voices from African experiences and scenarios and also the hegemonic Western episteme to trace an archaeology of absence, silence, passive resistance and finally positive articulation. His own texts and conceptual formulations are indications of this discursive articulation. This alone is no ordinary accomplishment. However, the question at this juncture is what are the possibilities of this accomplishment for articulating an emancipatory kind of politics? Without a cursory glance in this direction, his formulations might appear rather staid or over-determined to ideologues of the politics of authenticity in Africa.

Furthermore, Mudimbe's archaeological reconstructions frequently refer to Foucault whose critiques of the technologies of power are widely known. Thus, employing the Foucauldian paradigm of power/knowledge, he deconstructs the Eurocentric invention of Africa. The point would be to turn the basis of that same critique upon the work of Africans who carry out similar ethnocentric projects of invention and mystification. There are other ways of augmenting—not rewriting—Mudimbe's text.

Edward Said, the Palestinian critic also employs Foucault as a model of theorisation and emancipatory politics in relation to the question of Palestine. And with the work of Foucault complete and also largely situated within the Western epistemological field, Said becomes the heir apparent of that kind of emancipatory politics. His texts, notably *Orientalism* and *Culture and Imperialism* are also deconstructions of Western theories of otherness regarding the Orient. Nonetheless, other theoretical dimensions broaden the scope of his project. Meanwhile, let us return to Mudimbe.

Mudimbe employs an astonishing array of language games and discourses. The effect of this is that the field of African studies is enormously deparochialised with a powerful spirit of inventiveness. However such efforts at deparochialisation are never complete. For instance, in spite of his theoretical breadth he does not fully situate the African subject as a figure of pure agential counter-violence.[72] For some reason, Mudimbe's representations of the African subject or more precisely body are theorised into absence or as a sign of total lack. Instead of the presence and articulations of the body as lived consciousness as is so explicit in Senghor's interventions and in the discourse of African surrealists, the text in Mudimbe assumes the place of the absent body. The text becomes the frame and the skeleton. The body on the other hand retreats into infinity and the implications of its absence are not problematised.

There are yet other ways of augmenting in theoretical terms the epistemological field excavated by Mudimbe. There is a need to examine other technologies through which knowledge is constituted in contemporary times. For instance, the electronic media as opposed to print has become a very dominant mode in not only the constitution but also the dissemination of forms of knowledge. It has also led to the homogenisation of a plurality of cultural forms in such a way that the question of what constitutes identity has become exceptionally problematic. The creation of the mass society during the twentieth century is also central to this development.

Analysing the nature of forms of knowledge in postindustrial societies, Jean-Francois Lyotard distinguishes between two kinds of knowledge—one narrative, the other scientific. Narrative knowledge is classified as 'savage, primitive, underdeveloped, backward, alienated, composed of opinions, customs, authority, prejudice, ignorance, ideology'.[73] On the other hand, scientific knowledge:

> develops into a profession and gives rise to institutions, and in modern societies language games consolidate themselves in the form of institutions run by qualified partners (the professional class).[74]

The dichotomisation of forms of knowledge within post-Fordist contexts necessitates a rethink of the issue in postcolonial societies as well. This is because the dynamics of contemporary globalisation oftentimes result in powerful homogenising tendencies. The electronic media as a means of information have become global. Bourdieu and Baudrillard have demonstrated the far reaching consequences of the growth of new information technologies. Consequently, this is why specialists in postcolonial theorists working in the area of African studies must include other levels of problematisation based on the challenges brought about by the age of virtuality. This of course also applies to Mudimbe.

Binsbergen's own reading of Mudimbe should serve as an even more important avenue for further theoretical augmentation. The reason being that race, identity, globality and commitment under the searchlight of Binsbergen's reading are radically transformed by the present context of the cultural moment.

Re-reading Valentine

Binsbergen's reading of Mudimbe's *Tales of Faith* is almost parricidal even though the latter is not the former's philosophical father in the actual sense. Binsbergen in his paper, 'An Incomprehensible Miracle', writes that he wishes to 'concentrate on *Tales of Faith*, but connecting as much as possible to the rest of Mudimbe's work, and to his person to the extent that this transpires in the published texts'.[75] He continues, 'I will be very critical, not out of lack of respect and admiration, but because the fundamental issues of Africa and of African studies today manifest themselves around Mudimbe as a central and emblematic figure, and we need to bring out those issues'.

Binsbergen classifies Mudimbe's method as 'kaleidoscopic and eclectic'. More fundamentally, Binsbergen identifies the leitmotif of homelessness that runs through the text. On the question of Mudimbe's methodology or the lack of it he writes:

The insistence on the book review method suggests how Mudimbe identifies himself in his authorial practice. The effect of this method is the avoidance of a systematic conceptual framework, the avoidance of faithful submission to any established academic discipline except the discipline of literary studies whence Mudimbe seems to derive, as the main model of his intellectual products, the virtually unbounded conventions of the 'essay', with its generous allowance (ever since the emergence of the essay as a genre in eighteenth century Great Britain) of conceptual freedom, literary originality, and limited empirical expectations or requirements.[76]

Mudimbe's text discusses religion and politics in Central Africa, however Binsbergen charges him of not situating the topics according to current discursive practices. Instead, Mudimbe treats both religion and politics according to their original etymological connotations which in spite of all, greatly undermines his text's contributions to the history of ideas and also African religious studies. Furthermore, Binsbergen extends and recontexualises both the reality and metaphor of homelessness that he associates with Mudimbe.

Homelessness becomes not only an acute physical reality but also gets redefined as an instance of intellectual alienation. The metaphor of homelessness is thus extended:

Mudimbe does not explicitly, and unequivocally choose a constituency in Africa among the African masses and their cultural, political and religious expressions, neither does he consistently and compellingly choose a disciplinary constituency in North Atlantic academic life, apart from the lack of methodological and theoretical constraint which the literary form of the kaleidoscopic, collage like essay accords him.[77]

This interpretation of homelessness and textual (dis)inscription in the face of death—after the great French surrealists and more importantly Nietzsche—becomes once again universalised in the field of African intellection. As hinted before, Mudimbe's rootlessness is not merely physical, it encompasses spiritual and intellectual dimensions. In that way, personal circumstances and consciousness, Binsbergen explains, are projected into apparently rationalistic discourse.

Rather than conceptualising the structure of meaning, the ecstasy and eclecticism of release are set loose. This claim is corroborated when Binsbergen writes:

The book testifies to a great creative and scholarly mind who can afford to play with the canons of scholarship; first of all because his qualifications in this field are incontestable, secondly and more importantly because to him these canons are merely effective stepping-stones (the Wittengsteinian ladder he may cast away after climbing up), leading towards something even more valuable; the articulation of identity and personal struggle in the face of death and homelessness.[78]

Mudimbe's largely self-inflicted isolation turns him away from studying what would otherwise have been an interesting angle: "the African people", the formal political institutions which are to some extent shaped and challenged by these people have expressed themselves in precolonial times and which have in part persisted since the advent of Christianity in the region'.[79] Consequently, Mudimbe in spite of his Foucauldian theoretical orientation, in the final analysis subverts some of its most propulsive tendencies. For central to Foucauldianism is the active articulation of difference, otherness and silence. Mudimbe, in turning away from this crucial ideological posture, certainly casts away some of Foucault's key theses. Also, Afrocentricism which is in part a reaction of Eurocentricism 'is reduced by Mudimbe to a mere act of Freudian transference, i.e. distorted self-projection out of touch with reality'.[80] Instead he aligns himself with 'Kwame Appiah, another cosmopolitan African philosopher who has endeared himself to the North Atlantic audience by rejecting the essentialism of Africanness'.[81]

Thus Mudimbe, in spite of being 'the most applauded critic of North Atlantic and African constructions of Africa'[82] is not beyond parricide since his strident typification that 'Afrocentricism is sheer transference of an inferiority complex among today's African Americans'[83] is an unequivocal attempt to debunk an established ideological school which is a posture that is certain to draw a number of repercussions. Binsbergen interprets Mudimbe's stance not just in terms of cultural and geographical moorings. At a deeper level, it speaks of 'a profound methodological dilemma which attend the entire empirical study of African religion through, participant observation or through African believers' introspection'.[84] This dilemma we are made to understand is a product of Mudimbe's elaborate withdrawal from the palpable African socius.

Binsbergen makes two incisive claims about a scholar who he agrees has a truly great cosmopolitan mind. The thrust is that:

Mudimbe analyzes other people's Tales, Parables and Fables, Ideas and Inventions, but for his personal needs retreats to the bare and windy rocks of agnosticism. His Africa is not that of other people, it does not exist as a tangible reality for himself, but at best constitutes a context for contestation, a laboratory for the politics of the liberation of difference.[85]

Binsbergen's other claim is that 'the construction of self through the liberation of difference ... is a politics of textual performance, not of substance: asserting difference, not contents, seems to be the game'.[86] Finally, Binsbergen dwells on the idea of cultural métissité which he defines as 'the condition of being of cultural mixed descent'.[87] Obviously, with the current wave of global capitalism and surges of recolonisation (in the form of cultural reappropriation), this condition is going to mark and shape humanity profoundly. However, for all their differences Mudimbe and Binsbergen are connected by a common axiom which is 'the impossibility of reducing anyone, any human culture, to an immobile essence'.[88] Their trajectories as individuals and also as academics meet within the field of African studies even though their approaches and concerns may not always be the same. Thus the espousal of a basic anti-essentialism in their approaches and practices may reveal stimulating continuities. Conceived in this way, Binsbergen's reading of Mudimbe is also a mode of discursive augmentation.

At this juncture, it should be interesting to note some of the ways Binsbergen approaches the field of African studies. The issue of witchcraft has had a checkered history in terms of the disciplinary spaces it has inhabited. In the main, the disciplines of anthropology and philosophy have been responsible for reiterating and sustaining the debates on African witchcraft. However a major conceptual breakthrough was made when 'Winch argued that African witchcraft, like any other religious beliefs the world over, comes in where knowledge (the knowledge of members of an African society, but also the knowledge of cosmopolitan natural sciences) runs out. African witchcraft is no more a theory of the natural world than that of the Christian and Islamic dogma of Divine Providence is'.[89] In other words, 'African witchcraft is a way of speaking about the unspeakable'.[90] For Binsbergen, 'the study of witchcraft in Africa poses the same epistemological problems as any other attempt to study religious beliefs and practices with the concepts and theories which the social sciences have developed in the course of the twentieth century'.[91]

Another debunked anthropological and epistemological fallacy is the notion that 'African historic societies' (as Binsbergen terms them) were 'holistic, self-contained, bounded, integrated, locally anchored'. Paulin Hountondji and Kwame Appiah have done a lot to undermine this notion. And then Binsbergen demonstrates how the virtualisation of human experience under contemporary globalisation has rendered previous explanatory models—in terms of the analyses of social formations and fissures—unsuitable.

A crucial problem facing various categories of populations in Africa today is how to forge and sustain new links of community in the face of daunting political and economic obstacles. Binsbergen centralises this problem is a way that forces us to reconsider what community means in its broader epistemological sense. From the practices of various African communities we are encouraged to believe it is a way of coping, and also a primal response to solitude. Hence the rationalisation of the processes of constructing community and solidarity need not always be intelligible. Thus 'healing cults, prophetic cults, anti-sorcery movements, varieties of imported world religions and local transformations thereof, e.g. in the form of independent churches, struggles for political independence, involvement in modern natural politics including the recent wave of democratisation, ethnicity, involvement in a peripheral-capitalist cash economy'[92] are all various African avenues for forging and maintaining community.

The village used to be a locus for community within the African context but with the advent of the virtual village, this is no longer the case. The 'elite (for whom patterns of consumerism replace the notion of community through media transmission and the display of appropriate manufactured symbols)'[93] seem to have found other meaningful ways of constructing community beyond the locus of the village.

However, in spite of the virtualisation of experience and the dissemination of discourses of modernity, the preoccupation with witchcraft has not diminished, rather, it has assumed other interesting forms. Binsbergen argues that aspects of witchcraft may be read as a theory of evil.[94] More explicitly:

> Witchcraft is opposed to kinship, group solidarity, rules of kinship, incest prohibitions, avoidance rules concerning close kin, kinship obligations concerning redistribution of resources, the repression of intra-kin violence, and the acknowledgement of ancestral sanctions. Outside of the kinship order is the realm of witchcraft; and it is here that we must situate kinship, trade and the specialties of the bard, the diviner, the magician and the rainmaker.[95]

Binsbergen breaks interesting theoretical grounds when he supports the thesis that witchcraft is an instance of virtuality. Witchcraft has moved from the 'village' as a discursive terrain into the modern arena where 'many instances of competition over scarce resources, and many instances of the exercise of power'[96] have transformed it into a revised theory of evil. Thus 'witchcraft has offered modern Africans an idiom to articulate what otherwise could not be articulated: contradictions between power and meaning, between morality and primitive accumulation, between community and death, between the village and the state.'[97]

This reading of witchcraft, as a theory of evil and as an instance of virtuality offers discursive grounds for linking certain African primordial characteristics to the age of virtualisation. In spite of the hegemonic tendencies of global capitalism, theories of virtualisation alone cannot fully explain the complex amalgam of African realities. Furthermore, witchcraft as a theory of evil situated in the 'village' cannot account for the discourses of modernity in which the African continent as a whole has become enmeshed. The recognition of these realities and the adoption of an appropriate assortment of theoretical strategies by Binsbergen provide a generous opening for the future of African studies.

His employment of subjects like religion, anthropology and witchcraft as fields for constructing and understanding human experience centralises what technologisation and digitalisation are always on a quest to exclude. In that way, we are offered new ways of resistance, interpretation and perhaps also re-appropriation. Binsbergen describes his current research concerns thus: 'the articulation of philosophical problems of interculturality, and the suggestion of possible routes towards possible answers, specifically from the context of religion or, perhaps more generally, vaguely, and state-of-the-art-like, 'spirituality'.[98]

Derrida's recent work on religion merely reestablishes the centrality of issues concerning life, thought, truth, righteousness, sacrifice and violence in the history of ideas and action. Postmodernity, globalisation and the information age have not eroded their relevance. Thus if religion provides opportunities for constructing community it is not only imperative to study the source of such opportunities but also the complex of situations to which they give rise. Binsbergen claims religion allows people to create 'among themselves, a new social identity, new communities, which they would never have had without that religious expression; whilst creating a boundary between the chosen and the outside world. The diasporic religious situation seeks to efface boundaries among the chosen whatever their pre-existing differences in terms of class, gender, region, itinerary, age, etc.'[99] Furthermore, 'the alliance between Christianity, capitalism, and the scientific-technological complex of today'[100] provides methodological alternatives for the study of contemporary globalisation. These insights are what Binsbergen's work affords us, as the challenge of reorienting African studies in the 21st century confronts us.[101] In addition, we are provided new tools for examining identity, belonging, place and homelessness. Binsbergen's reading of Mudimbe locates the spaces of these questions in the latter's work and within the larger field of African studies.

What we see in Mudimbe's project within the context of Binsbergen's work and reading is that the former confronted by the sprawling spectre of exile and homelessness withdrawals behind the superstructure of the text. The text fetishised beyond measure in the African consciousness becomes an opaque sheet, the final severance from the African body which Mudimbe with all seriousness had sought to appropriate.

There are ways in which to construct yet edifying forms of community within and outside the context of post-Fordism and the digital age. Binsbergen's work on African scenarios and forms of subjectivity is in part a projection of some of these modes of collective inclusion and strategies of self-inscription. We are also led to revisit the deliberations within the field of African studies.

African studies, which, it can be argued, is in part a reaction to the hegemony of Eurocentricism and North Atlantic intellectual traditions is structured and galvanised by elements of a largely by-gone metaphysical philosophy—the essence of Being, God, justice, the Enlightenment and metanarrativity in general. Thus, its status ought to be defined within specific discursive geographies and specific locales. What does doing African studies as an African in the First World really mean? How do local peculiarities shape the field within the African continent itself? Practitioners of African studies should always endeavour to admit that their positionalities and their various discursive contexts are provisional and contingent. Through the mere articulation of this echo, our techniques for discerning difference should become sharper.

Traditional specificities of place and belonging have been eroded by virtualisation. Binsbergen demonstrates this in relation to Mudimbe and by his own example. Place and belonging become what we make of them through constructs of meaning and also through the construction of community. The constructs of meaning and the construction of community are different and yet are linked by the same complex of thematics: identity and postidentity politics, rootedness and alienation, text and context, contingency and universalism. Individual agency and chance as demonstrated by the separate yet related trajectories of Mudimbe and Binsbergen reveal a lot about how we create forms of community, belonging and also modes of severance. Any reading of rootedness and belonging carries within it decisive instances of exclusion and oftentimes it is these instances that give fuller pictures of our situationality.[102]

Notes

1. See his interview with Christian Hoeller in *Springerin Magazine*, Austria, 2002.

2. Ibid.

3. Achille Mbembe, *On the Postcolony*, Berkeley: University of California Press, 2001, p. 6.

4. Ibid. p.7.

5. Ibid.

6. Ibid. p. 4.

7. Ibid. p. 5.

8. Ibid. p. 14.

9. Ibid. p. 17.

10. Ibid. p. 26.

11. Ibid. pp. 31-32.

12. Ibid. p. 42.

13. Ibid. p. 44.

14. Achille Mbembe, 'An Essay on the Political Imagination in Wartime', *CODESRIA Bulletin*, 2, 3 & 4, p. 7.

15. Achille Mbembe, *On the Postcolony*, 2001, p. 52.

16. Ibid. p. 51.

17. Ibid. p. 52.

18. Achille Mbembe, 'Ways of Seeing: Beyond the New Nativism', *African Studies Review*, Vol. 44, No.2, p. 2

19. Achille Mbembe, *On the Postcolony*, 2001, p. 57.

20. Ibid. p. 68.

21. Ibid. p. 76.

22. Ibid. p. 77.

23. Ibid. p. 80.

24. Ibid. p. 93.

25. Ibid.

26. Ibid. p. 102.

27. Ibid. p. 103.

28. Ibid. p. 108.

29. Ibid. p. 110.

30. Ibid.

31. Ibid. p. 114.

32. Ibid. p. 118.

33. Ibid. p. 128.

34. Ibid. p. 145.

35. Ibid. p. 141.

36. Ibid. p. 160.

37. Ibid. p. 189.

38. Achille Mbembe has been calling for an internationalisation of African modes and types of academic production. See for instance, his editorial in *CODESRIA Bulletin*, Nos. 3 & 4, 1999.

39. Gilles Deleuze and Félix Guattari, *Anti-Oedipus: Capitalism and Schizophrenia* trans. R. Hurley, M. Seem and H. R. Lane, London: The Athlone Press Ltd, 1984, p. 9.

40. Ibid. p. 36.

41. This term is not employed in its usual sense.

42. I borrow this term very loosely from Alain Badiou.

43. Wim Van Binsbergen, 'An Incomprehensible Miracle: Central African clerical intellectualism versus African historic religion: a close reading of Valentin Mudimbe's *Tale of Faith*', paper presented at SOAS, 1 February 2001.

44. Ibid.

45. V. Y. Mudimbe, *The Invention of Africa: Gnosis Philosophy, and the Order of Knowledge*, Bloomington and Indianapolis: Indiana University Press, 1988, p. x.

46. Ibid. p. XI.

47. Ibid. p. 2.

48. Ibid. p. 4.

49. Ibid. p. 5.

50. Ibid. p. 17.

51. Ibid. p. 20.

52. Ibid. p. 35.

53. Ibid. p. 39.

54. Ibid. p. 41.

55. Ibid. p. 43.

56. Ibid. pp. 46-47.

57. Ibid. p. 50.

58. Ibid. p. 53.

59. Ibid. pp. 54-55.

60. Ibid. p. 76.

61. Ibid. p. 85.

62. Wole Soyinka, *The Burden of Memory: The Muse of Forgiveness*, New York and London: Oxford University Press, 1999, p. 97.

63. Ibid. p. 164.

64. V. Y. Mudimbe, *The Invention of Africa*, 1988, p. 92.

65. Ibid. p. 93.

66. Ibid. p. 94.

67. Ibid. p. 132.

68. Louis Althusser, *The Future lasts a long Time* trans. R. Veasey London: Vintage, 1993, p. 221.

69. V. Y. Mudimbe, *The Invention of Africa*, 1988, p. 140.

70. Ibid. p. 175.

71. Ibid. p. 185.

72. Although this point cannot be made in relation to his text, *Parables and Fables,* Madison: University of Wisconsin Press, 1991.

73. Jean-Francois Lyotard, *The Postmodern Condition: A Report on Knowledge,* Manchester: Manchester University Press, 1984, p. 27.

74. Ibid. p. 25.

75. Wim van Binsbergen, 'An Incomprehensible Miracle'.

76. Ibid.

77. Ibid.

78. Ibid.

79. Ibid.

80. Ibid.

81. Ibid.

82. Ibid.

83. Ibid.

84. Ibid.

85. Ibid.

86. Ibid.

87. Ibid.

88. Ibid.

89. Wim van Binsbergen, 'Witchcraft in Modern Africa as Virtualised Boundary Conditions of the Kinship Order', http://www.geocities.com/africareligion/witchtxl.htm.

90. Ibid.

91. Ibid.

92. Ibid.

93. Ibid.

94. Ibid.

95. Ibid.

96. Ibid.

97. Ibid.

98. Wim van Binsbergen, 'Derrida on religion: Glimpses on interculturality', paper presented at the Dutch-Flemish Association for Intercultural Philosophy, Research Group on Spirituality meetings, April and June 2000, http://www.geocities.com/nrv.f/derrwim.htm.

99. Ibid.

100. Ibid.

101. See Wim van Binsbergen, 1991, 'Becoming a Sangoma: Religious Anthropological Field-work in Franscistown, Botswana', *Journal of Religion in Africa* 21, 4.

102. See Wim van Binsbergen, ed., 1997, *Black: Athena Ten Years After Hoofddorp: Dutch Archaeological and Historical Society,* Special issue, Talenta: Proceedings of the Dutch Archaeological and Historical Society, Vol. 28-29, 1996–97 Wim van Binsbergen, Global Bee Flight (Forthcoming).

Conclusion

This volume has been primarily concerned with Kwasi Wiredu's project of conceptual decolonisation, and other forms of decolonisation, which has entailed analyses of a diverse range of other scholars. It has been necessary to rewrite the notion of conceptual decolonisation as conceived by Wiredu since I maintain that the very concept of decolonisation is a world historical process. Wiredu, having for several years influenced the course of philosophical deliberations in Africa, has once again managed to direct attention to an important problem, which we would do well to tackle. Consequently, this study addresses the challenges, as well as the limitations of his project as presently conceived, and then goes on to discuss vital issues that are related to it but which he fails to address. But it is also very much concerned about the overall state of African philosophy in various specificities and African and black diasporic studies generally.

I began by exploring the global implications of imperialism in the widest possible terms, which is something Wiredu neglects to do. The argument is that any project of conceptual decolonisation must also include a vibrant critique of imperialism in its various ramifications: political, economic and socio-cultural, technological. Other theorists of decolonisation such as Frantz Fanon, Edward Said, Stuart Hall, Cornel West, bell hooks, Ngugi wa Thiong'o and so many others have done this competently. Since decolonisation is 'a vast process' as Ngugi wa Thiong'o affirms and a 'world historical process' as Cornel West points out, we have to attempt to understand it on a global scale and from a multidisciplinary perspective, which is another task I have attempted in this study.

Furthermore, this study argues that Wiredu's project of conceptual decolonisation is rather narrow, since not only a robust critique of imperialism is absent but also because it fails to acknowledge related developments in other disciplines. In addition, Wiredu does not pay sufficient attention to authoritarianism in post-colonial African states. This is also necessary in any project of conceptual decolonisation.

Also, Wiredu's relation to the tradition of Western philosophy does not reflect current taxonomies that subvert its ethnocentricism, phallocentricism and, need one add, racism. Deconstructionist philosophy has demonstrated ways in which these excesses of Western philosophy can be addressed. If one has a 'conventional' relationship with Western philosophy as Wiredu posits, that is, if one goes on to examine philosophical concepts such as 'Mind' 'Truth' and 'God' using tropes that are still tied to a traditional philosophical vocabulary, then those very excesses of Western philosophy will be replicated in contemporary African philosophy. That is why post-structuralist theorising is important in explicating a more comprehensive version of decolonisation. This is an argument this study advances. We must note here that decolonisation is also a 'programme of violence', according to Frantz Fanon, so that the application of any philosophical method requires constant vigilance, a quality that is to be found in post-structuralist philosophy.

There are also concepts that Wiredu fails to situate adequately, most notably, identity in a post-colonial context. There are several works that have opened these discursive sites, which any discussion on conceptual decolonisation has to address. Instead, what this shortcoming evinces is a rather incomplete representation of the issues involved. In other words, the level of theoretical problematisation of conceptual decolonisation is rather restricted.

This study has taken all these issues into consideration, hence its importance. In addition to issues related to imperialism and post-coloniality, it also discusses topics such as Afrocentricity, as a vital response to Western manifestations of dominance and exploitation and emerging conditions and configurations in the African postcolony.

Mention must be made of the fact that language also poses a great problem to Wiredu's project. Even within a monolingual context, the problems of meaning, reference and representation are undoubtedly awesome. Similarly, within the annals of analytic philosophy, the philosophy of language has always presented some highly engaging problems. This study highlights some of them and then relates them to Wiredu's project. Wiredu's project of conceptual decolonisation involves a bilingual approach, and yet he fails to address problems of contemporary philosophy of language. This is a social reality we must address in order to go beyond Wiredu's restrictive appraisal of decolonisation. So in the final analysis, Wiredu's project of conceptual decolonisation has not addressed certain important philosophical issues and discourses that are germane to his project.

The major points made here are corroborated in the paper, 'The Problem of How to Use African Language for African Thought—On a Multilingual Perspective in African Philosophy' (1999) written by Kai Kresse. First of all Kresse states with telling relevance:

> I draw from an analogy to the field of literature where similar basic problems concerning the use of language for the mediation of thought occur, and have been intensively and with obvious consequences discussed for a much longer period. It seems likely that philosophy can gain from a reflection on this discussion.[1]

Clearly, this is an approach that this study has adopted.

Kresse also makes the same sort of criticism of Wiredu's approach—'Wiredu himself does not go that far'[2]—in relation to his project of conceptual decolonisation. This is because:

> reasoning independent of language cannot be imagined, so the independent grounds have to be searched in an area common to all languages. This seems to pose an unsolvable task for the philosopher and a valuable project for linguistic research.[3]

In the same article Kresse also discusses Ngugi wa Thiong'o in very favourable terms, making the point that 'The title *Decolonising the Mind* expresses Ngugi's agenda and can be seen as a literary predecessor to Wiredu's philosophical *Decolonisation of African Thought*'.[4] These are also among the strategies and attitudes this study has embraced to overcome Wiredu's shortcomings. Nonetheless, Kwasi Wiredu's reflections on conceptual decolonisation have provided a lot of inspiration for what needs to be done and have also pointed the way to generating even further thought on this persistent problem. Decolonisation entails both theoretical and practical work. It entails the task of 'keeping alive potent traditions of critique and resistance.'[5]

Notes

1. Kai Kresse, 'The Problem of How to Use African Language for African Thought-On a Multilingual Perspective in African Philosophy', *African Philosophy* Vol. 12, No. 1, March 1999, p. 27.

2. Ibid. p. 32.

3. Ibid. p. 33.

4. Ibid. p. 35.

5. Cornel West, 'The New Cultural Politics of Difference' in Russell Ferguson et al., eds., *Out There: Marginalization and Contemporary Cultures,* New York, Cambridge and London: The New Museum of Contemporary Art and MIT Press, 1990, p. 33.

Bibliography

Ahmed, Aijaz, 1996, 'Jameson's Rhetoric of Otherness and the National Allegory' in Bill Ashcroft et al., eds., *The Post-colonial Studies Reader,* London and New York: Routledge.

Aina, T. A. and Salau, A. T., eds., 1992, *The Challenge of Sustainable Development in Nigeria,* Ibadan: NEST.

Aina, T. A., *Globalization and Social Policy in Africa: Issues and Research Directions,* Dakar: CODESRIA working paper series 6/96.

Ake, Claude, 1979, *Social Science as Imperialism,* Ibadan: Ibadan University Press.

Ake, Claude, 1992, *The Feasibility of Democracy in Africa,* Ibadan: CREDU.

Ake, Claude, 1994, *Democratization of Disempowerment in Africa,* CASS Occasional Monograph No 1, Lagos: Malthouse Press Ltd.

Ake, Claude, 1996, *The Marginalization of Africa,* CASS Monograph No 6, Lagos: Malthouse Press Ltd.

Ake, Claude, 1996, *Democracy and Development in Africa,* Washington D. C.: The Brookings Institution.

Alkalimat, Abdul, 'eBlack: A 21st Century Challenge', http://www.eblackstudies.net/ebblack.html

Altbach, P. G., 1996, 'Literary Globalism: Books in the Third World' in Bill Ashcroft et al., eds., *The Post-colonial Studies Reader,* London and New York: Routledge.

Althusser, L., 1970, 'From *Capital* to Marx's Philosophy' in L. Alhusser and E. Balibar, eds., *Reading Capital,* London: New Left Books.

Althusser, L., 1990, *Philosophy and the Spontaneous Philosophy of the Scientists and Other Essays,* London: Verso Publishers.

Althusser, L., 1993, *The Future Lasts a Long Time* trans., R. Veasay, London: Vintage.

Amin, Ash, 1994, *Post-Fordism: A Reader,* Oxford: Blackwell Publishers Ltd.

Amin, Samir, 1989, *Eurocentrism,* London: Zed Books.

Amin, Samir, 1992, *The Empire of Chaos*, New York: Monthly Review Press.

Anderson, Benedict, 1983, *Imagined Communities: Reflections on the Origin and Spread of Nationalism*, London: Verso.

Appadurai, Arjun, 1990, 'Distinction and Difference in the Global Cultural Economy', *Public Culture*, 2.

Appiah, Anthony, 1985, 'Soyinka and the Philosophy of Culture' in P. O. Bodunrin, ed., *Philosophy in Africa: Trends and Perspectives*, Ile-Ife: University of Ife Press.

Appiah, Anthony, 1992, *In My Father's House: Africa in the Philosophy of Culture*, New York: Oxford University Press.

Appiah, Anthony, 1993, 'Europe Upside Down' in *Sapina Newsletter: A Bulletin of the Society for African Philosophy in North America*, Vol. V, No. 1. January–June.

Appiah, Anthony, 1994, 'Myth, Literature and the Africa World' in A. Maja-Pearce, ed., *Wole Soyinka: An Appraisal*, Oxford: Heinemann.

Asante, K. Molefi, 1990, *Kemet, Afrocentricity and Knowledge*, Trenton, N. J.: Africa World Press.

Asante, K. Molefi, 1996, 'Multiculturalism and the Academy', *Academe: Bulletin of the American University Professors*, May/June. Available at http://www.pc.maricopa.edu/departments/ss/phi101/supplementary/more/Molefi_Kete_Asante.htm

Ashcroft, Bill, 1996, 'Constitutive Graphonomy' in Bill Ashcroft et al., eds., *The Post-colonial Studies Reader*, London and New York: Routledge.

Bakhtin, M., 1981, *The Dialogic Imagination: Four Essays*, ed. M. Holquist, trans. C. Emerson & M. Holquist, Austin: University of Texas Press.

Bangura, Y., 1994, *Intellectuals, Economic Reform and Society Change*, Dakar: CODESRIA Monograph Series, 1/94.

Barthes, Roland, 1988, 'The Death of the Author' in David Lodge, ed., *Modern Criticism and Theory: A Reader*, Essex: Longman.

Baudrillard, Jean, 1981, *For a Critique of the Political Economy of the Sign*, trans. Charles Levin, St. Louis: Telos Press.

Baudrillard, Jean, 1975, *The Mirror of Production*, trans Mark Poster, St. Louis: Telos Press.

Bello, A. G. A., 1985, 'Truth and Fact: An Objectivist Reply to Wiredu's Anti-Objectivism', Ph.D. thesis, Department of Philosophy, University of Ibadan.

Bernal, Martin, 'Review of *Not Out of Africa* by Mary Lefkowitz' gopher://gopher.lib.virginia.edu/00/alpha/bmcr/v96/96-4-5

Bhabha, Homi, 1996, 'Sign Taken For Wonders' in Bill Ashcroft et al., eds., *The Post-colonial Studies Reader*, London and New York: Routledge.

Bhabha, Homi, 1996, 'Cultural Diversity and Cultural Differences' in Bill Ashcroft et al., eds., *The Post-colonial Studies Reader*, London and New York: Routledge.

Bhabha, Homi, 1996, 'Dissemination: Time, Narrative, and the Margins of the Modern Nation' in Bill Ashcroft et al., eds., *The Post-colonial Studies Reader,* London and New York: Routledge.

Binsbergen, W., 1991, 'Becoming a Sangoma: Religious Anthropological Fieldwork in Francistown, Botswana, *Journal of Religion in Africa,* 21, 4.

Binsbergen, W., ed., 1997, *Black Athena: Ten Years After,* Hoofddorp: Dutch Archaelogical and Historical Society, Special Issue, *Talenta: Proceedings of the Dutch Archaelogical and Historical Society,* Vol. 28-29, 1996=97.

Binsbergen, W., 2000, 'Derrida on religion: Glimpses on interculturality', paper presented at the Dutch-Flemish Association for Intercultural Philosophy, Research group on Spirituality, meetings April and June. http://www. geocities.com/nvu.f/derrwim.htm.

Binsbergen, W., 2001, 'Witchcraft in Modern Africa as Virtualised Boundary Conditions of the Kinship Order', http://www.geocities.com/africareligion/witchtxl.htm.

Binsbergen, W., 2001, 'An Incomprehensible Miracle: Central Clerical Intellectualism versus African historic religion: A close reading of Valentin Mudimbe's *Tales of Faith',* paper presented at SOAS, February http://www.geocities. com/africanreligion/mudi10.htm.

Binsbergen, W., 2003, *Intercultural Encounters: African and Anthropological Lessons Towards a Philosophy of Interculturality,* Hamburg: LIT.

Binsbergen, W., (forthcoming) *Global Bee Flight.*

Bloom, Allen, 1987, *The Closing of the American Mind,* New York: Touchstone.

Bodunrin, P. O., 1981, 'The Question of African Philosophy' in *Philosophy,* Vol. 56.

Bostrom, Nick, 1995, 'Understanding Quine's Theses of Indeterminacy,' unpublished MA thesis, LSC and Stockholm University, July. www.hedweb.com/nickb

Bourdieu, Pierre, 1999, 'The Social Conditions of the International Circulation of Ideas' in Richard Shursterman, ed., *Bourdieu: A Critical Reader,* Oxford: Blackwell.

Bourdieu, Pierre, 1973, 'The Three Forms of Theoretical Knowledge', *Social Science Information,* 14(6).

Chen, K., 1996, 'Post-marxism: Between/Beyond Critical Postmodernism and Cultural Studies' in D. Morley and K. Chen, eds., *Stuart Hall: Critical Dialogues in Cultural Studies,* London and New York: Routledge.

Comaroff, Jean, and Comaroff, John L., 1991, *Of Revelation and Revolution: Christianity, Colonialism and Consciousness in South Africa* Vol. 1, 1, Chicago: University of Chicago Press.

Comaroff, Jean, and Comaroff, John L., 1997, *Of Revelation and Revolution: The Dialectics of Modernity on a South African Frontier,* Vol. 2, Chicago: University of Chicago Press.

Comaroff, Jean, and Comaroff, John L., 1999a, 'Introduction' in *Civil Society and the Political Imagination in Africa: Critical Perspectives.*

Comaroff, Jean, and Comaroff, John L., 1999b, 'Alien-Nation: Zombies Immigrants and Millennial Capitalism', *CODESRIA Bulletin* Numbers 3 & 4.

Comaroff, Jean, and Comaroff, John L., 1999c, 'Occult Economies and the Violence of Abstraction: Notes from the South African Post Colony' in *American Ethnologist*, 26.

Comaroff, Jean, and Comaroff, John L., 1999d, 'Alienation: Zombies, Immigrants and Millennial Capitalism', Working Paper No. 9901, American Bar Foundation.

Comaroff, Jean, and Comaroff, John L., 2000, 'Millennial Capitalism: First Thoughts on a Second Coming', *Public Culture, 31.*

Crossberg, Lawrence, 1992, *We Gotta Get Out of This Place*, London: Routledge.

Crossberg, Lawrence, 1996, 'The Space Culture, the Power of Space' in I. Chambers and L. Curti, eds., *The Post-colonial Question,* London and New York: Routledge.

Crossberg, Lawrence, 1996, 'History, Politics and Postmodernism: Stuart Hall and Cultural Studies', in D. Morley and K. Chen, eds., *Stuart Hall: Critical Dialogues in Cultural Studies*, London and New York: Routledge.

Crowder, M., 1963, *West Africa under Colonial Rule,* London: Hutchinson.

Darwish, Ali, 1989, 'The Translation Process: A View of Mind', paper written for the post graduate students of the Diploma in Translation and Interpreting at Victoria College, Melbourne, Australia, http://www.surf.net.au/writescope/translation/mindview.html

Davidson, Basil, 1993, *The Black Man's Burden,* Ibadan: Spectrum Books Ltd.

Davidson, Donald, 1961, 'Truth and Meaning' in J. F. Rosenberg and C. Fravis, eds., *Readings in the Philosophy of Language*, New Jersey: Prentice Hall.

Davidson, Donald, 1984, *Inquiries into Truth and Interpretation*, Oxford: Clarendon Press.

de Man, Paul, 1988, 'The Resistance to Theory' in D. Lodge, ed., *Modern Criticism and Theory: A Reader,* Essex: Longman.

Deleuze, G., 1983, *Nietzsche and Philosophy* (trans. H. Tomlinson) London: Athlone.

Deleuze, G. and Guattari, F., 1983, *Anti-Oedipus: Capitalism and Schizophrenia,* Preface by M. Foucault trans. R. Hurley, M. Seem and H. R. Lane, London: Athlone Press.

Derrida, J., 1972, *Disseminations,* Chicago: University of Chicago Press.

Derrida, J., 1994, *Specters of Marx: The State of Debt, the Work of Mourning and the New International,* trans. Peggy Kamuf, New York: Routledge.

Derrida, J., 1973, *Speech and Phenomena,* Evanston: Northwestern University.

Derrida, J., 1976, *Of Grammatology,* (trans. by Gayatri Spivak) Baltimore: Johns Hopkins University Press.

Derrida, J., 1978, *Writing and Difference* (trans. by Alan Bass), Chicago: University of Chicago Press.

Diagne, S. B. and Ossebi, H., 1996, *The Cultural Question in Africa: Issues, Politics and Research Prospects,* Dakar: CODESRIA Working Paper 3/96.

Diawara, Manthia, 1998, 'The Song of Griot' in *Transition* 74.

During, Simon, 1996, 'Postmodernism and Post-colonialism Today' in Bill Ashcroft et al., eds., *The Post-colonial Studies Reader,* London and New York: Routledge.

Eagleton, Terry, 1988, 'Capitalism, Modernism and Postmodernism' in D. Lodge, ed., *Modern Criticism and Theory: A Reader,* D. Lodge, Essex: Longman.

Edim, O. O., 1990, *Berkeley and Wiredu on Knowledge and Existence,* Ph.D. Thesis, Department of Philosophy, University of Ibadan.

Ekeh, Peter, 'Colonialism and the Two Publics in Africa: A Theoretical Statement' in *Comparative Studies in Social and History*, Vol. 32, No. 4.

Fanon, Frantz, 1967, *Black Skin, White Masks* (trans. C. Van Markmann), New York: Grove Press.

Feyerabend, Paul, 1975, *Against Method,* London: New Left Books.

Foucault, Michel, 1967, *Madness and Civilization* (trans. by R. Howard), London: Tavistock.

Foucault, Michel, 1980, *Power/ Knowledge,* New York: Pantheon.

Foucault, Michel, 1972, *The Order of Things,* London: Tavistock.

Foucault, Michel, 1984, *The Foucault Reader,* Harmondsworth: Penguin.

Foucault, Michel, 1988, 'What is an Author' in D. Lodge, ed., *Modern Criticism and Theory: A Reader,* D. Lodge, Essex: Longman.

Foucault, Michel, 1977, *Language Counter–Memory, Practice* ed., D. F. Bouchard, Ithaca: Cornel University Press.

Fukuyama, F., 1992, *The End of History and the Last Man,* Harmondsworth: Penguin.

Gates, Jr., H. L., ed, 1986, '*Race', Writing and Difference,* Chicago: University of Chicago Press.

Gates, Jr., H. L., 1987, *Figures in Black,* New York: Oxford University Press.

Gates, Jr., H. L., 1988, *The Signifying Monkey: A Theory of Afro-American Literary Criticism,* New York: Oxford University Press.

Gates, Jr., H. L., 1992, *Loose Canons: Notes on the Culture Wars,* New York: Oxford University Press.

Geertz, Clifford, 1973, *The Interpretation of Cultures,* New York: Basic Books.

Gilroy, Paul, 1993, *The Black Atlantic,* London: Verso.

Gilroy, Paul, 1996, 'Route Work: *The Black Atlantic* and the Politics of Exile' in *The Post-colonial Question,* eds., I. Chambers and L. Curti, London and New York: Routledge.

Gilroy, Paul, 2000 *Against: Race : Imagining Political Culture Beyond the Color Line*, Harvard: University Press.

Gyekye, Kwame, 1997, *Tradition and Modernity*, New York: Oxford University Press.

Habermas, Jurgen, 1987, *The Philosophical Discourse of Modernity*, Cambridge: MIT Press.

Habermas, Jurgen, 1989, *The Structural Transformation of the Public Sphere*, trans T. Burger and F. Lawrence, Cambridge: MIT Press.

Hacking, Ian, 1982, 'Language, Truth and Reason' in *Rationality and Relativism*, Cambridge: MIT Press.

Hall, Catherine, 1996, 'Histories, Empires and the Post-colonial Moment' in *The Postcolonial Question*, eds. I Chambers and L. Curti, London and New York: Routledge.

Hall, Stuart, 1996, 'When was 'the Post-colonial'? Thinking at the Limit' in *The Postcolonial Question*, eds. I Chambers and L. Curti, London and New York: Routledge.

Hall, Stuart, 1996, 'The Problem of Ideology: Marxism without Guarantees' in D. Morley and K. Chen, eds., *Stuart Hall: Critical Dialogues in Cultural Studies*, London and New York: Routledge.

Hall, Stuart, 1996, 'Cultural Studies and Its Theoretical Legacies' in D. Morby and K. Chen, eds., *Stuart Hall: Critical Dialogues in Cultural Studies*, London and New York: Routledge.

Hall, Stuart, 1996, 'New Ethnicities' in D. Morley and K. Chen, eds., *Stuart Hall: Critical Dialogues in Cultural Studies*, London and New York: Routledge.

Hall, Stuart, 1996, 'What is this "Black" in Black Popular Culture?' in D. Morley and K. Chen, eds., *Stuart Hall: Critical Dialogues in Cultural Studies*, London and New York: Routledge.

Hancock, Graham, 1991, *Lords of Poverty*, London: Mandarin.

Hebdige, Dick, 1996, 'Postmodernism and the Other Side' in D. Morley and K. Chen, eds., *Stuart Hall: Critical Dialogues in Cultural Studies*, London and New York: Routledge.

Hountondji, Paulin, 1983, 'Distances' in *Ibadan Journal of Humanistic Studies*, No. 3, October.

Hountondji, Paulin, 1983, *African Philosophy: Myth and Reality* (trans. Henri Evans with J. Lee), London: Hutchinson and Co.

Hountondji, Paulin, 2002, *The Struggle for Meaning: Reflections on Philosophy, Culture and Democracy in Africa*, Athens: Ohio University Center for International Studies.

Hutcheon, Linda, 1987, 'Beginning to Theorize Modernism', *Textual Practice*, Vol. 1 No. 1 Spring.

Hutcheon, Linda, 1988, *A Poetics of Postmodernism: History, Theory, Fiction*, London and New York: Routledge.

Hutcheon, Linda, 1996, 'Circling the Downspout of Empire' in Bill Ashcroft et al., eds., *The Post-colonial Studies Reader,* London and New York: Routledge.

Irele, Abiola, 1981, *The African Experience in Literature and Ideology,* London, Ibadan, Nairobi: Heinemann.

Irele, Abiola, 1983, 'Introduction' to *African Philosophy: Myth and Reality,* Hountondji, P. J., London: Hutchinson and Co.

Irele, Abiola, 1992, 'In Praise of Alienation', inaugural lecture delivered at the University of Ibadan on November, 1982. Published privately in Ibadan as a monograph, 1987. Reprint in V. Y. Mudimbe, ed., *The Surreptitious Speech: Présence Africaine and the Politics of Otherness,* Chicago: University of Chicago Press.

Irele, Abiola, 1992, 'The Crisis of Legitimacy in Africa' in *Dissent* (summer).

Irele, Abiola, 1995, 'The African Imagination' in *Research in African Literatures,* Vol. 26, No. 1, Spring.

Irele, Abiola, 2001, *The African Imagination: Literature in Africa and the Black Diaspora,* New York: Oxford University Press.

Irele, Abiola, 1998, 'Toward Reconstruction in Africa', unpublished conference paper.

Irele, Dipo, 1993, *Introduction to Contemporary and Political Thinkers,* Ibadan: New Horn in conjunction with Critical Forum.

Irele, Dipo, 1993, *In the Tracks of African Predicament,* Ibadan: Option Books and Information Services.

Irele, Dipo, 1993, *The Violated Universe: Fanon and Gandhi on Violence,* Ibadan: Critical Forum.

Irele, Dipo, 1998, *The Public Sphere and Democracy,* Ibadan: New Horn Press.

Jahn, Janheinz, 1961, *Muntu: The New African Culture,* New York: Grove Press.

Jahn, Janheinz, 1968, *Neo-Africa Literature: A History of Black Writing,* New York: Grove Press.

Jameson, Fredric, 1984, 'Postmodernism, or the Cultural Logic of Late Capitalism' in *New Left Review,* 146.

Jameson, Fredric, 1988, 'The Politics of Theory: Ideological Positions in the Postmodernism Debate' in D. Lodge, ed., *Modern Criticism and Theory: A Reader,* Essex: Longman.

Jeyifo, Biodun, 1990, 'The Nature of Things: Arrested Decolonisation and Critical Theory' in *Research in African Literatures,* Vol. 21, No. 1.

Jinadu, Adele, L., 1980, *Fanon: In Search of the African Revolution,* Enugu: Fourth Dimension Publishers.

Kebede, Messay, 2004, *Africa's Quest for a Philosophy of Decolonization,* Amsterdam and New York: Rodopi.

Kotei, S. I. A., 1996, 'The Book in Africa Today' in Bill Ashcroft et al., eds., *The Post-colonial Studies Reader* eds. London and New York: Routledge.

Kresse, Kai, 1999, 'The Problem of How to Use African Language for African Thought—On a Multilingual Perspective' in *African Philosophy*, Vol. 12, No. 1 March.

Kuhn, I. S., 1962, *The Structure of Scientific Revolutions*, Chicago: University of Chicago Press.

Kundera, M., 1979, *The Book of Laughter and Forgetting* trans. by M. H. Heim, London and New York: Penguin Books.

Laakso, L. and Olukoshi, A. O., 1996, 'The Crisis of the Post-colonial Nation-State Project in Africa' in A. O. Olukoshi and L. Laakso, eds., *Challenges to the Nation-State in Africa*, Uppsala: University of Helsinki.

Laforest, H. Marie, 1996, 'Black Cultures in Difference' in I. Chambers and L. Curti, eds., *The Post-colonial Question,* London and New York: Routledge.

Lefkowitz, Mary, 1996, *Not Out of Africa: How Afrocentricism Became an Excuse to Teach Myth as History*, New York: New Republic and Basic Books. http://www.pc.maricopa.edu/departments/ss/phi101/supplementary/more/Not_out_of_Africa.htm

Levi-Strauss, Claude, 1963, *Structural Anthropology*, New York: Basic Books.

Lindqvist, Sven, 1996, *Exterminate all the Brutes,* trans. Joan Tate, New York: The New Press.

Lyotard, Jean-François, 1984, *The Postmodern Condition: A Report on Knowledge* (trans. G. Bennington and B. Massime), Minneapolis: University of Minnesota Press.

Mafeje, Archie, 1996, *Anthropology and Independent Africans. Suicide or End of an Era?* Dakar: CODESRIA Monograph Series 4/96.

Mamdani, Mahmood, 1996, *Citizen and Subject: Contemporary Africa and the Legacy of Late Colonialism,* Princeton: Princeton University Press.

Mamdani, Mahmood, 2004, *Good Muslim, Bad Muslim*, New York: Pantheon Books.

Mannoni, O., 1950, *Prospero and Caliban,* New York: Frederick A. Praeger.

Masolo, D. A., 1994, *African Philosophy in Search of Identity,* Bloomington and Indiana: Indiana University Press.

Mbembe, Achille, 2000, 'An Essay on the Political Imagination in Wartime', *CODESRIA Bulletin* 2, 3 & 4.

Mbembe, Achille, 2001, *On the Postcolony,* Berkeley: University of California Press.

Mbembe, Achille, 1992a, 'Provisional Notes on the Postcolony' in *Africa* 62, No. 1.

Mbembe, Achille, 1992b, 'The Banality of Power and the Aesthetics of Vulgarity in the Postcolony', *Public Culture,* 4.

McClintock, Anne, 1995, *Imperial Leather: Race, Gender and Sexuality in the Colonial Conquest,* New York and London: Routledge.

McGowan, J., 1991, *Postmodernism and Its Critics,* New York: Cornell University Press.

Mercer, Kobena, 1990, 'Black Hair/Style Politics,' in Russell Ferguson et al, eds., *Out There: Marginalization and Contemporary Cultures,* New York, Cambridge and London: The New Museum of Contemporary Art and MIT Press.

Minh-ha, T. T., 1996, 'Writing Postcoloniality and Feminism' in Bill Ashcroft et al., eds., *The Post-colonial Studies Reader,* London and New York: Routledge.

Miyoshi, Masao, 1996, 'A Borderless World? From Colonialism to Transnationalism and the Transnational Imaginary' in R. Wilson and W. Dissanayake, eds., *Global/Local: Cultural Production and the Transnational Imaginary,* Durham and London: Duke University Press.

Morley, David, 1996, 'EurAm, Modernity, Reason and Alterity: Or Postmodernism, the Highest Stage of Cultural Imperialism' in D. Morley and K. Chen, eds., *Stuart Hall: Critical Dialogues in Cultural Studies,* London and New York: Routledge.

Mudimbe, Valentine, 1988, *The Invention of Africa: Gnosis, Philosophy and the Order of Knowledge,* Bloomington/Indianapolis: Indiana University Press.

Mudimbe, Valentine, 1991, *Parables and Fables: Exegesis, Textuality and Politics in Central Africa,* Madison: University of Wisconsin Press.

Mudimbe, Valentine, 1994, *The Idea of Africa,* Bloomington and London: Indiana University Press.

Nagel, Joane, 2003, *Race, Ethnicity and Sexuality: Intimate Intersections, Forbidden Frontiers,* New York: Oxford University Press.

Newman, John Henry, 1969, 'The Idea of a University', *The Harvard Classics,* New York: P.F. Collier & Son Corporation, pp. 31-40.

O' Farrell, C., 1989, *Foucault: Historian or Philosopher?* Hampshire: The Macmillan Press Ltd.

Ofeimun, Odia, 1995, 'Africa's Many Mansions' in *ANA Review,* November.

Ojo-Ade, Femi, 1989, *On Black Culture,* Ile-Ife: Obafemi Awolowo University Press.

Ojo-Ade, Femi, 1996, *Being Black Being Human,* Ile-Ife: Obafemi Awolowo Univ. Press.

Oke, Moses, 1988, 'Wiredu's Theory and Practice of African Philosophy' in *Second Order: An African Journal of Philosophy* (New Series) Vol. I, No. 1.

Okolo, C. B., 1989, 'Democratic Aspiration Versus Tribalism in Africa: An Essay in African Social Philosophy' in *Philosophy and Social Action,* Vol. 15, June.

Okolo, C. B., 1993, *African Social and Political Philosophy: Selected Essays,* Nsukka: Fulladu Publishing Company.

Okpewho, Isidore, 1981, 'Myth and Rationality in Africa' in *Ibadan Journal of Humanistic Studies* No. 1, April.

Oladipo, Olusegun, 1991, *The Idea of African Philosophy,* Ibadan: Molecular Publishers.

Oladipo, Olusegun, 1995, 'Reason, Identity and the African Quest' in *Africa Today,* Vol. 42, No. 3.

Oladipo, Olusegun, 1995, 'Introduction' in Kwasi Wiredu's *Conceptual Decolonization in African Philosophy,* Ibadan: Hope Publication.

Oladipo, Olusegun, 1996, *Philosophy and the African Experience. The Contributions of Kwasi Wiredu,* Ibadan: Hope Publication.

Oluwole, Sophie, 1992, *Witchcraft, Reincarnation and the God-Head (Issues in African Philosophy),* Lagos: Excel Publishers.

Oruka, Odera, 1981, 'Four Trends in Current African Philosophy' in Alwin Diemer, ed., *Philosophy in the Present African Situation,* Wiesbaden: Franz Steiner.

Osha, Sanya, 1996, 'A New Direction in African Philosophy' in *Journal of Philosophy and Development* Ago-Iwoye: Ogun State University, Vol. 2, Nos. 1 & 2, January.

Osha, Sanya, 1998, 'Reflections on the Thought of Abiola Irele' in Aduke Adebayo and S. Adenuga, eds., *Literature, Ideology and Society,* Ibadan: AMD Publishers.

Osundare, Niyi, 1993, *African Literature and the Crisis of Post-structuralist Theorising,* Ibadan: Option Books and Information Services.

Owomoyela, Oyekan, 1987, Africa and the Imperative of Philosophy: A Poverty of Speculative', *African Studies Review,* 30, (1) 1987.

Palermo, James, 1997, 'Reading Asante's Myth of Afrocentricity: An Ideological Critique', http://www.ed.uiuc.edu/EPS/PES-Yearbook/ 97_docs/palermo.html

Parry, Benita, 1996, 'Problems in Current Theories of Colonial Discourse' in Bill Ashcroft et al., eds., *The Post-colonial Studies Reader,* London and New York: Routledge.

Pompa, L., 1981, 'Philosophy without Epistemology' in *Inquiry: An Interdisciplinary Journal of Philosophy and Social Sciences,* Vol. 24, No. 3, October.

Quayson, Ato, 1995, 'Orality—(Theory)—Textuality: Tutuola, Okri and the Relationship of Literary Practice to Oral Tradition' in S. Brown, ed., *The Pressures of the Text: Orality Texts and the Telling of Tales,* Birmingham: Centre of West African Studies, Series No. 4.

Quine, W. V. O., 1960, *Word and Object,* Cambridge, Mass: MIT Press.

Quine, W. V. O., 1969, *Ontological Relativity and Other Essays,* New York: Columbia University Press.

Rodney, Walter, 1972, *How Europe Underdeveloped Africa,* London: Bogle–L'Ouverture.

Rorty, Richard, 1998, *Achieving Our Country: Leftist Thought in Twentieth Century America,* Cambridge: Harvard University Press.

Rorty, Richard, 1978, 'Philosophy as a Kind of Writing' in *New Literary History* X.

Rorty, Richard, 1983, *Philosophy and the Mirror of Nature,* Oxford: Basil Blackwell.

Rorty, Richard, 1984, 'Habermas and Lyotard on Postmodernity' in *Praxis International,* 4 (I).

Rorty, Richard, 1988, *Contingency, Irony and Solidarity,* Cambridge: Cambridge University Press.

Rorty, Richard, 1993, 'Feminism, Ideology and Deconstruction: a Pragmatist View', *Hypatia* 8, No. 2 (Spring).

Rorty, Richard, 1999, *Philosophy and Social Hope,* Harmondsworth: Penguin Books Ltd.

Said, Edward, 1988, 'Crisis (in Orientalism)' in D. Lodge, ed., *Modern Criticism and Theory: A Reader,* Essex: Longman.

Said, Edward, 1994, *Culture and Imperialism,* London: Vintage.

Said, Edward, 1996, *Representations of the Intellectual,* London: Vintage.

Salazar, Phillipe-Joseph, 2002, *An African Athens: Rhetoric and the Shaping of Democracy in South Africa,* London and New Jersey: Erlbaum Associates.

Senghor, Leopold, 1976, *Prose and Poetry* (eds. and trans. J. Reed and C. Wake), London, Nairobi, Ibadan: Heinemann.

Shursterman, Richard, ed., 1999, *Bourdieu: A Critical Reader,* Oxford: Blackwell.

Smith, Sidonie and Watson, Julia, 1992, *De/Colonizing the Subject: The Politics of Gender in Women's Autobiography,* Minnesota: University of Minnesota.

Sogolo, Godwin, 1987, 'Translational Problems: Meaning and Reality in African Thought' in *Ultimate Reality and Meaning: International Studies in the Philosophy of Understanding,* Vol. 10, No. 1, March.

Soyinka, Wole, 1976, *Myth, Literature and the African World,.* Cambridge: CUP.

Soyinka, Wole, 1994, 'Nobel Lecture 1986: This Past Must Address Its Present' in A. Maja-Pearce, ed., *Wole Soyinka: An Appraisal,* Oxford: Heinemann.

Soyinka, Wole, 1996, *The Open Sore of a Continent,* New York: Oxford University Press.

Soyinka, Wole, 1999, *The Burden of Memory: The Muse of Forgiveness,* New York: Oxford University Press.

Spark, Colin, 1996, 'Stuart Hall, Cultural Studies and Marxism' in D. Morley and K. Chen, eds., *Stuart Hall: Critical Dialogues in Cultural Studies,* London and New York: Routledge.

Spivak, Gayatri, 1988, *In Other Worlds: Essays in Cultural Politics,* New York and London: Routledge.

Spivak, Gayatri, 1990, *The Post-colonial Critic: Interviews, Strategies, Dialogues,* London and New York: Routledge.

Spivak, Gayatri, 1993, *Outside in the Teaching Machine,* Routledge: New York & London.

Spivak, Gayatri, 1996, 'Can the Subaltern Speak' in Bill Ashcroft et al., eds., *The Post-colonial Studies Reader,* London and New York: Routledge.

Steiner, George, 1975, *After Babel: Aspects of Language and Translation,* London: Oxford University Press.

Stoler, A. L., 2002, *Carnal Knowledge and Imperial Power: Race and the Intimate in Colonial Rule,* Berkeley: University of California Press.

Strauss, Gideon, 'Does Africa exist? Racial Essentialism and Pan-African Solidarity in Postcolonial Cultural Politics', http://www.uovs.ac.za/lettere/essays/africa1.htm

Sundiata, Ibrahim, 1996, 'Afrocentricism: The Argument We're Really Having', *Dissonance,* September 30, http://way.net/dissonance/sundiata.html

Tal, Kali, 'The Unbearable Whiteness of Being: African American Critical Theory and Cyberculture,' http://www.kalital.com/Text/Writing/Whiteness.html

van Hensbroek, P. B., 2001, 'Introduction' *QUEST,* Special issue on African Renaissance and Ubuntu, Vol. XV, No. 1-2.

Ware, Vron, 1996, 'Defining Forces: 'Race', Gender and Memories of Empire' in I. Chambers and L. Curti, eds., *The Post-colonial Question,* London and New York: Routledge.

West, Cornel, 1993, *Keeping Faith,* Princeton: Princeton University Press.

Wiredu, Kwasi, 1980, *Philosophy and an African Culture,* Cambridge: Cambridge University Press.

Wiredu, Kwasi, 1983, 'The Akan Concept of Mind' in *Ibadan Journal of Humanistic Studies,* No. 3.

Wiredu, Kwasi and Kwame Gyekye, 1992, *Person and Community: Ghanaian Philosophical Studies,* Washington, D.C.: Council for Research in Values and Philosophy.

Wiredu, Kwasi, 1993, 'Canons of Conceptualisation' in *The Monist: An International Journal of General Philosophical Inquiry,* Vol. 76, No. 4, October.

Wiredu, Kwasi, 1995, *Conceptual Decolonization in African Philosophy: Four Essays,* Ibadan: Hope Publications.

Wiredu, Kwasi, 1996, *Cultural Universals and Particulars: An African Perspective,* Bloomington and Indianapolis: Indiana University Press.

Wiredu, Kwasi, 'Towards Decolonizing African Philosophy and Religion', *African Studies Quarterly,* Vol. 1, issue 4.

Wittgenstein, L., 1953, 2001, *Philosophical Investigations,* G.E.M. Anscombe trans. Oxford: Blackwell Publishers.

Wuthnow, Robert *et al.,* 1984, *Cultural Analysis,* London: Routledge and Kegan.

Yai, Olabiyi, 1977, 'Theory and Practice in African Philosophy: The Poverty of Speculative Thought,' *Second Order,* No. 2, July.

Zahar, Renate, 1974, *Colonialism and Alienation,* Benin: Ethiope Publishing Corporation.

Index

The Publisher

The **Council for the Development of Social Science Research in Africa** (CODESRIA) is an independent organisation whose principal objectives are facilitating research, promoting research-based publishing and creating multiple forums geared towards the exchange of views and information among African researchers. It challenges the fragmentation of research through the creation of thematic research networks that cut across linguistic and regional boundaries.

CODESRIA publishes a quarterly journal, *Africa Development*, the longest standing Africa-based social science journal; *Afrika Zamani*, a journal of history; the *African Sociological Review*, *African Journal of International Affairs (AJIA)*, *Africa Review of Books* and *Identity, Culture and Politics: An Afro-Asian Dialogue*. It co-publishes the *Journal of Higher Education in Africa* and *Africa Media Review*. Research results and other activities of the institution are disseminated through 'Working Papers', 'Monograph Series', 'CODESRIA Book Series', and the *CODESRIA Bulletin*.

Printed in the United States
48980LVS00006B/334-339